NO SOUND THE SILENCE MAKES

Christy Gerrell

Copyright © 2025 Christy Gerrell

All rights reserved.

No part of this book may be reproduced, stored in a retrieval system, or transmitted by any means, electronic, mechanical, photocopying, recording, or otherwise, without written permission from the author.

ISBN (Paperback): 979-8-9989661-3-2

Dedicated to: My beautiful daughter Amy Lynn Bac
that is in a war with an incurable disease
and she's only 16 years old – Amy died Oct. 14, 2018 to read her story:
Something's the Matter with Amy amazon.com

No Sound the Silence Makes

You came to me; your heart in your hand,
I accepted your betrothal ring and your wedding band.
But my heart wasn't free to love you because of guilt and shame,
And I never meant to hurt you or cause you any pain.

A cry in the darkness and an emptiness within,
I look in the mirror and see only sin.
Lost in the night and unable to see,
The only thing I can do is set you free.

In search of the truth, I gave you lies,
I thought I killed our love, and you let it die.
But you loved me pure and with all of your heart,
I love you too and won't let us part.

No sound the silence makes,
Quiet is the sun as it awakes.
I thought when I married you, I was taking you to hell,
You held me in your arms, and to heaven we fell.

Synopsis:

Cecily fell in love with Levi on the banks of Cherry Lake near Madison, Florida when she was still a girl. Levi is all Cecily's ever wanted as she's grown into a woman. But she cannot have him; Cecily's not free to be with Levi. Standing between these two star crossed lovers is a man bent on destroying them both, and it will be up to Levi to save Cecily from the silent world that she's forced to live in, a world that makes no sound. A love story of two lovers meant to be together that are instead torn apart by greed, jealousy and a lack of communication. Together Levi and Cecily struggle to overcome all obstacles that are keeping them apart so that they can have their happily ever after.

Chapter One

March 1897
Cherry Lake, Florida

She was going to be late. She had never been late for church in her whole life. And the past two years she had been sure to be early so that she would have a place in the front pew. She needed to be in the very front of the church every Sunday; God might better hear her prayer from there rather than the very back of the church. The double doors of the old frame church house were closed. She was late. Gathering a long deep breath, she opened one of the huge doors and tried to enter silently. She had no such luck. The door scraped the floor and creaked on its hinges, and several people turned around to stare at her, the old preacher stopped speaking his sermon in mid-sentence and looked back at her standing there alone and late in the doorway of his church.

Cecily Walker felt her face turn warm with a blush as the preacher stared hard at her, the Reverend Bidwell could stop a train with the look that he gave to her, and he knew that very well.

So here she stood, in the very back of the church knowing that she had to walk down that long aisle with the Reverend staring at her and half of his congregation staring at her, and the other half of his congregation staring at the good Reverend Bidwell.

And then, out of nowhere it seemed, a hand grabbed a hold of her hand, and she was pulled down into the very back pew. Cecily gasped loud in surprise and gave an even louder squeal as she was yanked down and sat hard on the lap of Levi Tucker.

"Sorry Cecily," Levi said as he put her from off of his lap and helped her to settle down beside him. Cecily's face was on fire when she finally sat facing the Reverend Bidwell and pulled her hand from Levi's gentle hold. Several children giggled while looking back at her and an old man laughed out loud at Cecily causing her to sink low down into the pew and wishing that she could hide. She shouldn't have even come to church today, she thought. All of her luck had been bad for so long. Too long, and now this incident just added to her humiliation.

"I would like to continue with today's sermon, if I may?" the Reverend Bidwell's loud almost booming voice filled the sanctuary and brought about complete silence from his congregation. Several people glanced back at Cecily and gave her accusatory looks. It just wasn't done, she knew, people were never late for church. She wished that she had stayed home and pretended illness. If she had felt safe at home, she would have stayed home, Cecily thought. But she knew home wasn't a safe place for her to be right now.

Cecily sat silent for a long few moments and stared at her hands folded in her lap as she regained her composure by taking long deep even breaths. She glanced up at Levi sitting beside her and then back down at her hands. She had known Levi all of her life. She had loved Levi for most of her life. He was a tall man, hard work and physical labor had made his body fine tuned and well muscled. He owned a two thousand acre tree farm and his own sawmill, he also had cattle and bred horses. Levi was a good man, and he had a full life. She grieved that she was no longer a part of his life. She both admired him and respected him. Levi had no idea what she really felt for him. She knew that Levi would never know her feelings for him.

Cecily glanced back up at Levi and saw him looking down at her. He gave her an easy smile. Levi always gave everyone an easy smile that was his way. They were neighbors. They had been neighbors all of her life, and Cecily's father thought a lot of Levi, almost everyone in Cherry Lake knew and liked Levi and thought that he was a good and fine man. Cecily looked at the Reverend Bidwell but did not hear the sermon. Her thoughts were on Levi Tucker. Her thoughts through the years had often been on Levi Tucker.

Levi's father had been a Yankee that had come south after the Civil War. Ethan Tucker had met Levi's mother, Lilly Harris and he married Lilly in order to save her father's farm. Lilly hadn't wanted to marry Ethan. Lilly hated Ethan because he was a Yankee. She only married Ethan Tucker for his money and nothing more. Ethan and Lilly's story was well known in the Cherry Lake area, Lilly hated the Yankee that her father had all but forced her to marry like any good southern girl should and Ethan had loved his Lilly at first sight. Ethan had waited for his Lilly to love him the story went. He made her love him with his kindness and his patience. And Lilly gave to Ethan two children, her whole heart and then died with him in a diphtheria epidemic more than thirty years after she wed him. Their story had put many little girls in Cherry Lake to sleep for years.

Levi's younger sister, Sarah was one of Cecily's best friends. Cecily hadn't seen Sarah in almost two years as Sarah had married Franklin Mathews and moved to the city of Madison, Florida a few miles south of Cherry Lake. Levi lived alone in the house that his father had built for his mother more than thirty years ago. Cecily only saw Levi at church on Sundays. Cecily loved seeing Levi at church on Sundays.

Cecily glanced back up at Levi and thought of how things had changed since Sarah had gone away. Cecily used to see Levi every day, she and Sarah and their friend Clementine they called her Clemmie Floyd, had been inseparable as children. Every spare moment they had, the three girls had been in each other's company, and Levi had often been around watching them, sometimes even joining the girls on picnics or horseback riding.

Cecily had only been fourteen years old, Levi nineteen when she knew that she loved him. He had been chasing after all three girls at the lake. They had all been laughing and giggling and running from Levi, and then she had turned, and she saw him running only after her and she stopped and stood still, smiling up at him as he ran to her and stopped before her as though he were seeing her for the very first time, the same way that she was seeing him and she knew. She loved him, she would love him always. He was no longer Levi. He was always in her mind from thereafter known as her Levi. He belonged to her and she would always belong to him.

Every year at church in the spring there was the box social, the girls and women would make boxes with lunch inside them, and the boys and men would bid at auction on a box, and then they would not only enjoy the boxed lunch, but they were able to have the girl that made the box share the lunch with them. Every year since she was sixteen, Levi had bid and won Cecily's box. And unbeknownst to Levi, all these years, Cecily had been in love with him. He was kind to her, often through the years he had shown her attention, but he was five years older than she was and she had been a child when he was a man. And then when she became old enough for him to notice her, she was in too much trouble to even think of him or any other man. She could never think of loving or marrying Levi now she would ruin any man she chose to love. She wasn't free, she would never be free, and Levi Tucker was lost to her before he ever had the chance to find her.

Sadness filled Cecily's eyes as she sat and thought of Levi. He would never want her now even if she were free to give him her heart. Two years ago, when she was only seventeen years old, Bernard Calhoun had appeared to everyone in the community to be courting her, and it appeared as well that she was allowing him to court her. Bernard was not a good man. He was not a well-respected man as Levi was. And she had wanted nothing to do with him. Everyone in Cherry Lake had thought, and many had expressed that Cecily Walker was a fool for giving a man like Bernard the time of day she had known that she was a fool to give Bernard the time of day and she had never wanted anything to do with the evil scoundrel. But Cecily had done what she had to do. She always would do what she had to do. It was too late for regret, except where Levi was concerned. She had lost the only man that had ever mattered to her, the only man that she was certain she would or could ever love she had lost all of her hopes and dreams of Levi Tucker. And Bernard Calhoun had complete control over her life, and he had for more than two full years.

Levi Tucker always sat in the very back pew of the Baptist Church, and he was one of the first people to leave the building every Sunday after services. He liked to stand alone in the churchyard and watch his friends and neighbors file outside, most of all he liked to watch Cecily Grace Walker come out of the double doors, her beautiful crystal clear blue eyes often met his eyes, and she would smile that sweet, gentle smile he adored. Often he would go to her, and they would talk, he ached to be near her in any way that he could be near her.

Today Levi had gotten truly blessed, today he had Cecily sitting beside him, and he could look down at her all through the church service. He had even been able to hold her hand for a moment, her hand was soft, and he knew he could have held her hand for hours.

Levi thanked the good Lord that the Reverend Bidwell seemed to have a lot to say and that church was lasting longer than it usually did. He felt that it was right and wonderful to have Cecily sitting beside him. He wanted Cecily beside him always.

Yet, Levi knew that Cecily rarely noticed him beyond anything other than as a good friend these days. Even though they had lived within a mile of each other all their lives, and their parents had been best friends for more than thirty years, she never gave him any indication that he could or should attempt to court her. He used to see her every day until his sister married and moved away, now he would only see her after church and pray that she might speak to him, even if for only a moment. Cecily was always polite to him, always distant, but Levi wanted more from Cecily than her good manners, he wanted Cecily to see him as a man, as a man that was in love with her and wanted to spend every waking hour in her company.

Levi looked down at Cecily and lost himself in his thoughts of her. he wished that she knew just how much he did think of her. Her father's property and his property met at both the south and west and even to the north part way between the lake and a grove of trees. Even though Daniel Walker was thirty years older than Levi, they got along well as Daniel bred some of the finest horses in North Florida and Levi knew and loved horses. Cecily's father had a lot in common with Levi, and they spent time together talking. Levi had wanted to see more of Cecily than of her father, but the sad fact was, he never saw Cecily away from church. She kept to herself, and he felt like she was avoiding him, and all he wanted was Cecily, all he wanted was to see her, to talk to her, to love her, he could love her a lifetime and longer. She could be everything to him.

Levi would never forget the moment that he knew that he was in love with her. They had been down at the lake with his sister and Clemmie Floyd. The girls were only thirteen and fourteen years old. He had been chasing them with a garden snake, teasing them and playing and Cecily had run away from him, her hair loose from her braid and long down her back. She had turned and looked at him with a huge smile on her face and he had stopped, he had stared at her and then he had walked up to her throwing the snake on the ground, and he stood over her smiling at her as she was smiling up at him. And he knew in that instant that he would wait, he would wait for Cecily to grow up, fall in love with him and marry him.

The Reverend Bidwell finally wound down his sermon on damnation, and Levi stood with Cecily to leave the church. She blushed when she reached the doors and shook the Reverend's hand, the Reverend gave her a warning to not be late to church again in his booming loud voice, and she turned an even brighter red.

Levi followed Cecily from the church and once outside, she turned around to wait for her father to join her. Her father had been on time, and Daniel had sat in their usual place in the front of the church. Cecily saw Levi standing very close and didn't move, nor did she offer him a smile; she only stared at the man that she had loved for most of her life. A man that she knew she could never have for her own.

Levi saw the sadness that touched Cecily's face when she saw him, and he felt his heart twist inside of his chest. Cecily should never be sad, he thought. She was too beautiful to be sad. Her heavy dark brown hair was artfully arranged on top of her head. Her heart-shaped face had high cheekbones, and she had wide beautiful crystal clear blue eyes, her eyes were framed by the longest lashes that Levi had ever seen on anyone. And Levi knew that he could stand here like an idiot for the rest of his life and stare at Cecily Walker. He loved her. She was the only woman that he had ever loved and that he ever wanted to love.

"I'm so sorry that I embarrassed you, Cecily," Levi said as he took a step toward her thinking that the sadness on her face was his fault for having made her look like a fool in church this morning.

A smile touched Cecily's beautiful sweet face as she took a step toward Levi, his heart slammed into his chest to have her so near to him. "I made myself embarrassed, Levi. I won't be late for church again." Her soft southern voice filled Levi's ears. He loved even the sound of her voice. "How have you been?" she asked as the cool March wind brushed against her face causing a thick strand of her long hair to fall free and down her back.

"I can't complain, Cecily," Levi answered in his deep husky voice and twirled his hat in his hands nervously. He did not want her to leave him. He liked talking to Cecily. He could talk to Cecily all day every day because she was the love of his life. "How have you been?" was all he could think to say to her and felt dumb, but then, Levi knew he was dumb.

"I'm just fine. Daddy told me that you had a big shipment of timber go out east on the train last week." Cecily could see that Levi was nervous and she hoped that she hadn't embarrassed him earlier in the church by falling into his lap, of course, she would not have been in his lap if he hadn't pulled her there, she thought.

"Hard work never hurt a man," Levi said and felt like kicking himself for saying something so stupid to Cecily. He knew that Cecily was smart, that she loved to read and read a lot of books while he could only deal with numbers. He had tried to learn to read all through school, but he just could not seem to learn. And now words on paper just didn't seem so important to him when he had someone that he trusted to make out orders and read for him while he did the accounting and physical work.

"One of your cows got into my garden last week," Cecily said, bringing Levi's attention back to her and away from his fault. "She ate nearly half of my greens before I could chase her out."

"I'm sorry, Cecily," Levi said and sounded truly upset. He never wanted to be the cause of any trouble for Cecily. He wanted to make her happy. He wanted to make her his wife.

"It doesn't matter," Cecily said and reached out taking a gentle hold of Levi's hand, a smile on her face meant only for him. "There's still plenty of time for me to plant more greens and the cow liked them better than Daddy does anyway." Levi stared down at her hand touching his, Cecily was touching him, and he felt a heat spread throughout his whole body, her smile was taking his breath away when he looked upon her face. "Besides, I milked the cow real good after I got her out of my garden and Daddy does like cream," Cecily continued to speak and smile as she looked up into Levi's deep dark blue eyes.

Levi hardly heard a word that Cecily said to him after she took a hold of his hand. Her hand was soft and small in his own large and calloused hand, her skin pale while his skin was dark. Levi thought that even Cecily's hands were beautiful. And Cecily had never touched him before, nor had he touched her, except in his dreams.

"The next time one of my cows gets into your garden, you can keep it Cecily," Levi said forcing his eyes back to her face.

"Levi, if I kept every one of your cows that got into my garden, I would own your whole herd inside of two years," Cecily gave a soft laugh and let go of his hand while taking a step back and away from him. She could not love him. She could not have him. Touching him was causing her heart to burn with the pain of her reality, Levi Tucker was forbidden to her always.

"My cows bother you that much Cecily?" Levi asked in surprise and in disappointment that she had let go of his hand and stepped away from him. "I didn't know. I'll pen them up." Levi looked so serious in what he said that Cecily had to laugh.

"You have more than fifty cows, if you penned them all up," she broke off speaking and gave him another small laugh while shaking her head. "Let the cows alone, Levi. I'll milk them, and I don't mind running them out of my garden. If you were to pen anything up, I suppose that it should be my garden." Cecily watched the play of emotions on Levi's handsome face and sighed. He was so nice, both to look at and in personality. He was too good for her. If only she hadn't been a fool she might even now be his wife and know his love. But a fool is what she had been and she had to stop thinking of Levi in the way that she always seem to want and need to think about him.

"How's your sister?" Cecily asked trying to dismiss her private hopeless dreams of Levi Tucker. She could never have him. She had lost all hope of ever having him and dreaming of him only caused her heart to ache inside of her chest.

"Sarah's good now," Levi spoke of his sister and relaxed a little, he did like talking to Cecily. "The baby had her worn out some the last time I was down in Madison for a visit, but she was happy. She named her little boy, Frankie."

"The next time that Daddy goes to Madison, I'm planning on going with him and visiting Sarah," Cecily looked into Levi's dark eyes and thought that they were the most beautiful color that eyes could be, the blue almost seemed black, they were so dark. Once he had been a good friend to her, she missed his friendship, she missed what she could have had with him, but Levi deserved better than her. Levi deserved a wife that was not only beautiful but smart as well. She was not smart, not after she had allowed herself to be used as she had.

"Hello Levi," Daniel Walker said as he joined his neighbor and daughter standing outside the church.

"Mr. Walker," Levi said and shook the older man's hand. His time alone with Cecily was up, Levi knew, and he wondered if he would be alone with her again anytime soon. He wished that he could have her alone to himself for a lifetime. He felt like he had wanted her for a lifetime. Cecily didn't seem to want him any other way beyond a friend. If only, he thought.

"I heard that you had a big shipment of timber go out the other day. I told Cecily I have never known a man with your business sense. Timber, cattle, horses and the sawmill. You must stay busy." Daniel looked from his neighbor to his daughter. He knew that Levi Tucker was deeply fond if not completely in love with his beautiful Cecily and he knew his daughter was and had been for a long time, in love with Levi Tucker.

"I bought some land up in Brooks County, Georgia last week," Levi said. "I have men planting it in pine trees right now. If I rotate the trees like I plan too, I'll always have plenty of pines ready to cut. That shipment that I sent out last week was of trees I had to thin out so that the smaller ones could grow."

"You're a smarter man than your Daddy was, Levi. Ethan cut today all that he could and had nothing for tomorrow. But then, your Daddy had his beef and horses, and they were his first love," Daniel said as he took Cecily's arm and pulled his daughter close. "Come over and see us sometime, Levi. You're always welcome. Maybe you could come to supper one night this week?" Daniel looked down at Cecily's head and felt it was up to him to get these two together. He wanted that for his only child, she would be safe in Levi's care. "Are you free on Tuesday night?" Daniel asked not seeing his daughter blush and very aware of the smile on Levi's face.

"Yes, I'm free. If it's alright with Cecily that I come," Levi looked down into her crystal eyes and thought he could drown in the pool of those beautiful large eyes.

More than anything in this world, Cecily wanted Levi to come to dinner. It was just dinner, not like they were courting. She knew he was forbidden to her, but just to be in his company, to listen to her father and Levi talk, to get to know him better, there was no harm in that. "Yes, please do come," Cecily said softly knowing that she could only be his friend and yet wanting so much more.

Levi took her hand and smiled into those eyes that melted his hear. Then he looked at her father with a wide grin. "Thank you, sir." Daniel shook his hand and said he'd look forward to dinner Tuesday night before he guided his daughter to their buggy in the far corner of the churchyard. Cecily looked back over her shoulder at Levi, and he was smiling at her, she did not return the smile, the sadness was touching her eyes again, Levi thought. She had been such a bright and happy girl, Levi thought, her laughter was often heard in their little circle of friends. Then she took up with that no good Bernard, and after he left her, she lost her laughter and her smile. Levi wondered if she was still in love with Bernard, that was one of the main reasons he'd not made the move to court her, was that sadness for the man she had lost and still loved?

Levi lifted up his hand to wave as his eyes met and held Cecily's. He almost lost his breath when her small hand lifted up to wave back. She was so beautiful he thought as he watched her father lift her up and into their buggy. For a brief moment it hit him that he might not be smart enough for Cecily, she wasn't just beautiful, she was bright and witty and intelligent. Would she want a dumb man like himself for a husband? Levi mounted his horse with a frown and started toward his home, he may be a dumb man, but he knew how to work, and he did work hard. He also had money enough to take care of himself and any woman that he chose for a wife for two lifetimes. And he wondered if he could keep the fact that he couldn't read a secret from her forever. He hoped he could he knew he would try.

Daniel walker looked at his daughter's bowed head as he guided their buggy home. Cecily looked tired and too sad, she was also nervous and anxious, and Daniel had to reach out and take a hold of her hand. He felt anxious himself. He could not save his Cecily anymore than he could stop what was happening to her. They were both trapped by the evil of Bernard Calhoun.

"Did you leave the money where he would be sure to find it?" Daniel asked his daughter, and Cecily nodded her head. "Well, he has almost all of our money now." Cecily again nodded her head. "Maybe he'll leave us alone for a little while at the least."

"Let's not talk about it, Daddy. Please." Cecily turned her large crystal clear eyes onto her father's face. Daniel forced a smile for her sake. He could not let her see what this situation was doing to him. He could not let her see the pain that he was in from their endless trouble. Daniel knew that his daughter was scared, that she had been scared for a long time. He was scared for her. He was scared for himself.

"I think that Levi would like to court you, Cecily." Daniel saw his daughter shake her head hard from side to side. "Levi likes you, and a lot. He's a fine man sweetie.

"Daddy," Cecily's voice sounded like she was crying and she leaned her head against her father's shoulder. "If only things were different." Her father rested his cheek on the top of her head and thought the same thing. "Levi is a wonderful man, Daddy and I've always liked him so much, but as things are, my feelings for Levi can do neither him nor I any good." She knew that she would only bring trouble to Levi, she never wanted to give Levi her troubles, she loved him, with all of her heart and all of her soul, she could no more hurt him then she could hurt herself.

"I'll find some way out of this mess for you, Cecily." Her father had said these words many times before to her. She knew that he would never find a way out of this mess that she had made. She was trapped, and so was her father. She had trapped them both with her naivety and stupidity her trusting nature had forced them into a world of terror for the past two years.

"There is no way out, Daddy. You know that and so do I. And I can't even think of Levi, I'm not free to be anything more to him than a friend. If I tried to be more to him, I would destroy him as I'm destroying you. And in the end, I'll be ruined and unable to show my face to anyone ever again."

"But if Levi really loves you and cares for you, he might could help," Daniel said as he pulled his daughter closer and felt her head shaking against his shoulder.

"No, Daddy. Levi would pay the same price as you for my stupidity. And anything that Levi feels for me would soon turn to disgust once he saw what I have done. He would hate me, Daddy. I couldn't stand it if Levi hated me," not when I love him as much as I do, she silently added to herself

"You didn't do anything wrong, Cecily," her father said in an angry voice. Cecily knew her father wasn't angry with her. He never had been. Her father understood what had been done to her. Her father knew that she was not bad. He made her believe that she was still good. Cecily wanted to be good.

"Yes, Daddy, I did do something wrong," Cecily said after a few moments thought. "I trusted someone that I never should have trusted, and it has cost you and me almost everything that we have and more than we could have afforded." Cecily hid her face against her father's shoulder and let him comfort her. He had given her comfort often these past two years, and she was so thankful to have him standing by her in this storm, to be supporting her and not blaming her. His love was as any father's love for his child should be – unconditional.

"The only mistake that you made was trusting the wrong person. I'll find some way out of this mess for us both, daughter. I promise you that I'll find some way out of this sorry mess." Daniel held his daughter tighter.

"There is no way out. And you're almost broke from paying for my stupid mistake." There was nothing that her good, brave father could do to save her, except pay all of his money and then sell all that he owned and pay more. Two years ago they had a cook and a maid and farm help, now she and her father did those jobs. And her father, in the past two years, his hair had turned white as snow, he was far too thin, and he looked as sad as she did most of the time.

Daniel's money was almost all gone in his attempt to save Cecily, and he was breaking his back doing work that he hadn't done since he was a young man. Daniel needed more money if he didn't find some and soon, he would not be able to go on protecting his daughter. Her mother's jewelry had been sold long ago. Half of his horses were gone as well, soon there would be nothing left. If Levi's cows didn't get into the garden every week, they wouldn't even have milk.

Cecily thought of Levi Tucker and mourned for what more was lost to her. She could have loved Levi forever, and she could have made him a good wife, they would have been happy together, she was certain of that. Now she had only her father and work and fear. Cecily closed her eyes and thought of the goodness and beauty of Levi. She saw his handsome face with his wide mouth and the dimple in the center of his chin and when he smiled his eyes seem to light up with his inner beauty. His hair was a deep dark brown parted on the side with bangs that fell wistfully to the side of his forehead. She could have loved Levi until she died. Now he was lost to her and to even think of a life without him hurt so much that she wanted to cry her heart out.

Cecily looked up at her father, and she knew that she was ruining his life. She had already ruined his life. She closed her eyes and thought her father would be better off if she were to leave him, but she had nowhere to go even if her father were to allow her to leave him. And she knew, her Daddy could not save her, no one could save her, not even Levi Tucker, a man that may well love her at this moment, but he would hate her when what she had done became public. And her sin would become public if she were to run out of money.

Her father stopped the buggy and held her close within both arms when he heard her sob…

Levi rode home alone and lost in his thoughts. Cecily Walker was every dream he had ever had. He knew that one day he was going to marry Cecily and spend the rest of his life looking into her crystal eyes. When Cecily had turned seventeen, he had meant to make his move toward his goal of having her for his wife, but Bernard Calhoun had started calling on her and Levi had to back off and wait and hope that whatever was between the two would fade and Cecily would notice him. Everyone in the county had feared that Cecily would marry Bernard Calhoun, she was sweet and kind and good, and Bernard was a bully at best. Then one day, Bernard had up and moved his business to Madison and stopped courting Cecily and she had seemed truly heartbroken, so Levi held back and waited for Cecily to forget Bernard, and she had drifted further and further away from him, and Levi didn't know how to bridge the gap that was between them.

Cecily was nineteen years old now. She was alone and seemed to want to be alone. And Levi noticed no other woman. He wanted only to court and wed Cecily. He had fallen in love with her more than five years ago, he had waited for her and today, when she had taken his hand in the churchyard he knew that he had to have her, the time had come to make his move, and he would take her any way he could get her. She would be his wife. He loved her so much.

A cool spring breeze blew the hair off of Levi's forehead as he kicked his horse into a faster pace. The road to his home was red clay, and towering oak trees lined the road to become a canopy as their long branches met in the center. The wind blew through the bright yellow-green leaves, and it sounded as though a thousand people were whispering or perhaps it was the voice of God. The sound was beautiful. The sound filled him up, this place was a glorious place to be, Levi thought as he trotted along thinking of Cecily, he wished to remove the sadness that always seemed to be on her face and make her smile always and smile for him and because of him.

Levi's thoughts turned to his mother, a southern born woman that had hated all Yankees. His father Ethan Tucker had come south after the war because he had fallen in love with the land. Ethan had met Lilly Harris and fallen in love with her right away. Ethan was determined to win the love of the southern beauty that had hated him for having fought on the wrong side of the war.

Ethan had his work cut out for him right from the start. Lilly had hated him at first sight, or so Levi had been told by his father. When Lilly's father was going to lose his farm for back taxes being owed, Lilly had married Ethan Tucker so that he could save her father's farm and preserve her families way of life. Ethan knew that she hated her Yankee husband, but he was determined to win her love. He had to court his Lilly after their marriage, and he had thanked God that they had married in the late summer as he was able to bring her wild flowers he picked himself for her every single day.

"The only reason to ever make a fool of yourself is over the love you have for a woman," Ethan had told Levi years ago. He then assured his son that he had made a fool of himself trying to win the love of his Lilly. "Your Mama has that deep dark hair the color of yours, Levi, and she wore her hair in a long braid down her back. She has those eyes like yours as well, deep dark pools of innocence. I love her eyes. I wanted your Mama to love me so much that I thought I would die every time she turned me away." Ethan had looked at Levi's mother in the telling of their story, and the couple shared a smile.

Levi could close his eyes right now and see his mother's gentle, sweet smile. He could never imagine his mother hating anyone, and certainly not his father. "Do you love Papa now?" Levi remembered worriedly asking his mother this question long ago when he had been a boy.

"With all my heart, Levi," she had answered him while staring at her husband. "Remember always my darling son what I tell you now. Love and hate are both strong emotions. Without love there can be no hate. And besides, when I married your father, I didn't really hate him, I was just lost in my own troubles, and I needed to save my Papa's farm. And Levi, you Daddy, he is a good man, one day you'll be a good man too, and some woman will love you like I love your father. With all of her heart and all of her soul and for all eternity."

Levi had loved his parents more than he could ever say and he missed them still every day. He kept remembering their love when he thought of Cecily Walker. He wanted a love with her like his parents had. Today in church, he had made a fool of himself over her, and he knew that now he had to have her. He also knew he could not rush her. He had to wait like his father had waited for his mother. One day Cecily would love him, and he would marry her in the name of love. He had never liked the fact that his mother had married his father for his money.

Levi smiled thinking of having Cecily for his wife. They could ride horseback on these beautiful tree-lined clay roads. He would race her and jump fences with her and see her smiling at him as he let her win their race, he knew how well she handled horses. He would take her down to the lake to swim and kiss her and make a part of the lake their own special place. He would hold her hand in church, he would lift her in and out of the buggy, and he would come up behind her while she cooked his dinner and kiss her neck and they would forget the food and make love instead. His smile grew as he thought of their one day having children, sitting on the porch in the dusk of the evening watching their children play, a little girl that was just like her mother and a son so much like him. His dream might seem simple, but for Levi, it was a dream he wanted to come true.

Chapter Two

Cecily stood looking at the sunrise beyond the fields to the east as the wind blew the few clouds in the sky away to the west. She loved the sunrise and the morning, all of her life she had been up early and waiting to see the moon leave the sky and the sun enter that same sky turning the world orange and bright. She wished that she were free to enjoy the world as she used too. She wished that her father was free with her. She wished for some way out of the mess that she had made of her life, but she knew, wishing was like dreaming. Dreams never came true, and wishes blew away in the breeze too soon and forgotten in the day. Living was too difficult sometimes to care about a wish, Cecily thought.

Cecily turned to see her father standing stooped over in the yard just beyond the house, and she started to walk toward him. Her father had always loved the dawn of the day she had learned her love of a sunrise from him. She knew that her father was scared for her and that he was worried. They were without money now, all he had was his few horses, and those horses would not last much longer. She thought of Levi and almost moaned out loud. If only she could be sure of Levi's love for her, she would go to him now and tell him everything. Then she stopped and stood still. Reality was cruel, Levi could never love her with the truth, any love that might be between them would be based on a lie because she knew that she could never tell him the truth. She was alone in the truth.

Money was Cecily's only salvation. Money was the answer to all her prayers and wishes. And she had no money. Her father had lost everything because of her. She had brought about his ruin with Bernard Calhoun controlling her. And here her father stood in their yard looking far older than his fifty-seven years of age. She hated what she had done to him. She hated what Bernard had made her do to her father.

"Daddy," she said gently and touched her father's arm. "Daddy, please, don't pay another cent, let this end for you at least." Daniel gasped and turned to face his only child while shaking his head.

"Your whole life would be ruined here if I don't pay, Cecily. No, I cannot let," his daughter covered his mouth gently with her hand to stop his words.

"Listen to me, Daddy. Let him do his worst to me. Let this end now. I don't care about myself anymore. I love you. I'd rather be ruined forever in this life than see you hurt the way you are by all of this. Daddy, listen to me. I know who and what I am, what Bernard did to me didn't define who I am. And you know my truth. Please, Daddy. You're all I have in this whole world that really matters to me. You mean everything to me," Cecily looked deep into her father's eyes. "I love you, Daddy. Thank you for trying to save me all these years, thank you for being here for me. But it's time for you to stop hurting and allow me to take my punishment and be done with this waiting and being afraid all the time." Daniel grabbed his daughter's hand and forced it away from his mouth so that he could speak sense to her.

"Ah, Cecily, my sweet child," Daniel said as he brushed her hair back from her face with a pained expression on his face. "You are my world. You mean more to me then all these simple earthly goods I've ever known. You always have. You're my only child. I'd die to keep you safe." A tear fell from his daughter's clear crystal eyes, and he brushed the tear away with the pad of his thumb. "I was just standing here thinking. Of everything that I've done in this life, of everything that I am, you are the best part of me. You're the only thing in this whole world that I want. Let's sell this place, Cecily, let's sell out and go away from here for good. Whatever Bernard might do to you won't matter. We won't be here to care."

"Daddy," she said his name before she fell into his warm embrace. "You're the best Daddy ever." Daniel clung to his child and squeezed his eyes shut tight thanking God they had one another, that's all they really ever had needed.

"I bet that Levi would buy this place and be happy to have it," Daniel said as he looked out at his land over his daughter's head. "We have some fine trees, Levi would probably give us a thousand dollars if I sold him my horses also. I want you safe more than anything else, sweetie. And I'm not too old to start again. We would make out just fine I know we would." Daniel looked back down into his daughter's eyes.

"I can find a job too," Cecily said as she looked back up at her father trying to give him a smile. He pulled her to him, and she hugged him tight with a real smile for the first time in a long time.

"That's my good girl," Daniel hugged his daughter closer.

"I'm so sorry for everything, Daddy," she almost whispered, she spoke too low with the shame that she felt. "Please, forgive me."

"There is not one thing to forgive you for Cecily. What was done was done to you. You didn't ask for any of this to happen any more than I did. Besides, it could have happened to any trusting, gently bred girl. My only regret is that I didn't take you away from here two years ago. I never should have waited as long as I have. I let that no good bastard bleed me dry and scare you night and day with his threats. But that's all over with now. We'll sell out to Levi and go away from here as soon as we can. No more fear." Daniel thought of Levi and wished things had gone another way for Levi and his Cecily.

"No more fear, Daddy." Cecily tried to smile again, but instead, she felt like she wanted to cry. This was the only home she'd ever known in her whole life, and she loved it here.

"Then you don't mind leaving? You don't have regret over not giving Levi a chance?" Daniel pulled his daughter from his arms so he could look down into her face and read her thoughts. Cecily looked away from her father and closed her eyes for brief second thinking of Levi, her heart crying out for him and what might have been. Regret touched her face, and Daniel saw that regret in her eyes when she opened them again. He knew that his daughter loved Levi. He had known of her feelings for years. Cecily looked up at her father and tried to smile into his loving, kind face. Levi was a dream that could never come true her father must know that as well as she did. "I see," Daniel read his daughter's mind. "Levi is coming to dinner tomorrow night. I'll ask him to buy this place from me. Then, I'll even let him name the price. He's a good man. He won't cheat us. He would have been a good husband for you too, Cecily," and a good son to me, Daniel added to himself.

"Would have been," Cecily said softly. "But it's too late, Daddy. And besides, Levi is too good for me the way that I am now." Cecily turned to leave her father, but Daniel reached out and grabbed a tight hold of her arm and forced her to look back at him.

"Let me go to Levi right now Cecily." His daughter started shaking her head and didn't stop. "Please, daughter. Let me tell him everything. He'll know what to do to stop this madness. He's young and strong, and he can protect you in ways I cannot."

"No, Levi can't know anything about this Daddy. He'll hate me. I can take anything in this world, but I cannot stand even the thought of Levi knowing about this. I can't stand the thought of Levi hating me Daddy. Let's just sell this place and go away, never come back, start over new somewhere."

"If I had been any sort of a man, I'd have taken a gun and killed Bernard for what he did and is doing to you," Daniel grieved.

"You're a Christian man, Daddy. A good and kind man that I admire and love; you wouldn't and couldn't harm anyone." Cecily was glad that her father was the way he was, she herself could never do harm to another as well.

"But Levi," Daniel tried to argue.

"The only way to stop Bernard is with money. Bernard has taken all of your money daddy; if Levi were to get involved, he would lose all of his money as well." Cecily shook her head again, and her father listened to her. "No, Daddy. We are leaving here, and I promise I'll find some way to make up to you for what I've done."

"You haven't done anything, sweetie," her father said sadly. "But I'll do as you ask. Tomorrow we'll sell this place to Levi and leave here. Tomorrow." Daniel let his daughter go and stood thinking of Levi Tucker and his daughter. Daniel felt certain that Levi loved his daughter and he knew she loved Levi. He wouldn't tell her, he'd quietly saddle his horse and in the morning ride over to Levi's sawmill. Once there he would talk to Levi and not about buying this place. He would tell Levi everything; he would ask for Levi to help him in trying to protect his daughter. He should have done this at the start. He'd also go to the Reverend Bidwell and inform him of all that was being done to him and his Cecily tomorrow. Cecily might have some shame to bear over this, but she wouldn't lose her home, and if Daniel explained it the right way to Levi, he just might still love Cecily.

Daniel felt tired and old. He didn't want to die and leave Cecily unprotected. He wanted to leave her safe; he wanted to leave her happy. She would be both of those things with Levi. Their only hope was Levi, and he was a good man.

Cecily stood on the porch and saw her father still standing in the yard lost deep in his thoughts. She knew that he had always hoped that she and Levi would someday marry. Because of one second in time, she would never have her Levi, and her father's hopes were at an end, along with all of her dreams. The truth of what she had done must never be known; the truth of Cecily Walker was ugly and dirty and a terrible shame. The truth would make Levi turn her away in pure horror; she would rather leave here than lose the only man that she had ever loved in her life with the truth of what she had done. If only she could go back in time, Cecily thought. She would have stayed away from Bernard Calhoun and run to Levi when she had been seventeen and hope that he would take her for his wife. She thought that he might have. But it was all too late now. She would miss Levi forever; she hoped that he might miss her as well.

Cecily saw her father grab a hold of his right arm and stumble forward a step. When her father turned pale her first thought was that he was ill, and then Daniel fell down, and Cecily gave a cry of alarm. She ran to her father calling out his name, but he didn't move, and she fell to her knees beside him.

"Daddy!" she screamed as she fought to roll her father over onto his back and she nearly fell on to him doing so. "Daddy, what's wrong?" she cried and pushed and finally her father was on his back, and she could see his face.

Daniel Walker's lips were turning blue; a spittle ran from the corner of his mouth and down his chin. His eyes were open wide, and Cecily could see, her father saw nothing, his eyes were open wide. Her father was dead. "Oh Daddy," Cecily cried out and fell onto her father's chest crying. This could not be happening, she had heard of people falling down dead, but not her father. Her father could not just drop dead, not now when they were leaving. They were selling this place and leaving; they were going away, they were going to be safe. Her father could not die; she needed him to keep her safe. She needed his understanding and his love. Without her father, she would be lost and alone for the rest of her lie.

"Don't leave me," she cried and begged and shook her father's too still body. But it was too late. Daniel's life was over; her father was safe from the terrible trouble that she had brought into their lives. "Please," Cecily cried as she laid her head on her father's chest. "Please, Daddy. I can't live without you. I need you." Cecily cried deep soul-wracking sobs. In one second she had lost her father, she had lost the only thing that stood between herself and the certain ruin of her life. She was on her own now, and she was afraid. She had been afraid for more than two long years. A terrible trembling took hold of her body as she sat back on her heels and screamed at her father not to leave her. She shook him and begged him to come back. This was a bad dream she was having. Daniel Walker couldn't be dead. Despite her screams, despite the cries of his only child, Daniel Walker was dead, and at last, he was safe from this world.

Grant Whittaker was the foreman of Levi's sawmill; he was also courting Cecily's best friend, Clemmie Floyd. Grant saw Levi coming into the sawmill and went to him. "I don't suppose you've heard the news?" he asked his boss and best friend. Levi shook his head before asking,

"What news?"

"Daniel Walker died yesterday," his words caused Levi to take a step back in shocked surprise, he was supposed to be having dinner with Cecily and Mr. Walker tonight.

"Cecily?" Levi managed to say the name of the one he was most concerned about with hearing this news.

"She's pretty bad off, Levi. Clemmie and I were out for a buggy ride yesterday morning and heard her screaming. I left Clemmie with Cecily and went for the doctor. Poor Mr. Walker, the doctor said he died in an instant, never knew what hit him. Cecily is devastated as you can imagine." Levi heard the pain in Grant's voice; he knew his foreman was still hurting over the loss of his own father and telling him about this couldn't be easy.

"I'll go get cleaned up and go over there," Levi said to Grant and hurried from the sawmill thinking only of his Cecily and the suffering pain she must be in right now. Cecily loved her father like Levi loved his own father; death was too final.

Grant watched Levi walk away before he turned toward the breeze and let the wind touch his face. He knew that Levi loved Cecily. He was Levi's best friend, and he had known for years how Levi felt about Cecily Walker. Grant thought of his own father dying just weeks ago and felt a rush of tears sting his eyes. He hadn't told Levi how he and Clemmie had found Cecily lying on top of her father and crying herself sick begging Daniel to come back to her. Just remembering how they had found Cecily yesterday made Grant feel sick with grief. He had found his father; his grief was too raw, too deep.

A mockingbird cried constant from a nearby tree, and Grant looked up, his brown eyes allowed his tears to fall, tears that he quickly brushed away and he glanced around to make sure no one saw him crying. Maybe some good would come from Daniel Walker's death. Maybe Cecily would see Levi loved her and wanted her. Maybe she would give Levi what he wanted. Grant knew, what Levi wanted was Cecily.

Grant took a deep breath before he went to his horse. Clemmie was still with Cecily, Clemmie had been his lifeline these past weeks, and he needed her. He would go to Cecily's house and wait to see Clemmie. Maybe she would let him hold her and take away his pain. He hated death; he hated graveyards. Grant loved Clemmie.

Levi went into his house and changed his clothes. Ollie Tool, his housekeeper, stopped his mad dash out the front door by gently grabbing a hold of his arm and he turned his deep dark blue eyes onto his maid as she gave him a sympathetic look. Ollie knew that Levi had thought a lot of Daniel Walker and that he cared for the daughter, the poor daughter that was alone now that her father had passed. "It ain't right for you to be going over there empty-handed Mister Levi," Ollie said to a man that she had helped bring into this world and raise, he meant the world to her. "I got one of the stable hands hitching up the buggy right now boy, and a ham and some beans and freshly made rolls all packed up to go over to Miss Cecily's house." Levi nodded his head and took a deep breath to help slow himself down. "Half of the town will probably be over there about right now, and the other half is on the way — folks to feed. You come to help me get this food in the buggy," Ollie ordered.

"Thank you, Ollie." Levi went with her and helped as she had told him to do, thankful he had her to make things run smoothly in his home. When he climbed into his buggy, food was on the floor at his feet covered in heavy pots and wrapped tightly into baskets with clean cloths.

"If Miss Cecily needs anything," Ollie called after him, "You be sure to see that she gets it, Mister Levi. I always did love that little gal." Ollie saw Levi lift a hand in a wave and knew that he had heard her. "And you tell her I'm keeping her in my prayers!" She yelled out louder before Levi took a turn in the road and disappeared.

Mister Levi should have married Miss Cecily years ago; Ollie thought as she made her way back inside the house. And he would have if that no good Bernard Calhoun hadn't come around Miss Cecily and made her not notice Mister Levi. Bernard Calhoun was gone now and so was Miss Cecily's father, maybe now Miss Cecily would let Mister Levi court her. Maybe Mister Levi would soon have a wife for his home. Ollie decided to pray for the happy event as well as for Miss Cecily's sad loss.

Levi was shocked by all the buggies that filled up Daniel Walker's yard. Ollie had been wrong, he thought, the whole town was here now. He pulled his buggy near a tree and got down, knowing that Daniel Walker was well known and well liked in the community it really came as no surprise that the yard was so full. Daniel had often loaned people money and horses at planting time, he had been a good neighbor, a loving parent and above all, a God fearing Christian man. Levi's own father had been one of Daniel's best friends, the men thought alike and often would pray together for others suffering in their community, he wished he was more like his father and Mr. Walker, his faith wasn't as strong, and he had the weakness of being unable to read. Levi felt a deep sense of loss as he had been so close to Daniel Walker all of his life, he made his way to the house hurting for Cecily and for everyone in their community that they'd lost this fine man.

"Hello Levi," Jamie Liston took Levi's hand in a firm shake when they met in the front yard. "I see your buggy is loaded with food; your Ollie is a good cook. Want me to help you get it to the house?" Levi nodded his head as they moved back to his buggy, his head turned to look at the porch of the house.

"Have you seen Cecily?" Levi asked Jamie as he took the pot of beans and the basket of bread from the buggy leaving Jamie to grab the rest of the food. Levi saw the crowd on the porch and even inside the house through the window.

"The women have her surrounded in the kitchen," Jamie said as Levi put the food on a long trestle style table in the dining room. "Clemmie's been with her since yesterday morning. Grant had taken Clemmie out for a ride, and they came over here and found Mr. Walker dead. Clemmie said that Cecily lay on top of her father and was screaming bloody murder at him to not leave her. Grant went and got the Doctor even though he knew it was too late to do anything for Mr. Walker and half of the women in town followed him back out here. They've kept Cecily safe from the crowd ever since this morning."

"Grant told me she was devastated," Levi said while looking at the closed kitchen door and wishing that he could be with Cecily for just a few moments.

"The doctor said Mr. Walker died right away. I heard Clemmie tell some of the folks that Cecily didn't sleep a wink last night."

Jamie followed Levi back into the yard as he spoke, many of the people in the crowd had said Levi's name in greeting and reached out to pat his shoulder or touch his hand. Levi was well liked also and admired, people knew that he would help anyone in need, even give the shirt off his back if need be. Jamie lit a cigarette offering one to Levi. "They got Mr. Walker all laid out in a coffin in the parlor. I saw him, and he looks real good."

"He's dead, Jamie," Levi said as he smoked the cigarette. "I doubt the man cares now how he looks."

"Well, I'm sure his looking good matters to Cecily," Jamie said before he tossed his cigarette away into the grass beyond the buggies. "I wonder what she'll do now that her father is dead."

"I guess we'll just have to wait and see," Levi said before leaving Jamie under the tree in the front yard and going to the stables. He had known Jamie all of his life, along with Grant and Jon Hyde they had all gone to school together and now Grant was his foreman at the sawmill and Jamie was his crew leader for cutting the pine trees and seeing the wood was dried out properly. Jamie was a small man, but he was built sturdy and worked hard. The only thing that Levi didn't like about Jamie was that he talked too much. No secret was safe with Jamie Liston.

Levi entered Daniel Walker's stables and saw that the stalls had not been cleaned out nor had the horses been given feed and fresh water since the day before. He took off his jacket and reached for the pitchfork. He wanted to do something for Cecily; he would take care of these few horses for her.

After Levi had finished his chore, he went and patted the best horse that Daniel Walker had owned on the neck. The horse was a stud right out of Kentucky, a beautiful animal with a deep dark red coat and a black mane and tail. This horse had been Cecily's father's pride and joy. Levi wondered if Cecily would consider selling him the horse now that her father was gone.

The horse nudged Levi, and he reached into his pocket and pulled out a sugar cube that he held in the palm of his hand. The horse took the sugar and Levi patted the animal's strong neck. He knew he would give Cecily a good price for the horse if she wanted to sell; it was one of the best to be had in the state. He wanted Cecily more than he wanted her horse; Levi thought before he reached for his jacket and left the stables.

Cecily slipped out the back door of her house, Levi saw her as he came out into the yard. He watched her hurry across the field and wondered where she was going, and then he felt himself move and knew, he had to be with her, he had always needed to be with her. His heart was in his throat as he moved swift and sure behind her, she was his dreams; he loved her more than anything.

Cecily walked with her head down, and with no destination in her mind, she just needed to be away from the house for a few moments and try to think what she was going to do. She still could not believe that her father had died. This was some kind of horrible nightmare, and any moment now she would wake up and her father would be there with her, and everything would be all right. Well, maybe not all right, Cecily thought; but certainly not so all wrong. She took a deep breath and almost yawned, she had not slept at all the night before, and the ladies were after her to eat something. Cecily knew that she couldn't eat, she had too much on her mind, and worrying seemed to be easier than trying to force down food right now.

Cecily touched her throat with her fingers and tried to swallow; her throat hurt when she did that, her eyes felt thick and sore, she ached all over and wanted to find someplace where she could hide and gather her thoughts. She was alone now. She was too afraid. She had to run away before it was too late and Bernard Calhoun tried to hurt her worse than he already had.

Levi hurried after Cecily across the green field and hoped that no one would see them together and come after them. He had to be alone with her, just for a little while. Right before they entered the trees he spoke her name, and she stopped, slowly she turned around and faced him. Levi was shocked at the sight of Cecily's face, she appeared far too frail, broken and her eyes looked too large in her small face, those eyes were filled with sadness. Without thought, Levi hurried to Cecily and took both of her hands into his own and held them tight.

"I'm sorry, Cecily," he saw her bottom lip tremble as he said these words.

"Oh, Levi," Cecily breathed his name before she fell against his firm hard chest and he folded her into his loving arms and held her close, his cheek coming to rest on the top of her head. "My Daddy's dead, he's dead," she cried piteously. Levi sighed and knew that Cecily was where she belonged; she felt right being held in his arms. And Cecily almost felt safe. She wouldn't be safe if Levi knew the truth about her.

"I'll do anything I can for you, Cecily," Levi said in a choked voice. He never wanted his Cecily to hurt like this again; he never wanted to let go of her. He wanted to take her home with him and take care of her always. She was his; she would always be his, he adored her.

Cecily knew that she had to let Levi go before he got the wrong idea about them, they could never be anything more than friends, he had to know that, she had to let him know that. For her to be anything more to him would cause them both nothing but certain pain. She knew that he was lost to her; she had to move away from him now.

Levi held her tighter and Cecily took a deep breath; she could smell him, his scent was special, and she would remember this smell always. He was everything to her, but he could be nothing to her. She had to see to his safety; he would not be safe with her; her father hadn't been safe because of her. She pulled herself regrettably from his arms, but he reached for both of her hands, and she let him hold them. "I want to thank you, Levi, you've been a good friend to me and to my Daddy." She looked up at him with those large hurt crystal clear eyes. "I do need to talk with you. Will you walk with me?" Levi nodded his head and let go of her hands; he held the one still though as they walked and Cecily allowed him too even though she knew that she should force him away from her. She had to force him away from her forever.

"Your father was a fine man, Cecily." Levi finally said after they had walked a little way in complete silence.

"I had the best father in the world," Cecily said and stopped to look out at the sun starting to sink to the earth, soon it would be dark, and she would be all alone. "Daddy liked the quiet of the sunrise and the sunset. He was always up early because he said that he liked to watch the sun wake up." She fell quiet for a long few moments, and Levi stood quiet beside her.

And then, she turned and looked up into his dark blue eyes, her wide crystal clear eyes swimming in unshed tears, tears in her eyes because she knew she couldn't be with Levi, she couldn't openly love him or have him love her in return, and she wanted Levi so much, she wanted him for her family now that her father was gone. "Daddy wanted to sell this place to you, Levi. He was going to talk to you about it tonight when you came for dinner." She heard him take a deep, sharp breath and saw him shake his head in denial. "He did want to sell," Cecily said firmly. "We were going away, as soon as possible."

"Why?" Levi asked when he was able too; she had been quiet for some time.

"Because we wanted to start again somewhere new, Levi. Daddy wanted you to buy this place, and now I'm asking you to please buy it from me." Cecily saw Levi's head shake.

"No," Levi said in a haggard voice. "You can't leave me, Cecily. I won't let you go."

"Listen to me, Levi," Cecily said and reached out to hold both of his hands while trying to keep the tears in her eyes from falling, hot, thick tears for her loss of him. "I have to go." Levi stood shocked and silent before her, and she begged him to understand. "Please, Levi. Understand, I have to leave here; I can't stay." His hands tightened on hers as she looked up at his handsome face, she wanted to memorize every part of his face and take the memory with her holding him in her mind's eyes for the rest of her life. He was the most handsome man she had ever known, he was beautiful in her eyes, and he was a man she could never have and would always love.

"I don't want you to leave me, Cecily," Levi said, and she reached up and put her hand on his cheek.

"There can never be anything between us, Levi. I can't hurt you. Please, I'm begging you, please. Don't make me hurt you." He shook his head at her words and held her eyes with his own. She could see that he really did want her; he wanted her as much as she wanted him. Cecily knew that her heart had just cracked right down the middle. "Levi, listen to me, I'm not good enough for you. You deserve the very best."

"The very best for me is you, Cecily," he whispered and leaned his face into the palm of her hand, Cecily held his face tenderly, and he knew that she felt something for him, he could see her caring and concern in her eyes. She had to love him; he needed her to love him more than anything in his life. "I'm not fit for you to wipe your boots on, Levi Tucker. If you only knew what I have done, you would hate me, and I would let you."

"Oh, Cecily. If you are trying to tell me that you gave more to Bernard Calhoun than was correct, I don't care." Cecily removed her hand from his face and looked away from Levi's eyes. "I don't care what you did with Bernard, darlin'. That was over more than two years ago. You can be mine now, now and forever. I love you, Cecily. I've always loved you. I won't ever leave you."

Cecily felt the tears fall from her eyes. Levi had just said the words to her that she had heard him say in her dreams. And she had to turn him away; she must turn away from him. "Bernard used my feelings for him against me, Levi." Cecily wiped her face before she looked back up into his dark eyes.

"Not all men are gentlemen, Cecily. But I am. I fell in love with you years ago, and I love you still. I'd honor you, darlin', you have my word. And I would be honored if you'd have me for your husband."

Cecily gasped at Levi's words; he was killing her with his words. She couldn't be his, and she couldn't have him. "I can't marry you," her voice broke, and the tears rushed from her eyes. "I can't marry you." Levi pulled her into his arms, and she wrapped her arms around his waist and laid her head against his firm, solid chest.

"I love you darlin'. I don't want to live without you. And I don't think that you want to live without me." Cecily shook her head against his chest, and he held her tighter in his arms. She couldn't pull away from him.

"Levi," Cecily said his name as he rested his head on the top of her head. "Love doesn't matter in my situation. I cannot marry you and loving you has nothing to do with the reason why I can't marry you. And please, don't ask me to explain my situation to you because I can't and I won't."

"I'll make you love me, Cecily. I'll make you love me so much that nothing else will matter but our love." Levi felt her head shaking again. He could not lose her, not now when he was certain that she wanted him and needed him as much as he wanted and needed her. He didn't care what he had to do to get her; he knew only that in his heart; he could not let her go; she had to stay with him."

Cecily pulled away from Levi's arms and turned to look at the sinking sun. She should tell him that she didn't love him and never would. But she could not say those words any more than she could reach out and touch that sinking sun that seemed to be within arm's reach. She could never marry Levi; she could never be his wife, to do so would be to destroy him, to earn his hatred for all time when he learned the truth of her and to ruin him as she had ruined her father. He had to see that she meant to sell this place and leave here. He had to see that she could not stay and would not stay. "I can't marry you, Levi." Cecily turned back toward the kindest man that she had ever known. "I can't marry you," she whispered and saw the look on his face, she was hurting him with her words, and she never wanted to hurt him. Better this pain than the other she would bring to him as his wife, she thought. "I'm sorry," she whispered again and took his cheek in the palm of her hand. "Please, you must forgive me."

"I won't let you go, Cecily. I won't buy this place, and I'll keep at you until you agree to marry me. I won't let you go." Cecily gave a sigh when Levi turned his face into her hand and placed a gentle kiss on the palm of her hand.

"Don't make me hurt you," Cecily cried as she turned from him with her palm fisted, his kiss held tight in her hand.

"Then don't leave me," Levi pleaded with her before Cecily turned and walked away from him. She was walking away from her heart, Levi held that organ in his hand, he would have her heart throughout all time and she knew that she would have his heart as well. Levi did love her, and he would have married her, she had lost more than she had known she would lose.

"I have to leave here, Levi," Cecily said as she turned back and saw him still standing where she had left him. The look of pain on his face nearly brought her to her knees. "I cannot stay here," she cried out in an agony over having to hurt him.

Levi lowered his head; he could not watch Cecily walk away from him. And then, he grabbed a deep breath as she flung herself back into his arms. "I'm sorry. I'm so sorry," she said over and over as he pulled her close, she only fell silent when his mouth covered her mouth.

Cecily let Levi kiss her; she knew that she was going to take the memory of this kiss with her wherever she went. His teeth touched hers as his tongue entered her mouth and she moaned deep within herself, that moan going down Levi's throat and feeling as though it gave to him his very life breath. He held her so close that there was not even a tiny space between them, his hands at the small of her back, her arms around his neck. The kiss went on and on, her moans and his moans mingled and became one, he didn't want to ever let this moment end, and he knew he loved her more than he'd ever know, she was in his blood, he couldn't live without her, it was Cecily that made his heartbeat.

After a few long moments, Cecily fought to pull away from Levi, her hands on his chest pushing hard and she was shaking all over as was he. "I have to leave you," she cried. "I can't marry you. I can't love you. Don't make me, Levi. Please, don't make me love you. I cannot love you." Cecily begged of him before she turned and ran away from him.

"Cecily!" he cried out her name, but she didn't look back. She ran from him when he knew that she wanted to stay.

Levi put his face in his hands and stood still for a long few moments; the sun was going further down in distant sky in its quest for another part of the world in which to bring the light of day to. She loved him, he thought. She couldn't leave him. She wanted him as much as he wanted her. Surely once she saw things more clearly after her father's funeral tomorrow, she would come to him again and they would talk, and everything would be as it should be. He would not lose her. He could not lose her. He would take her any way that he could get her. And he would make her love him; he knew he could.

Twilight filled the early night sky, and Levi went to his buggy with thoughts of Cecily and Bernard Calhoun. He had long suspected that Cecily had been more to Bernard than Levi had wanted her to be. Bernard was a charmer; Levi could see how Cecily would fall in love with a man like that even though he wasn't thought much of. And he could see why she gave herself to Bernard if she truly had thought that she loved the no good skunk. Levi had always hated Bernard; now he hated the man even more for what he had been to Cecily and for what he had taken from her. But he hadn't kept her; she could be Levi's. Levi pushed the jealousy that consumed him away with superhuman strength. All he wanted was Cecily. He had never loved anyone like this. He never wanted to be with anyone the way he wanted to be with Cecily Walker.

Levi thought of Bernard Calhoun again; the man had come from a bad home; his parents used others and never had anything that wasn't given to them. They weren't hard working, God-fearing people, Levi knew as did most in the community. Levi thought at the time when Bernard was courting Cecily that he was doing so to make a better name for himself, showing that he had one of the best girls in the county at his side. Bernard was out of Cecily's life now; he had been for more than two years. He didn't believe that Cecily was pining away for Bernard, not when she had kissed him the way that she just did. Levi wouldn't let what Cecily had done with Bernard matter to him. It had nothing to do with Cecily's feelings for him; he would make her see that. She needed him; he would make her see that as well.

Levi was just fixing to get into his buggy and go home when Grant hurried to him and grabbed his arm. "Cecily is asking for you Levi," Levi felt his heart lodged in his throat. "The ladies have been after her to eat all day long and she just told Clemmie that she would eat if you will come in and eat with her." Cecily wanted him, Levi sighed in relief. She would marry him; he would have her soon, this was going to work out, Levi thought and felt hopeful for the first time.

"I guess I had better go in and get something to eat then," he said and stepped away from his buggy. He wondered if Grant heard the strain in his voice and the hope that filled his heart. He tried to calm down; he felt anything but calm. Why did Cecily want him to come in and eat with her? He wondered. She had just run away from him, and now she wanted him. "Oh, please God," he begged in a silent prayer of his Lord and Savior before he entered the house, "please let her marry me."

Levi wiped his sweating hands on his trousers and realized that he was nervous; he was almost scared. He had waited for Cecily for too long. He was anxious in his wait; she had to want him. She could not turn him away. He couldn't live if she did. But nothing mattered right this moment. Cecily wanted him; Cecily wanted him to eat with her.

Several ladies stepped away from Cecily as Levi handed her a plate of food and sat down on the sofa beside her to eat, he had sat beside her in church on Sunday as well. He had to convince her to stay by his side for all their lives. He looked down and saw that she was not eating, she looked worried, she looked scared, and she had taken a hold of his hand and was hanging on for dear life. He followed her eyes into the crowd of people and saw what she saw. Bernard Calhoun was standing across the room and staring at them both. Levi frowned and wondered what this man was doing here. And was Bernard the reason that Cecily seemed to be afraid? Levi looked back down at Cecily and thought, she is afraid of Bernard Calhoun.

Cecily had panicked when she had come back into the house after running away from Levi and found Bernard there waiting for her. She had immediately looked for Levi in the crowded house; she needed him. She was scared; her father was gone, her father wasn't here to protect her any longer; she had no one. No one but Levi, Levi could protect her. When she had told Clemmie to have Grant find Levi and have him come in and eat with her, Clemmie had been so glad that Cecily had said that she would eat that Clemmie had hurried to find Grant so that he could go and find Levi, but not before Bernard had gotten to Cecily. Not before Bernard had terrified Cecily again.

Cecily felt herself start to shake all over when Bernard came toward her and Levi; she felt almost sick with fear and squeezed Levi's hand hard. Levi looked down at her, but she did not notice, her eyes saw only Bernard Calhoun and her heart was lodged in her throat where it beat out of control.

"Hello, Bernard," Levi said when Bernard came to a stop before him and Cecily. Levi's eyes had narrowed as he looked at the man and worried about Cecily's reaction to Bernard.

"Levi," Cecily's old boyfriend, stared hard at Levi, Levi stared just as hard right back at Bernard. "Cecily tells me that you may buy this place from her." Levi looked at Cecily's frightened face again and wondered what was going on here. "She tells me that she's planning on leaving us," Bernard added and Levi looked back up at Bernard and away from Cecily.

"I'm trying my best to persuade her to stay," Levi said and looked back down at Cecily, she was white as a ghost. "I don't want her to leave me, ever."

Bernard smiled at Levi's gently spoken words and saw Cecily's hand being held by Levi. "Are you trying to say that you and Cecily might have some plans for the future Say wedding plans? I hadn't even heard that you two were courting." Bernard's words brought Levi's eyes back up to stare at him.

"I don't see where anything that Cecily or I either one do is of any concern to you, Bernard." Levi's eyes turned cold and hard as Bernard continued to stare at Cecily's hand being held in Levi's hand.

"Well, if you do marry her, I wish you both the very best. No one is better than our Cecily." Levi watched when Bernard turned away and left them with those parting words and felt like killing the man for insulting Cecily.

"Why did you want me, Cecily?" Levi asked gently and looked back down into her crystal clear blue eyes. "Was it because you were afraid of Bernard?" He saw her head nod, and a tear fell into her roast beef on the plate in her lap. "I won't let him bother you, darlin'," Levi said firmly. "Try and eat something before your food gets cold."

She may not want him, she may not even love him as much as he loved her, but she did need him, Levi thought as he sat still beside Cecily and tried to eat some of his own food. This was a start; she had needed him, he would and could make her want him and then she would marry him and be his. Levi felt more sure of himself, and a smile touched his lips. He had hope, a lot of hope.

Cecily looked up at Levi as she forced herself to eat and wished that he could keep her safe from Bernard Calhoun. But Levi could do nothing more for her than what he had just done, and she felt too deeply for him to be involved in her troubles. Besides, he may learn of what she had done, and he would be sick just at the sight of her, it was hard enough to face herself each and every day. Her father had been brought to ruin because of her; she was standing at the door of certain pain if she leaned on Levi too much. And she would not hurt him; she could never hurt her dear handsome Levi.

"I owe you my thanks, Levi," Cecily finally said. "I was afraid that Bernard would say or do something that would start more gossip about he and me, you know how he can be. I didn't want to be near him alone. I knew that you would help me."

"I'd do anything in the world for you, darlin'," Levi said in a passion-filled voice. "Marry me, let me take care of you for the rest of our lives. Bernard could never hurt you as my wife." Cecily pulled her hand free from Levi's hand, and he fell silent. He could not push her, he would not rush her, and he knew that he was; he couldn't help himself. He hadn't even courted her as he wanted too. He would court her, and she would let him, he would give her the world, and she would accept his world. He turned his attention back to the food on his plate, but he tasted nothing that he attempted to eat. All he could think about was making Cecily see that she need him as he needed her.

Levi left after Cecily had eaten and Clemmie insisted that she needed to lie down for a while. He knew that Clemmie was right, Cecily looked worn out and heartsick. He wanted to pull her back into his arms and take her to bed with him; he wanted to give her all of himself and take all of her in the bargain. She was a fire that burned through his veins. One day he would lose himself within her, and she would let him. He just had to slow down and allow her time to deal with her grief.

Levi went back outside and knew that he should be going home, but he stopped in the yard and lit a cigarette while he looked up at the star-filled sky. The wind blew through the trees, and the leaves made a haunting noise above his head. He was doing as his father had told him to do; he was making a fool of himself over Cecily. Ethan had told him that the men in their family loved only one woman and they loved her with more heart and soul than the average man, the Tucker men were romantics. Levi may not be able to read, he may well be dumb, but he knew how to love, his whole body was consumed with that emotion. And in the name of that emotion, he would do whatever he had to do to get what he wanted. He was certain that he would have Cecily; his hope was consuming him.

Bernard watched Levi standing alone and smoking a cigarette. It was late, and almost everyone had gone home. Bernard smiled when he saw Levi finally climb into a buggy and disappear down the road and into the darkness. Cecily would do like Bernard had told her to do; she had been following his orders now for years, her and her father. She would do like he told her to do always, Bernard thought and smiled. Cecily was going to marry one of the richest men in the whole State of Florida, Cecily was going to marry Levi Tucker, and then Bernard would have some of Levi's money, and he doubted that Levi would ever know. Daniel Walker had paid to protect Cecily; now Cecily would marry Levi and pay to protect herself. Bernard rubbed his hands together and nodded his head. Bernard was fixing to get rich.

"Please, leave me alone," Cecily begged of Bernard as she made her way to the outhouse. She knew that he had been out here waiting on her the second that she saw him and he had called out her name. She knew also that she could not take his threats; she had no way to pay him to keep those threats from destroying her life.

"Marry Levi," Bernard ordered, and Cecily stopped and stood still.

"No, Bernard. I'm selling this place, and I'm leaving here and never coming back. You can do whatever you want to do to me; I won't be around to care. You can't hurt or threaten me anymore." Bernard grabbed a hold of her and shook her so hard that she felt like she was going to fly apart if he didn't stop. When she cried out only then did, he hold her still.

"You'll do like I say, Cecily," Bernard gave her an order and expected her to obey. "You will sell this place to Levi and give me the money that he gives to you. Tell him that your father had debts that must be paid. And then, you will marry him, and I'll leave you alone except for a few times every year." Cecily shook her head hard. "Levi will give you money for things that you need; he'll never have to know that you are giving that money to me. Your secret will stay a secret. And any fool can see that Levi wants you, though why he does, I don't know. You're skinny and pale, and your face is all eyes." Cecily stood shaking her head. "If you don't do like I say, I'll make what I have on you public at your father's funeral tomorrow. Do you hear me, Cecily? I'll ruin you and your father in his grave. He'll have died for nothing." Cecily stopped shaking her head and went weak all over. Bernard would do as he threatened; she knew that he was truly evil. She would never be free of him.

"Please, don't do that. I'll sell this place and give you all the money I get for it, I swear. And then I'll find a job and pay you forever every penny I can. Please, Bernard, don't pull Levi into this, he's never done anything to you. Please, I'm begging you."

"Shut up, Cecily. I want Levi's money," Bernard hissed.

"Why?" Cecily nearly cried out and tried to step away from Bernard, but he would not let her go. His hands were bruising her arms with the hold he had of her.

"Because the bastard's got plenty of money, you stupid woman. Now, I want you to marry Levi as soon as you can. The sooner, the better. But first, get him to buy this place from you and give me the money that he pays you. If you're good Cecily, you just might get to live happily ever after."

"I can't marry Levi. I won't. You can't make me." Cecily was crying now, and Bernard laughed at her, right in her face.

"You'll do as I say, Cecily. Your father's funeral is at four tomorrow; I'll give you until noon to become engaged to Levi." He heard her gasp and his smile grew wide on his handsome face. "Levi wants you, give him the word, and you'll be his. Noon, Cecily or what I have becomes public knowledge, and you're ruined for the rest of your life." Bernard let her go, and she stepped away from him, she heard his harsh laugh as he reached out and pushed her hard almost causing her to fall down. "Noon tomorrow or the cat is out of the bag. I wonder what Levi will think of you when he sees what I have," Bernard laughed out loud before he turned and left Cecily.

The tears fell in earnest down Cecily's face while she stood alone in the night and worried for herself and for Levi. She had to run away. She had to leave here right now, tonight. She could not stay. Reality was cruel when it took a hold of Cecily. She had nowhere to go; there was no place to hide. Her father was gone, and he couldn't keep her safe any longer, all their money was gone, and Daniel was in an early grave because of Bernard. She had nothing to support herself with if she ran away, she was completely alone. Marry Levi; her head ached with the thought. If she married him, every moment of their marriage would be based on a lie and on her fear. She could never trust Levi with the truth, never. And he would hate her if her secret was known. Levi would not protect her from Bernard if she were honest with him. If she went to him and told him the whole story, he would hate her, and it would destroy her to know that he knew. She would drag Levi into hell with her if she married him. She would be his hell. And Levi would be loving her when he should be hating her.

"Cecily," Clemmie Floyd called her name out in the darkness. "Where are you?" Cecily wiped the tears from her face with the back of her hand. She had known Clemmie all of her life; they had been best friends since they had learned to walk and talk as babies. But even Clemmie, her own dear friend, did not know Cecily's secret shame. Clemmie must never know, no one must ever know. She had to make sure that Bernard never showed anyone what he had on her.

"I'm over here, Clemmie!" Cecily called out, and Clemmie reached her in the darkness that was relieved by the soft glow of the half moon and the stars that filled the cloudless night sky.

"I was starting to get worried about you," Clemmie said to her friend. "You've been out here for some time now."

"I'm in terrible trouble, Clemmie," Cecily whispered. "I owe a man a great deal of money, and I have no way to pay him with Daddy gone."

"What are you going to do?" Clemmie's concerned voice filled the silence of the night. "And why do you owe anyone money?"

"It's a long story, Clemmie and I can't tell it to you." Cecily lowered her voice; she was half afraid that Bernard might still be close by and listening to her. "Levi asked me to marry him today."

"Levi has money," Clemmie said and spoke in a low voice as Cecily had. "He can pay your debt."

"Clemmie, oh Clemmie," Cecily breathed as she looked up at the sky. "I can't marry Levi for his money."

"Well, why not?" Clemmie asked, and Cecily looked at her shadowed face. "Levi's mother married his father for money, everyone around here knows their story, it's the nicest love story ever. And Levi is so nice; he is one of the nicest men we know. He would help you, Cecily."

"I can't do it, Clemmie. I just can't marry Levi for his money. I don't know what I'm going to do." Cecily felt like she might start to cry again. All she had done for the past twenty-four hours was cry. If she married Levi, she knew that she would cry forever for doing him so wrong.

"Then go to Levi, tell him you need help. He'll help you, Cecily. I know he will. He cares about you; we've all been the best of friends for all our lives. He would never want anything bad to happen to you."

"I just could not use him like that Clemmie. I don't know what to do." Cecily stood still and tried to think of some way out of this mess; she knew that there was no way out of this mess, there hadn't been for more than two years.

"Cecily, listen to me. Women marry for security all the time, what choice do we have? We can't provide for ourselves. We have to let our men take care of us. We have to let them give us everything, they know they have to provide for us, and they do. Go to Levi, tell him what you feel you can marry him if he'll have you and let him pay off your debt." Cecily stayed quiet for so long that Clemmie tried to convince her further. "I don't know what's going on with you, Cecily and I'm surprised that I don't since I thought that we told one another everything and you don't have to tell me now if you can't. But go to Levi, lean on him; let him take care of you as men do for we women."

Cecily listened to Clemmie; she listened to herself. Levi did want her, and she could try and make him a good wife. Every day she would have to work hard to make up for using him as she was going to use him, but he would never have to know any of the truth, she would somehow find a way to keep her wolf at bay and protect herself and Levi as well. He would never know what she had done two years ago. Her shame would still be her own. The shame would be only on herself. He would never know, she would die before she let him find out.

Could she really do this? Cecily asked herself. Could she marry Levi for his money? She almost groaned out loud. She would be cheating him, she would probably have to steal from him, and if her past should ever become known, she would not be ruined alone. People would look down on Levi for his having been her husband. But she could trust no one. Levi couldn't know of anything that was happening to her; she would see that he never knew. And in order to assure that no one ever knew her secret, she knew she had to do as Bernard said. She had to pay Bernard until he was dead or she was dead. The only way to do that was by marrying Levi.

"I'll go to Levi first thing in the morning," Cecily finally said, more to herself than to Clemmie. She fought not to cry any longer. Clemmie kept silent and waited for Cecily in the stillness of the night so that they could go back to the house together.

Cecily needed Levi, Clemmie thought. And Cecily did care for Levi, Clemmie was certain of that, and they both could be happy. Levi and Cecily would be a good couple. And Levi was Grant's best friend and Cecily was Clemmie's best friend, they would always be close and almost like family.

Clemmie heard Cecily crying and fought her own tears. Cecily had known too much sadness. Levi could take that sadness away. Levi's easy smile and tender ways would keep Cecily safe, and she would be blessed to have him. Levi would be blessed to have her, Clemmie thought. Cecily was a sweet, kind person; she would never fail Levi.

Chapter Three

The stillness of the dawn surrounded Cecily while she stood on her back porch and watched the sunrise in the quiet of the day. Even the birds in the trees were silent and the wind that blew made no sound. The stars left the sky one at a time as the moon seem to fall away from the earth, and the sun took possession of the sky and brought about the day.

Cecily had slept for a little while and been haunted by her dreams; Bernard was smiling his cruel, mean smile at her while showing the whole town her sin and shame right inside the church, her father's open coffin filled with evidence of what she had done. Her father had sat up in his coffin, gave a horrified scream and then died all over again. Levi had been by her side in the front pew, and he had stared at her, she could see his hatred and disgust in those deep dark eyes. When Cecily had left her nightmare and awoke she was wet and shaking all over. She knew what she had to do. She could not delay what had to be done before noon this very day.

Cecily would go to Levi; she would not risk being ruined. And when she married him, she would make sure to always be careful to never love him too much because if or when he learned her secret she would not be the only one hurt by Bernard. She could not allow herself to love Levi more than just a little because there would always be the threat that she could lose him or worse, have him hate her if her secret became known.

Cecily worried, she paced in his front yard. This was so wrong; she knew that in her heart, but she had no other choice. One day, if she failed to satisfy Bernard, Levi would learn the truth about her, and she would lose him. He would have ample grounds with which to divorce her, and divorce he certainly would do, of that Cecily, had no doubt.

Taking a deep breath and truly hating herself for what she was about to do to the nicest man she had ever know besides her father, Cecily went and saddled her horse and headed for the home of Levi Tucker. She was going to Levi with the full knowledge that she was about to ruin his life; she had already ruined herself. But she had no choice. She was giving Levi no choice by holding back the truth from him, a truth he must never ever know.

Levi answered Cecily's knock on his front door himself, and she saw his eyes grow wide when they fell onto her face. He had not even dreamed she would be at his door and she felt evil and wicked and sick; she was fixing to take Levi to hell, her mistake could someday be his greatest grief. And if she did not pay Bernard Calhoun, they would both be ruined together once he married her. This was all she kept thinking, all she had been thinking since she woke up from that nightmare. She could ruin Levi.

Cecily took a deep breath and stepped away from the door. If she did this to Levi, she would be throwing his money away. No, she thought, she would be saving herself. She had to save herself.

"Cecily," Levi said her name. "What's wrong darlin'?"

"I have to talk to you," she choked on her words and Levi stepped aside for her to enter his home. Cecily stood still and thought of the last time that she had been inside of his house. Sarah had been getting married. A happy time, this was not a happy time; this was a time filled with deception. She was deceiving this good and kind man, and he meant her no harm, he only meant to love her. "May we talk out here, please?"

"Of course," Levi answered her and left his house. When Cecily moved into the yard, he moved with her. He could not begin to imagine what she wanted and his head was spinning in wonder, and his heart was crying out for hope.

Tell him everything! Cecily's mind screamed at her long and loud when she came to a stop in the yard. She was not able to turn and face Levi just yet. Tell him nothing! Her heart ordered. He'll not save you!!! Her heart warned her. Her mind was begging that she not lie to him; her heart was pleading with her to never trust him or anyone with the truth. Cecily knew what she had to do. She knew what she was going to do. She followed her heart and ignored her brain.

"Levi, I – my father and I had a big debt that I must pay," she turned and faced him; her face was burning with the heat of the lie she must tell him. 'I have no choice but to sell the farm as quickly as I possibly can." Levi stared at Cecily in surprise; she could see the surprise on his face; if it were possible, she hated herself more than she thought she ever could. "I could never come to you with this debt hanging over my head, Levi." These words made her feel physically ill; she grabbed a deep breath to keep from vomiting on his boots. She may already be in hell, but this that she was doing to Levi was sending him down into the deepest darkest corner of that fiery pit right along with her.

"Your situation," Levi said, remembering her words to him the day before while they had been in the field together. "You mean you couldn't marry me because of money that your father owed?" Levi smiled, and Cecily wished that he would not, his smile hurt her heart all the more. She was doing him wrong if he found out…. Cecily forced herself to stop thinking and listen to what Levi was saying to her. "I'll pay your father's debt, darlin'. I love you. No debt should stand in the way of our happiness."

"Yes, Levi. My debt is all that stood in the way," she lied. "I was too ashamed to tell you," she nearly began to cry and looked quickly away from him. She could not look at his beautiful face and do this terrible thing. "But I want to pay my father's debt. You buy the farm from me, and I can come to you, free of all burdens." He would be paying her debt forevermore when he married her; she was doing more than lying to him, she was deceiving him and using him, he would hate her if he knew what she was doing to him. She hated herself.

Cecily burst into tears and covered her face with both hands; she could not do this to Levi. She could not ruin this man that she had loved for most of her life. But she had no choice if she did not marry Levi; Bernard would show the world her sin at her father's funeral today. She could not allow Bernard to destroy her after all her father had paid to save her. And here Levi stood before her trusting her and believing in her and willing to help her.

Levi grabbed Cecily and held her close in his arms. "Do you love me, Cecily?" he asked, and she clung to him tighter. It was not safe for her to love Levi as much as she did, not now. He may someday put her from him in sorrow that he ever even knew her. "Do you love me, darlin'?" he asked again as he gently kissed the top of her head.

"Yes," she said against his chest. That was the answer that he needed to hear; that was the answer she had to give in order to be safe. And then she thought of a new threat and took a deep breath before asking him what she had to ask. "May I ask you a question?" she started in the hopes that he would not think her mad for his money. She was desperate for his money, and she could only pray that he had enough to save her.

"You can ask me anything, Cecily. You can tell me anything. I told you yesterday that I loved you and I knew that you love me also. You should have told me then why you wouldn't marry me." Levi pushed her away from himself and looked down into those crystal clear blue eyes that he had loved for so long. He could get lost in those eyes. Soon he would be able to look into those eyes every morning when he woke and every night as he made love to her, she would always be his.

"Losing Daddy had me confused," Cecily said as an excuse for not having told him that she needed his money yesterday to pay a debt. "And I was ashamed to tell you that I needed money. I thought if I said that I loved you in one breath and that I needed your money in the very next breath that you would think I was lying to you and only wanted you for your money. So I turned you away. But I can't turn you away Levi. I need you. You have no idea how badly I need you." She hid her face in the shirt that covered his chest; if she had not, she was certain he would see her wickedness in her eyes and all over her lying face. The word wicked should be stamped onto her forehead for him and all to see.

"You would never marry me for my money, Cecily. You aren't that kind of person." His words caused her to go pale against him. He didn't know her. He was willing to give her everything, not just his heart, but his trust and she hated him for trusting her, she knew she would never trust him. Standing here agreeing to marry him was the worst thing that she had ever done in her whole life. If she lived to be a thousand years old, she would never forgive herself for what she was doing to Levi, and at Bernard's demand. She had no choice; she was doing this to save herself. And the ugliest truth of all, she was, in fact, marrying Levi, a man she could love forever, only for his money. She had to have his money. "You said that you wanted to ask me a question," he reminded her, and she pulled away from him and met his eyes which held so much innocence, they were beautiful eyes and blind to her sin. She thanked God that Levi did not know of her sin.

"After we are married will you give me any money of my very own?" Levi raised his eyebrows above those beautiful innocent eyes, and Cecily looked away from him. What could she say to explain her reason for this question? "What I mean is; I don't want to have to come to you for everything that I may want or need. I'd like my own money to see to my own needs, like the allowance that Daddy gave to me." She was becoming good at lying, too good, she thought and looked back at Levi's face.

"With all my worldly goods, I thee endow," Levi answered his Cecily in his soft husky, tender voice. Cecily bit her bottom lip and prayed that he gave her enough money to satisfy Bernard. She had to keep Bernard Calhoun silent. She had to keep silent herself.

"Thank you, Levi." Cecily looked quickly away from him. "I know I'm not deserving of you, but I promise; I'll do anything and everything to make sure that you never regret having married me." He didn't know how serious her words to him were, Levi was too grateful for the gift of herself to him.

"Hush Cecily," he said firmly. "I've wanted to marry you for a long time. And so you know, I'm not pure either. I really don't care what you did in the past with Bernard, that has nothing to do with us or right now. All that matters to me is that you are going to be my wife and let me love you and take care of you for the rest of our lives.

He wanted her, just as Bernard had said and he was going to take her any way that he could get her. And he believed that she loved him and would love him always. "I'll try and make you happy, Levi," she said softly while still looking up into his eyes. Levi touched her face, and she had to close her eyes. She could not take what she was doing to him, and to herself. And she had to have his money; if he failed to give her enough money to keep Bernard away, she might as well be dead.

"I want to kiss you, Cecily," Levi said softly, and Cecily nodded her head. His lips touched hers, and he knew that he had wanted to kiss her again since yesterday. He had to have her. Soon he would lay her down on his bed and kiss all of her, and she would let him. She was so soft, he thought, too warm, his very dreams were coming true, and the best thing of all was that she loved him and he loved her. He pressed his lips more firmly against hers and with his tongue, he gently forced her mouth to open and entered the cavity of her mouth and dove deep, his tongue touching hers and almost dancing with her tongue inside of her mouth. He pulled her closer to him; he could feel her heart beating against his chest and was on fire just by a simple kiss.

Cecily felt Levi's hands on her back as he pulled her so close to his own body that she couldn't tell where she started and he stopped. He wanted her, and in every way that a man wanted a woman. For one moment she was afraid of what he would do to her after she was his wife, and then his tongue touched hers and she tried to gasp as her whole body seemed to turn to liquid flames within his arms. She was melting into a puddle of hot liquid fire, and she put her arms around his neck and tried to pull him closer. She moaned into his mouth, a sound of agony as she couldn't get him close enough and he echoed her sound as she trembled in his arms.

And then sanity returned to Cecily; she could not want Levi like this, she could not love him, she could never need him for anything other than his money. If she did, when and if he found out her secret truth he would put her away from him, and she would lose more than she already had. She could not love him; he could never mean anything to her, she would be destroyed for ten lifetimes if she were to allow him to see her heart if she were to allow her heart to feel what it was feeling now.

Cecily pulled her arms from around Levi's neck and placed them on his chest where she shoved hard against him. When he let her go, she fell back, as did he and she saw that they were both breathing hard and fast, her heart was totally out of control, the burning fire he had started within her was leaving and as it left she began to shake all over. What had he done to her? And just with a kiss?

Levi saw the wild and frightened look in Cecily's eyes as she stood away from him gasping for every breath and he knew that he had put that look into her eyes. He ran a hand through his hair and tried to calm himself down. He saw her eyes lower and almost went to his knees when he realized what she was looking at. He was ready for her; he wanted her; his body was almost demanding that he take her now. His need was so great that it was almost impossible to ignore. The terrified look she was giving his lower body was enough to make him regain all of his senses and quiet his urge for her.

"Dear God," Levi breathed and closed his eyes to take a deep, steadying breath. "I'm sorry, darlin'." He opened his eyes and saw that her eyes were now on his face. "You just lost your father, and here I am practically taking advantage of you in my own front yard." Cecily heard the regret in his voice. He knew that he had frightened her. She knew that her reaction to his kiss had frightened her more than he ever could.

"I need time," Cecily said in a near hysterical voice. She needed time to understand what he had just made her feel. She needed time to learn not to love him as she did. She wanted to hide from him, she was using him, and he thought that she loved him only, that she wanted him only. Not his money and but for his money, she wouldn't be here now.

Levi moved the few steps that separated them and pulled his Cecily close. "I'm not a smart man, Cecily. I know you are sick over losing your father. I know you need time to deal with your grief. And I all but used you in a way that would dishonor you, and I swear darlin', I'll never dishonor you."

Cecily carefully put her arms around Levi's waist. If only she had not made that mistake two years ago, she thought. She could have been happy with Levi; she would have wanted more of what he had just done to her in his yard. Now she was betraying him; she was using his heart and his love for her to get the money that she had to have. She was a bad person, she was horrible, and she knew that too. Levi did not deserve this that she was doing to him. He would never deserve the evil that she was going to bring into his life. She felt like she could die right here in his arms for what she was doing to him. She knew in her heart that God might well understand and forgive her all of this, God knew the whole truth as her father had, God had seen. Levi would never believe the truth; no one would.

"Give me a few minutes darlin', and I'll saddle my horse and see you home." Levi pulled away from her, but not before he placed a light kiss on her forehead.

"You don't need to do that Levi," Cecily said as she took a step back and away from him. "I really need to be alone for a little while anyway." She started toward her horse, and Levi followed her. "I want us to marry as soon as possible. I need to sell the farm right away and get things settled. I feel in a hurry to settle everything."

Levi looked up at Cecily after she had mounted her horse. Dear God, she was in a hurry, if she only knew of the hurry that he was in to have her. He grabbed a deep breath thinking that he could have her in his home and in his bed within just a couple of weeks. "Anything you want, Cecily," Levi said in a strained voice. "You name the day and the time and anything else, I'll be there."

"Thursday," Cecily said, and Levi almost lost his breath. "If the Reverend Bidwell is available." Cecily thought to add and saw the look of pure joy on Levi's face and felt herself begin to shake again. Soon she would be his wife, and he was glad. He would want her in his bed; he would do that thing with her that husbands did with their wives and she was certain that she did not want that with him. He would make her heart feel with his body as he had done with the kiss, and she could not feel anything for him, it was too dangerous.

"Forgive me, Levi," Cecily said as she started her horse for home. If Levi only knew what she had done to him and would be doing to him, he would never forgive her, and she would understand his feelings completely. She would never forgive herself for using Levi like this. But there had been no other way, her heart told her, and she knew that her heart spoke the truth. To tell Levi the truth would have not set her free, the truth told to Levi would ruin her.

Bernard Calhoun met Cecily's eyes from across the room of her father's parlor, and he saw her head nod. She was standing beside Levi Tucker and listening to something that Clemmie was saying to her. Bernard looked from Cecily to Clemmie and thought that Clemmie was nearly as beautiful as Cecily was. Clemmie's hair was jet black and curly, her eyes were a deep dark green, and her skin was almost as pale as Cecily's skin. Bernard liked women with pale skin.

Levi looked down at Cecily and saw her worried frown, then he followed her eyes across the room and saw Bernard watching them. Bernard saw Levi looking toward where he stood, and Bernard's face broke into one of those charming smiles that Levi just could not like. Levi narrowed his deep dark blue eyes at Bernard as he stared hard at the man and Bernard, seeing the look that Levi gave to him, turned and left the house by way of the front door.

"Excuse me for a few moments, Cecily," Levi said, a forced smile on his face. "There is something that I must do." Levi left the house the same way that Bernard had and found Bernard standing in the yard under the big oak tree. Levi did not hesitate for one moment; he left the porch and went to where Bernard stood. "You don't belong here Bernard; you need to leave now. And I want you to leave Cecily alone," Levi said, and Bernard looked at him with that charming smile again on his face.

"I haven't even spoken to her Levi," Bernard gave Levi a satisfied look and Levi took a step forward forcing Bernard to have to look up as Levi was a good six inches taller than Bernard. "What's wrong Levi? Are you jealous because I had her first?"

"No, and I'd never be jealous of you," Levi said firmly. "Your presence here is upsetting Cecily, and I want you to leave. Now." Bernard gave a loud laugh, and Levi stepped even closer to Bernard while Bernard stood still.

"She doesn't love you, Levi," Bernard said while still laughing.

"No, Bernard. Cecily doesn't love you," Levi's voice was hard, his hands were fisted at his side, and his face was turning red with anger. Only the people close to Levi knew how bad his temper was, and they knew never to force him to anger. Levi did not forgive, and he never forgot, once he was made with someone, he was mad forever with that person.

"You'll never know what Cecily feels for me, Levi. I have had a part of her that you'll never get." Bernard leaned closer to Levi and lowered his voice. "She has the firmest little breasts you've ever seen. Just a mouth full Levi and she taste like milk and honey."

Levi didn't think; he reacted to Bernard's words as any lover would. His fist was at his side one second and the very next instant they were both flying into Bernard's face knocking the smaller man to the ground. Bernard put his hand to his bloody mouth and stared hard up at Levi who was still red in the face and feeling like he could really hurt Bernard Calhoun.

"You just made a big mistake," Bernard whined like an angry child as he jumped up and plowed into Levi with his head like a bull.

Levi was on the ground for all of one second, then he was on top of Bernard and hitting him with both fists. Levi did physical labor every day of the week, and besides being taller than Bernard, he was also thicker and had a much firmer body giving him twice Bernard's strength. Bernard was a photographer and owned a shop in Madison; the smaller man never got outside in the sun and was pale as well as weak. Bernard was losing the fight right from the start; he was no match for Levi.

Jamie Liston, Jon Hyde, and Grant Whittaker were all standing together on the porch and saw Levi hit Bernard. A long few seconds passed before any of them moved, and when they did, they all moved together and went out into the yard. Cecily did not need something like this on the day that she buried her father and rumor had it that she was engaged to Levi and here Levi was beating up her old boyfriend in her front yard.

Levi fought both Grant and Jamie as they pulled him off Bernard while Jon helped Bernard to his feet. "For God sake, Levi," Grant hissed into his best friend's ear. "Calm down. Half the damn county is standing on Cecily's porch watching you."

"You broke my nose, you son of a bitch!" Bernard screamed as he held a bloody handkerchief to his face.

"If you come near Cecily again, I'll do more than break your nose," Levi said in a low and deadly voice as he tried to take a step toward Bernard, Grant held him back.

"You're going to pay for this, Levi," Bernard whined as Jon helped him up onto his horse. "You'll be sorry you ever laid a hand on me."

"I'm already sorry," Levi said seriously. "Your blood has soiled my clothes, and your stench is gagging me." Jon slapped Bernard's horse hard, and the animal trotted off so fast that Bernard had to cling tight to the horse in order to stay on.

"You're a mess," Grant said looking at Levi's torn and blood covered clothes. "I think you still have time to get home and get cleaned up and changed before we leave for church if you hurry. Take my horse." Levi looked down at his shirt and knew that he would have to do as Grant told him too; his shirt was covered in blood as well as dirt.

"Is Cecily on the porch?" Levi asked Grant not looking back toward the house.

"Yes, she's right out front," Grant answered, and Levi groaned out loud

"One of ya'll tell her that I'm sorry," Levi said as he went to Grant's horse. "That stinking little worm never even hit me, not once," Levi said as he got on to Grant's horse shaking his sore and bruised hand.

Cecily stood on the porch shaking from head to foot as she watched Levi ride away from her house. Dear God, what had Bernard said to him to make him leave? Levi wasn't a violent man; she knew Levi. He was calm and good and kind. She felt like running after him and begging him to tell her what Bernard had said to make him fight like he had. But she couldn't run after Levi, all she could do was stand on her front porch with the crowd and be sick with worry and fear and pray Levi would be back and tell her what had caused the fight. She felt dizzy and lightheaded in her fear and fought to breathe.

"Levi said to tell you that he's sorry, Cecily," Jamie Liston said as he and Grant and Jon came back to the porch. "He's gone home to get cleaned up; he'll be back as soon as he can." Cecily sagged in pure relief of these words. Levi would be back, her mind screamed, he didn't hate her.

The Reverend Bidwell caught her, thinking that she meant to faint and she let him support her. "One of you younger fellows help her into the house," the Reverend Bidwell called out in his booming voice, and Grant moved up the steps to Cecily. He lifted her into his arms, and she let him, holding on to this dear friend as he carried her inside and laid her on the sofa.

"Here, Cecily." Clemmie bent down beside Cecily with a glass of water while she told everyone to leave and let Cecily catch her breath. "Are you all right?" Clemmie asked when they were alone, and Cecily nodded her head. "Levi sure beat the stuffing out of Bernard," she said, and Cecily leaned back on the sofa looking pale and worried for anyone to see.

"Why? Why did Levi beat up Bernard?" Cecily more moaned than spoke.

"Levi will tell you later, I'm sure. Did you go talk with him this morning?" Clemmie took the empty glass of water and sat it on the floor beside her while she looked at Cecily.

Yes. He said that he loved me and wanted to marry me." Cecily covered her face with both hands and wondered again what Bernard had said to Levi.

"I'm happy for you Cecily," Clemmie said as she reached to pull Cecily's hands from her face. "Everything will be fine from now on, you'll see. Levi is a good man; he'll stand beside you always and support you. I do wonder what made him so mad that he beat Bernard up like that. I've known Levi forever, and I've never seen him fight anyone before today. Grant told me that Levi tries never to get mad at anyone because he can't forgive and he won't forget, but he said Levi never is violent." Clemmie saw Cecily's pale face and forced a smile. "Don't worry," Clemmie said again. But all that Cecily Walker could do was worry.

Levi sat quietly beside Cecily in the buggy on the way to the church. She looked too thin and too frail, he hadn't noticed how thin and frail she was before this very moment. She looked like she would break into a million pieces at any time, or that she already had. He took a hold of her hand wanting to give her any comfort that he could, and she held onto his hand but said nothing. She was locked up inside of herself, withdrawn from him. He didn't know what to do for her, and he wanted to do something for her. It was killing him to see her like this.

The church service was long as the Reverend Bidwell went on and on of the goodness of Daniel Walker. Levi stood beside his Cecily and wished the blasted preacher would finish speaking. Cecily looked awful, and he didn't know how much more she could take. After more than an hour of the Reverend Bidwell's sermon and kind words, everyone left the church and went out into the graveyard. People surrounded Cecily from all sides offering her words of comfort, and she became separated from Levi.

Levi stood to the side of the graveyard and watched Cecily, she wasn't crying, but she might as well have been. She looked terrible, worse than she had on the buggy ride over here. When the Undertaker started to lower the coffin into the ground, Cecily wished that it was she that was dead and about to be buried. Her father had a good life until she had destroyed that life and now she was going to destroy Levi. Levi saw Cecily standing near the open grave when the dirt beneath her feet gave way; he was there and grabbed her from behind. Cecily gave a cry as Levi pulled her against his chest and she held tight to the arm that he had around her waist. She didn't notice all the people that were staring at her with sadness and concern; all she saw was her dear darling Daddy being taken from her forever.

"Levi," Cecily breathed his name and went weak against him. He picked her up into his strong arms and carried her to his buggy, her arms around his neck and her face turned into his shirt. She had to trust someone, Cecily thought. She had to trust that Levi would take care of her; if he did not, they would both go to hell together. She wished again that it was she in the grave. Her best luck would be if she were to die. But Bernard didn't want her dead; Bernard needed her alive so that he could torment her.

"You're safe, Cecily," Levi gently placed her into his buggy before he got in beside her. "I won't let anything hurt you again, darling.' You'll be safe forever." Cecily knew that Levi lied to her. He could not keep her safe. No one could

After they left the cemetery and had gone down the road for a few moments, Levi looked down at Cecily and found that she was no longer crying. "I owe you an apology," he said in his kind way. "I didn't mean to fight with Bernard today. But I saw that he had upset you, so I followed him outside and told him to leave you alone. He wouldn't listen to me." Levi refused to repeat what Bernard had really said to him in the yard earlier today. The man was not a gentleman. Bernard was filthy, and Levi hoped that Bernard never came around Cecily or him again as long as they all lived. Cecily's name should never even be on that man's foul lips.

Cecily pinched her lips together and squeezed her eyes closed tight. She knew that Bernard had said something awful and ugly about her to Levi. Otherwise Levi would never have been forced to violence. She had to know what Bernard's words had been to Levi. "What did Bernard say to you, Levi?" she finally worked up the courage to ask and to even open her eyes and look up at Levi to await his answer.

"Nothing darlin'," Levi said gently, the lie he told was lost in the easy smile that he gave to her. "He just acted arrogantly and mean, and something inside of me snapped. I don't get mad, Cecily because I know I can't forgive easy and I never seem to be able to forget a wrong. So I always avoid any kind of conflict." Cecily's eyes grew wide as she looked up at him and he gave her a quick soft kiss on the lips. "Don't you worry darlin'," he said lightly. "I'll never turn my anger on you. I love you too much to ever cause you any pain. You're my life."

"If you ever do get mad at me Levi," Cecily said softly, "I want you to know that I'll always forgive you. You are the finest man I've ever known in my whole life other than Daddy. And my Daddy liked you a lot too; he wanted me to marry you. He knew how I felt about you; he's always known." Well she thought, she had finally told Levi something that was true. She was so use to deceiving him that the truth seemed small and unimportant.

"Your father was a good man, Cecily," Levi said with a wide smile. She really did want to marry him; he felt like the luckiest man in the whole world. "I've been thinking about your father's farm. He still has that stud out of Kentucky and some fine mares. I'm going to give you two thousand dollars for the farm and the horses before we marry and another two thousand will be deposited into an account in your name in the bank in Madison. Does that sound fair to you?" He looked down when Cecily sat still and silent beside him for a long time; he found that she was crying again. "Don't cry, darlin'. Please."

"Daddy said that we would only get about a thousand dollars for the whole place," Cecily finally spoke. She laid her head on Levi's shoulder and fought the guilt that consumed her. But she was relieved also. She needed that money. And Levi; she was more certain than ever that she was not deserving of this man, he was far too good for her and innocent of how she was using him. She was doing him wrong, and he was being good to her.

"Will that cover your father's debt, darlin'?" he asked Cecily, thankful to God that she was with him, that her head was on his shoulder, that she smelled like sunshine and the world around her smelled of spring. He could see their happy future together, the children they would have, how he would add on to his home and she would make it the way she wanted. Life was so sweet; he kept thinking, now that Cecily was with him.

"It's enough, Levi." For now, she added to herself and thought that she would need more before the good Lord saw fit to take Bernard from this earth. "Forgive me, Levi. Please, forgive me," she begged softly, and he put an arm around her to draw her closer.

"I'll never have any reason to forgive you anything." Levi almost laughed at her seriousness. "Cecily, don't cry anymore. If there is anything to forgive you for it's for being too beautiful for me. I know that we're rushing things and I've not even courted you like I wanted too. I promise, once we are married, I'll slow down and give you the time you need to get over the death of your father. We're going to be so happy together; you just need time to grieve."

"Thank you, Levi. For everything that you're doing for me." His lips touched hers when she looked up at his face, and she let him kiss her, she wanted him too when Levi kissed her nothing seem to matter in the whole world beyond the fact that Levi was kissing her. She closed her eyes, and the feather softness of his lips brushed against her own. "Oh, Levi," she breathed and leaned into him, when he kissed her she felt almost safe, if only she could trust him and tell him what was being done to her, if only she could believe that he wouldn't hate her she would tell him everything in less than a second and without hesitation. But the truth would lose him; she could not take any chance of losing Levi, not now, he was all she had in the world.

Levi heard Cecily say his name and pulled her closer deepening the kiss, his tongue going into her mouth and taking her moans deep into the back of his throat, it was as if she were breathing life into him. He knew in his heart he had to court her, he had to be gentle of her, she had just lost her father, and it had been a sudden unexpected death. He would spend time kissing her and petting her and loving her before making her one with his body. He heard her gasp as he moved his mouth to her cheek and then her ear, his tongue going into her ear and circling it, his hot breath going down the back of her neck. She gasped again, and he knew he had to spend time loving her and showing his love.

The horses ran off the road, and the buggy jerked to a stop as the horses stopped, only then did Levi look up from Cecily, he still held the reins in one hand. "I forgot the horses," Levi breathed against Cecily's cheek. "You make me forget everything when I'm with you."

If only he could make her forget Bernard, Cecily thought as he maneuvered the horses back onto the road. Bernard was mad at Levi for having beaten him up as he had. She looked back up at Levi and wondered what he would have done had he known the truth of what Bernard had been doing to her and her father. Maybe, he could have found a way to put a stop to the madness of Bernard. Maybe he would have hated her forever when he found out what was going on. She shook her head hard and thought that right now, Levi was her savior, she had no one and nowhere to go, she was alone in this world without Levi. Her only family was now buried in the church graveyard. Levi was her savior. If she told him what was happening, she would be alone, ruined for all time and she might as well just be dead. She leaned against Levi and prayed that the money he gave to her for her father's farm would last a long time; it was a great deal of money. She had to keep Levi from finding out the truth. She had to keep safe with Levi. She had to keep Levi forever; she wanted him always.

"I've wanted you forever, darlin'," Levi breathed against the top of her head; the horses had stopped again and were standing still in the road. They had both been so lost in their own thoughts and desires they hadn't noticed anything around them. "Cecily," Levi said her name, and she looked up at him. "I've waited for you," he touched her cheek, "I've waited for years for you to grow up and I've watched you grow up more beautiful every single time I saw you for the past five years. I knew that I would wait for you forever if I had too. You were meant to be mine. I love you more than life itself." He touched his lips to hers again, and she pressed closer into his rock hard body wondering what he was doing to her, wondering why she felt as though she were liquid fire when he kissed her. She was on fire now and burning up with Levi.

When she moaned into his mouth, Levi let go of the reins and turned in the buggy seat to pull her closer. He had never dreamed she would kiss him like this, that she would have this effect on him. He knew he wanted her, but he never dreamed she'd know how to kiss him back like this. He moved his mouth back to her cheek, and she followed his lead kissing his cheek. "I'll try my best to be a good wife," Cecily breathed against his cheek and Levi thought to himself as long as she kissed like this, he didn't care what sort of wife she turned out to be.

"You can burn the house down, darlin', as long as you keep kissing me like this," Levi moved to her ear, and she moaned and fell against him. She wasn't kissing him like anything, Cecily thought; all of this was his doing. Until Levi, the only man she had ever kissed in her life was her Daddy. "I thought after Sarah married and moved away," Levi breathed as he kissed her neck, "that I had lost you. I only saw you after that in church on Sundays, we hardly ever talked and then if we did talk, it wasn't anything I wanted to hear. Remember how it used to be? You use to tell me all your secrets, and I wanted to hear those secrets. You would laugh; it was a sound better than piano music. We had fun too, riding and fishing together and picnics down on the lake. Sarah, Clemmie, Grant, you and me, we were always together. And then you grew away from me," Levi looked down into her liquid crystal clear eyes and Cecily knew he was thinking of Bernard and how he thought Bernard was courting her. "Promise me nothing will ever come between us again, Cecily. We have no secrets; we belong together, more than lovers, but also best friends." Cecily looked up at him wishing what he was asking was something that she could give to him without hesitation, wishing that life were as simple as Levi was making it sound.

Levi saw the tear that fell onto Cecily's face, and he quickly moved to kiss the tear away. "I didn't mean to make you cry again. I never want to make you cry."

Cecily buried her face against his shirt and swallowed hard. His words were killing her. He loved her true and pure and with all open honesty, and she could make him no promises of forever. To keep from speaking, she pressed her mouth to his and waited for him to kiss her as he had been the past two days and she followed his lead, her tongue darting into his mouth and dancing with his own. If he learned her terrible secret, he wouldn't want her like this or any other way. He would put her away from him and gladly. She could not let her heart feel too much; she had to protect herself from her uncertain future. And she had to protect Levi. Telling him her truth now would not be protecting either of them.

"I'll try and make you a good wife, Levi," Cecily said again and held perfectly still when the kiss ended, her forehead resting on his chest. She stopped thinking and said a silent prayer to God to protect her, to help her find a way out of this horrible mess with Bernard so she could be free to love Levi for the rest of her life. In her heart she knew, loving Levi Tucker was her own personal hell.

Clemmie came to Cecily's house after the funeral with the intention of staying for a few days at least. Her parents didn't mind; they knew that Cecily Walker was a good Christian woman and they trusted their daughter Clemmie. Cecily's house was a mess, so many people had been coming in and out the past few days that the floor was covered with dirt and the house was cluttered with empty dirty dishes that had to be washed and returned to their owners. Clemmie fell in with Cecily, and they went to work setting everything right.

"When do you and Levi plan on getting married?" Clemmie asked Cecily as she swept the floor and Cecily washed a huge pot at the sink.

"Thursday, a week from now," Cecily said without turning from her task to look at Clemmie. "I talked to the Reverend Bidwell since it's so soon after daddy's death and he said it was right and good for me to marry quickly, I don't need to be living out here alone. I was surprised, Clemmie. I would have thought the Reverend would have wanted me to wait until a year of mourning Daddy. He said it was more important that I have the protection of a man." Cecily looked out the kitchen window and wished that she didn't need to marry Levi; she wished there was no Bernard because then she would want to marry Levi and there would be no need involved.

Clemmie shook her head before she spoke, "I think it's sad that here we are almost in the twentieth century and we still must rely on men for everything. We can't even own land or cattle or do anything fun. We need a husband or a father, or if we have neither of those, then we have to turn to our brother."

"Clemmie, we can't have a real wedding like I always dreamed of," Cecily said softly as she realized that many of her childhood dreams were lost to her. "But will you come with me on Thursday? I know Levi has asked Grant to come with him. We need two witnesses and you're my best friend in the whole world."

"I'll go with you, Cecily. I'll always be here for you; you know that. We're almost like sisters." Cecily tried to smile knowing that her secret was between her and Levi and had also been between her and Clemmie, it was like a wall separating them. She wondered what Clemmie would think of her if she had told her what Bernard had done and was doing to her. She couldn't risk losing her friend; she couldn't risk anyone knowing now that Daddy was gone, she thought. She had to be silent, always silent. "Cecily," Clemmie interrupted her thoughts, "you're not afraid of Levi, are you?" Cecily turned from the sink and faced Clemmie. "Well, you know what I mean, of the wedding night?" Clemmie turned a fiery red and felt her face was going up in flames, some things you just didn't speak of, she knew. "Forget I asked that Cecily." Clemmie went back to her sweeping the floor where she had already swept.

"No, I won't forget," Cecily almost laughed out loud. She hadn't laughed in a long, long time. "I'm not afraid of Levi," I'm afraid for him, she added to herself and the smile faded quickly from her face. "Levi promised to give me time to deal with having just lost Daddy. He said he wouldn't rush me; Levi would never lie to me." She caught herself at the last words and realized that she had lied to him; she grabbed a deep breath and felt sick to her stomach.

You are so blessed, Cecily. Levi's a really good man, and he's so handsome. Daddy still can't believe that he beat up Bernard like he did today. Levi's such a calm laid back easy going person. But Daddy said he is glad Levi won the fight; Bernard has never been a nice person, most people can't stand him, though he has his photography business and I've heard he takes very fine photos." Cecily dropped a cup that she had been washing, and it cracked against the sink. "I shouldn't have said that, Cecily. I know that at one time you really liked Bernard a lot. I was afraid you would marry him, and I just couldn't learn to ever like him and not for your husband. Why did you stop seeing him?"

"Daddy didn't want me to see Bernard anymore," Cecily lied and attacked another dirty pot with her scrub brush.

"Is Levi going to pay that money you said you owed?" Cecily went still over, Clemmie didn't seem to notice.

"Clemmie, please," she almost begged turning around again to face her friend and letting the pot fall into the sink. "Don't tell anyone about that. Levi's bought Daddy's farm from me, so it's all over and now, no more debt, no more trouble." She was lying so much that the truth was getting lost in the lies. She hoped that she could keep everything straight in her own mind and not do or say anything wrong at some later date.

"You know I'll never tell anyone, Cecily. We've been sharing secrets forever, and I've never told anyone anything that you didn't want me to tell. Did I tell you that Grant kissed me last night?" Cecily gave a sigh of relief and turned back to the dishes in the sink thinking if Clemmie knew the kisses that she had shared with Levi, she would be shocked. Cecily felt the heat spread throughout her body just thinking of Levi's kisses and felt she could live forever lost in kissing the man she could have loved for ten lifetimes.

Clemmie talked on of Grant and Cecily listened with half an ear while she finished the dishes and tried not to think about what she was doing to Levi. She would give Bernard the two thousand dollars that Levi gave her for the farm and hope the other two thousand Levi put in the bank for her lasted a good long time. She would never be free of Bernard; she knew that she wouldn't, and once she married Levi, he would be paying forever and not even know. No matter what happened she had to keep Levi from knowing the truth; she would lie and even steal if she must to keep Levi safe from learning what she had done. She had no honor, she was full of dishonor and shame, and Levi couldn't know of that either. She would lose him; she didn't deserve him; she had no right to marry him and pull him into this terrible situation with her.

Cecily began washing another pot and thinking while Clemmie chattered on. If she had to kill Bernard to protect herself and Levi and the whole community from learning what Bernard had on her, she would. She should have killed Bernard two years ago, then her darling Daddy would be alive right now, not turning cold in his grave, the farm would still be running smoothly, Bernard had ruined her life; she couldn't let him ruin Levi's life. She would find some way to pay him, and if she couldn't, she'd find another way to protect herself. She wondered if she could kill Bernard. Her father had wanted too, but he was a Christian man, and it made Cecily stop and think of the Ten Commandments, and thou shall not kill, she wondered what God would think of her desire to do Bernard in since God knew what Bernard was doing to her.

If only she could trust Levi and tell him the truth. If only she could tell someone what was happening to her, but she was trapped in a world of silence with her secret, and the silence must make no sound. She was also trapped in a world of fear she could not let go of, her future so uncertain. She took a long deep breath and hung her head over the sink and asked God to again help her; she needed His help. For two years God had seemed to ignore her, she prayed now begging Him to not ignore her any longer; she needed help.

Levi knocked on Cecily's kitchen door the Sunday following her father's funeral and smiled at Clemmie when she opened the door. "Good morning, Clemmie. Is Cecily awake?" he asked, and Clemmie returned his easy smile.

"She's in the parlor," Clemmie said. "I'll just take a walk so you can be alone with her, Levi." Clemmie started to pass him, and Levi moved out of her way still looking into her eyes.

"I think I might have brought someone with me who would want to take that walk with you," he winked right before Clemmie looked up and saw Grant in the yard. "I guess I'll see you later," he said as he watched Clemmie hurry past him and into Grant's waiting arms.

Cecily was in the parlor polishing the furniture when Levi entered the room. "Hello beautiful," he said, and she looked up at him to see his easy, sweet smile and bright eyes. "You didn't come to church this morning," he said lightly as Cecily put down her oil and rag. She blushed as she remembered last week and how she had fallen into his lap at church and then all the kisses since then and how he made her feel, that liquid fire spreading even now throughout her body as she looked up at Levi.

"I forgot it was Sunday," she said softly. "And the house needed to be cleaned."

"We'll go together to church next Sunday, darlin'. I actually came over to invite you to my house tonight for dinner. Grant is taking Clemmie home to her folks for dinner, and I thought you could spend some time with me. Ollie will be there, and she's cooking now."

"That would be nice, Levi. Give me a few moments to get cleaned up."

Cecily had been to Levi's home many times in her life. She had played there with Clemmie and Sarah while her mother had visited with Levi's mother. She knew the house like her own home. And his house had been a home filled with love and laughter; she prayed that she would not destroy that image of his home with her secret and lies.

Levi helped Cecily out of the buggy knowing that in less than a week's time he would have her living in his home. He held her hand while they walked up onto the porch, the porch wrapped around the whole house, there were doors leading to the porch from almost every room in his home. The house was painted white with dark green trim and was a single story home; you could walk into the front door, and down a long hall, the living room and dining room and bedrooms were all off that long hall and at the far end was the kitchen. They entered the kitchen now, and Ollie turned to speak to Cecily as Cecily looked around the room, Levi had added all the modern connivances to the kitchen with a new stove, the walls were solid limestone, there were hooks drilled into that limestone so that pots and pans could hang on the wall. "Come look, Miss Cecily," Ollie took her hand and pulled her to the sink. "Mister Levi has added both hot and cold water to run to the sink," she put Cecily's hand under the water and grinned. "Mister Levi," Ollie called him, and he stepped to where they stood, "you go show Miss Cecily the rest of this house while I get dinner on the table. It's been a while since you were here last, honey." Ollie pinched Cecily's cheek and gave her a quick hug; she'd always been fond of Cecily and Clemmie and was glad that soon Levi would no longer be alone.

Levi held Cecily's hand as he pulled her from the kitchen; he loved holding her hand. He couldn't keep his hands to himself when she was around. And the best thing was that Cecily didn't seem to mind his holding her hand. For one brief moment, he thought of Bernard Calhoun touching his Cecily and kissing her, and the jealousy ate away at his whole being. He wouldn't think of that, Levi told himself firmly. The past was in the past, Bernard wasn't a part of their relationship, and Cecily made it clear she didn't like Bernard any longer when she had asked him to eat with her, and he'd felt her tension and fear of Bernard.

They walked together into the dining room, and Cecily saw the high walls, the ceiling was so high up that not even Levi who was well over six feet tall could reach it with his arm extended. There were soft blue curtains hanging on the windows which were open wide to let in the gentle breeze that was blowing. Levi had added screens to the window and the doors to keep out the bugs and snakes and lizards. Cecily turned and smiled at the portrait that hung high above the credenza, Levi's parents looked down over the room from that portrait and Levi at about the age of five stood between them, even as a little boy he had been beautiful, Cecily thought as she stared up at the painting.

"That was done the year before you and Sarah were born," Levi said as he looked up at the painting with Cecily. "I was mad as fire at the man that had painted it. He said something about my hair being a mess all the time. I still can't think of that man without my gut burning. Mama and Ollie sat me down and cut my hair; I didn't want my hair cut. That's why I'm pouting in the painting. I refused to smile at that man."

"I never knew you to be stubborn, Levi," Cecily stated and looked at Levi standing beside her.

"I'm not generally. I don't know what's wrong with me; I'm hard I guess. If I get mad at someone, I just stay mad; I can't get over it. Mama said I was unforgiving and use to lecture me and read bible verses on forgiveness. I've struggled through the years with that side of my temper."

"It sounds to me like you're stubborn, Levi," Cecily said with a soft laugh that was almost forced, she hoped with all her heart that if he learned of her secret, he would forgive her. Levi looked down at his future bride and gave her one of his easy smiles. "And getting mad over a comment on your hair being a mess, that's just unreasonable."

"Five-year-old boys are never reasonable, darlin'," Levi pulled her from the dining room to the huge front parlor. One wall was covered with a limestone fireplace; the oak mantle above the fireplace was thick and heavy. The walls in the rest of the rooms were a knotty pine paneling as was the ceiling and floors. Doors stood at the front and the side of the room and were open leading to the porch outside. The furniture was dark and heavy with a high shine. It was a beautiful room. Cecily smiled as she saw another painting of Levi and his sister Sarah. Levi was about 16, and Sarah was about 11, she almost lost her breath looking at the painting, Levi had been so handsome, it was no wonder as a little girl she had adored him.

"I can remember our parents visiting in this room," Cecily said as she looked away from the painting of her beautiful Levi.

"Everything is just as my mother had it before she passed away. If you want to make any changes to the house, Cecily, please feel free to do so." Levi pulled her into the hall that ran from one end of the house to the other the walls, ceiling and floors here were also made of the knotty pine wood. Cecily could remember running up and down this hall with Sarah and Clemmie as a child, often afraid of the shadows in the day time. The doors on each end of the hall were wide open now and a photograph of Levi with a serious expression frozen on his face for all time banged against the wall in its beveled glass frame as the wind blew through the hall.

Levi opened the door leading into the master bedroom, that bedroom was at the very front of the house. Like the parlor it had double doors leading off and onto the porch, and the furniture was heavy and dark and shone bright. This room needed no changes, Cecily thought. The whole house was perfect. Too perfect for her.

They moved to Sarah's old bedroom, and Cecily saw one of Sarah's dolls on the center of the bed. The curtain and the canopy on the bed were a soft pink, the same as she remembered when she had been a child. When she had been a young girl just on the verge of becoming a woman, she had lain in this bed with Sarah and Clemmie and had dreamed of one day marrying Levi and living in this house. She turned and looked at him and knew, her dreams were about to come true. If only she could be happy over the fact that she was marrying the man of her dreams, she thought. Cecily felt anything but happy at the moment. She had no right to this home. She had no right to Levi. She was coming to him the way that she was now which was in need of money. The only thing that mattered was money and Levi had money, otherwise, she would never have married him as things were right now.

"I use to sit and listen to you and Sarah and Clemmie play here from my bedroom," Levi said. "You were such silly girls. Grant and I would laugh in those days at how we thought you all were just prissy girls. And now look at us. Grant head over heels in love with Clemmie and I'm fixing to marry you."

"Things change," Cecily said as Levi took her past his own bedroom.

"That's my bedroom, and it's not picked up, so I won't let you see it," Levi said, and Cecily blushed. The other bedrooms were all simple; they had handmade quilts on their beds and braided rag rugs on the floor. The furniture was pine and light. "If my mother had had more children, these rooms would have been fancier. She had two stillborn daughters between myself and Sarah and lost a little boy after Sarah." Levi closed the door on the last bedroom, and Cecily thought of her own mother who had died trying to have a baby. There had been other children born to Daniel and Amelia Walker, but all had only lived a short time. Cecily had been their only child to survive childhood.

"You have a beautiful home," Cecily said as Levi took her back into the dining room. Ollie Tool had the table set, and dinner was waiting for them "I don't think that I'll bring anything from my father's house over here. I'd like to know that home is where I left it," Cecily said, and she took a bite of her chicken once she and Levi were seated at the table and their plates were filled with food.

"I'd like my home to be your home now, Cecily," Levi said softly, and Cecily looked up at him beside her. "I'm sorry, Levi. This will be my home once we are married." Cecily tried to eat, but she could taste nothing despite the fact that she knew the food was good. She kept thinking of all the valuables that had been in her father's home, valuables that had to be sold in order for her to be safe from Bernard and the constant threat of ruin. She had wreaked and ruined her father's home trying to buy Bernard Calhoun's silence. She did not want to destroy Levi's home; it was too perfect. She squeezed her eyes shut tight and fought the battle within herself. She had to marry Levi. She had too. Cecily shook her head hard; could she really drag him into this mess that she had made of her life? She should leave here now, take the money he'd given her for the farm and run away and let Levi be safe. If she cared for him at all, she would run now.

She had nowhere to go, Cecily thought in despair. This was her only choice. She didn't want to be alone in the world with no support and no place to live. She didn't want her friends here in Cherry Lake to know what she had done. She wanted to love Levi; she didn't want to leave him. Cecily opened her eyes and looked up into Levi's face, all her whole life she'd wanted to be with him, and she was going to bring shame to him and sorrow, by marrying him she was sentencing him to the hell she'd been living in for the past two years.

Levi saw Cecily shake her head and close her eyes tight, he wondered what she was thinking, was this grief for her father? Was this grief for leaving her home? "Cecily," he said her name softly, and she opened those beautiful crystal clear blue eyes that were now too bright with unshed tears. "Cecily," he said her name again.

She could not do this! Her mind screamed. She could not bring about the demise of this man, of Levi. She had known for days she couldn't tell him the truth, she never could. She really could not do this; she could not marry this man for his money when she loved him as she did. She had to get away from here now. She had to allow Bernard to carry out his evil threat and see herself destroyed rather than destroy this wonderful man. She would rather live a life of shame throughout all time than to hurt Levi. She could not hurt Levi.

Levi watched Cecily's face go pale, her eyes turned even brighter, and he frowned. Then, without a sound, without any warning, she jumped up from her chair and ran from the dining room. Levi jumped up from his own chair so quickly to follow her that it crashed to the floor. "Cecily!" he called out her name as she left the house and he left the house close behind her.

Cecily lifted up her skirt and made a mad dash down the red clay road toward her own home. She was scared to death. She had never been so totally alone before. She knew what she had planned to do to Levi was wrong. And she didn't know what to do. She only knew she had to save herself and she would not hurt Levi in the saving of herself. She begged God to help her. She was too afraid to even think straight. Her sin would become Levi's sin!!! Her mind screamed at her. She could not stay here. She had nowhere to go; her heart was pounding these words inside of her head over and over.

Levi reached out and grabbed Cecily's arm, and she gasped for breath. "Don't touch me, Levi!" she yelled, and he let her go. "Oh God," she more prayed that cried. "I can't marry you. I thought that I could, but I can't." She was sobbing now, and Levi reached out and turned her to face him, her face was buried in her hands as she sobbed.

"What's the matter, Cecily?" he asked her in his soft voice, and she looked up at him, he had that kind expression on his face, he wouldn't be so kind when he learned the truth about her. Her face had a tortured look on it, and Levi felt worried sick for her, "Talk to me, darlin'. It's alright; you can tell me anything, anything at all."

She couldn't tell him anything; if she told him what she couldn't tell him, he would hate her for all time and beyond. "You don't know me, Levi. You don't know what I've done. I'm not good and honorable and kind as you are. I'm none of those things. I'm bad, Levi, really bad," Cecily looked up into his eyes and assured him of this, she wanted him to at least know this truth of her.

Levi grabbed her and pulled her into his arm thinking that she really believed these words that she said to him. He felt Cecily lay her head on his chest as she begged him to believe her and Levi rocked her gently and held her close, knowing that he would never believe anything bad of her.

"Hush Cecily," he finally said right before she fell silent. "This is grief and pain talking. And I know you're ashamed for having given yourself to Bernard. But that doesn't matter to me. Honestly it doesn't. I won't let it matter. All I want is to make you happy and safe and to love you with all my heart. I could never be ashamed of you." He felt her sag against him and Levi took a deep breath of relief; she was hearing his words. He didn't understand what was happening to her; all he knew was that he had to have her and anyway that he could get her. And he didn't want her to hate herself for giving herself to Bernard. She had made a mistake, she was sorry for the mistake, they both may wish she hadn't done what she did, but he knew you couldn't turn back time. And Bernard was out of her life. "You do love me, don't you darlin'?" he asked suddenly afraid that she still might feel something for Bernard Calhoun. He felt her head nod against his chest and sighed in relief. "Then we can overcome anything once we're married. I'll forgive you anything, Cecily. Always, you have my word."

Cecily lifted her tear-streaked face and looked up at Levi, and he put his forehead onto her forehead. She was blessed that he did want her; she thought and felt him kiss her forehead and pull her close again. He was all that she had in the world. If she ran from him now, she would have nothing, and she would be nothing. She might as well be dead.

"My life is worthless without you Cecily," Levi said, and she took a deep breath to hear these words and then sighed. "You are mine now. Nothing can hurt us or separate us ever." She looked back up at him and hoped that his words were true. She felt guilt and shame consume her, then his lips touched hers, and she put her arms around his neck and held on for dear life. She needed him, and she knew she would do what she had to do, the only thing she could do.

Levi felt Cecily move closer to him as his mouth covered her mouth. He heard her moan and dove deep within her mouth with his tongue. "Dear God in heaven," Levi prayed as he came up for air. "I want you so much darlin', and I feel you want me too," he took her mouth again and felt her body mold into his, his knee going between her legs and him pressing his knee against her softest place.

Cecily almost shattered apart when Levi moved his leg between her thighs, she cried out and held on to him as his mouth took on her cry of pleasure. What was he doing to her? She tried to think and then couldn't think at all. He had her bent back in his arms and was kissing the life's breath from her body; she was on fire and burning up in his arms. "Help me," she whimpered when he let go of her mouth and covered her ear, his tongue diving into the hollowness there. "Levi," she breathed and gasped and shook apart all at the same time as his hand took a hold of her breast and squeezed gently. He was making her feel too much; he was killing her, Cecily thought and knew she shouldn't allow him this, they weren't married. But it was too late; if he pulled away from her right this second, she was certain she would die.

Levi felt Cecily respond to his touch and he gloried in the fact that she wanted him as much as he wanted her. He pushed his knee into her and felt her shaking apart; he heard her gasping for every breath and knew he'd given her pleasure. He pulled her back upright into his arms and saw her questioning look into his eyes, she may have slept with Bernard, but Bernard had never done to her what he just had done.

Cecily didn't understand what had just happened, her body was trembling inside and out still, she was liquid fire, and she never felt such a release of throbbing tension. Levi had her upright and was looking down into her eyes with a very satisfied grin on his face. "We shouldn't be doing this Levi," she almost cried, and the grin on his face faded quickly away.

"Forgive me darlin'," Levi said in a breathless whisper. "I didn't mean to rush you. I can't help myself; I've waited so long for you to be mind."

"I'm scared, Levi. I'm just so afraid."

"You aren't afraid of me, are you Cecily? What we just did; you wanted me." He saw her shake her head and took a deep breath. He was rushing her, he hadn't even courted her, and here he was making love to her in his own front yard.

"I'm afraid I won't make you a good wife," Cecily whispered, and Levi realized in that moment that she was afraid he would be bothered by the fact that she had given in so easily to him after having been with Bernard. "I don't want to fail you, Levi. Please, understand," she begged. "Promise that once we are married, you'll give me time to get over losing Daddy. You'll give me time before I come to you as a real wife," she turned a bright red in her face as she spoke; "I'm not ready."

"I've waited for you for five long years Cecily; I can wait until you say you're ready for the marriage bed. And I'll court you like I should have and wanted too." And he knew, he would make love to her with his mouth and with his eyes and his hands, when they finally came together as one, she would be more than ready, and any fears or doubts she might have will be long forgotten. "I know you're grieving your father; we have all the time in the world."

Levi gave her one of his easy smiles and took her hand, once they were living together, she would settle down, and before long there would be a baby in his home. "Come back inside with me; I have something for you." Levi pulled her gently by the hand back up the steps and into his house.

Once they reentered the house, Cecily saw Ollie give her a worried look and forced herself to smile at the kind old maid. "If you need anything, Miss Cecily," Ollie reached out and hugged her while looking hard at Levi, "you give this child time to get over losing her Daddy and try and remember she's leaving her home to come here, her worlds gone upside down, you be gentle with her." Levi nodded his head and smiled at Ollie knowing she was right in her advice to him.

"I want you to have this," Levi said as he pulled out a small velvet covered box from a larger wooden box he had sat on the table. Cecily took the box from him and opened it up. "That was my mother's betrothal ring. I want you to have it."

"Levi," Cecily said his name as she looked from the beautiful diamond to his beautiful face.

"Let me put it on your finger." Levi took the box from her and removed the ring as she held out her hand for him. "Will you marry me?" he asked as Cecily watched him slip the ring onto her finger and knew there was no going back from here. She would marry him. She nodded her head while looking up into his eyes and knew; she would be tormented with the reason why for the rest of her life, but she would marry him. She looked down again at the beautiful ring and knew that she may have to part with this ring in order to protect him, and herself. She did not want Bernard to have his mother's ring. She wanted to keep this ring all to herself. She knew that hoping and wishing that she would keep this ring was useless, Bernard would see it soon and take it from her, he was taking everything from her.

Levi called on Cecily every evening and often stayed until well after dark. He always brought Grant with him so that Clemmie would not be alone; Levi knew that Grant was glad to come along. On Wednesday he brought her another gift and Cecily opened it shyly and exclaimed over the lovely broach that she held in her small hand. Levi saw her worried look as he penned the broach on her lace collar at her throat and smiled.

"Don't worry, darlin'," he said lightly and tapped her chin so she would look up into his eyes. "If you lose it, I'll buy you another one."

Cecily wasn't afraid that she would lose her lovely new broach. She was afraid that it would be taken from her, by Bernard Calhoun.

"I promised not to kiss you again until we are married," Levi said with a light tease to his voice. "But may I?" he saw Cecily's eyes close and she leaned in closer, he wanted to make love to her again with his mouth, he wanted to hear her gasp and cry out in his arms again, but he knew he had to wait. His mouth came gently over her mouth, and he lost himself in the kiss, even becoming more lost as her tongue pushed past his lips, she was killing him with his desire for her, and he wondered if she knew. "We have to stop, or I won't keep my promise," Levi breathed against her cheek.

"What promise?" Cecily asked as his mouth covered her mouth again and she was pulled closer. They would be married soon, she assured herself.

Cecily slipped out of the house late on Wednesday night and waited in the darkness. She had the money that Levi had given her for the farm and knew that Bernard would be here soon to meet with her. She had thought about only giving him half of the money that Levi had given her for the farm, but thought better of doing that. If she gave Bernard the full two thousand dollars now he just might leave her alone for a long time to come. She could only hope that he would but felt sick with worry that he might not.

"So, you're here," Bernard said as he came up behind Cecily in the darkness and she nearly cried out as she whirled around to face the devil that he was, her very own personal devil. "You do follow orders well, Cecily." Bernard laughed, and Cecily took a step back and away from him, his breath stank and made her feel sick.

"Here Bernard," she thrust the envelope full of money at him, and he took it from her trembling hands with another sharp and cruel laugh.

"How much did good old Levi give to you?" he asked as he looked inside the envelope, but he could see nothing as it was far too dark a night out.

"Levi gave me two thousand dollars. Please, Bernard, I beg you please, let me alone for a little while." He laughed again, and Cecily hung her head. He would never leave her alone for long; she knew that. His greed drove him back to her time and time again. He would bleed her dry of any and all money she could get from Levi. And she would let him bleed her dry. She had to let him; she was afraid of his threat; she was afraid that his threat may someday be carried out.

"Your future husband messed up my face for a lifetime, Cecily. Levi broke my nose in two places." Cecily gasped when the moonlight shone full on Bernard's face. His once handsome nose was totally wreaked and ruined, Cecily saw. Bernard's nose was crooked and bent and swollen as were his eyes. Levi had hurt Bernard bad, far worse than she had known. "Levi will pay for what he did to me, Cecily." Bernard turned to leave, and Cecily stood still not seeing when he turned back to her. "By the way," Bernard said, and Cecily looked over to where he stood. "Good luck in your marriage." He laughed out loud, and Cecily fought not to shake apart in her fear of him.

Cecily stood alone after Bernard had left her; the darkness around her was not calming. She needed Bernard Calhoun to drop dead as her father had, she thought. That would bring good luck to her marriage. But then, Cecily knew, good luck was something that she hadn't known in a long time. The only luck that Cecily had was bad.

Thursday afternoon came too soon for Cecily and not soon enough for Levi. She had sent a trunk of her clothes over to Levi's house early that morning with Grant, everything else that she had, she left in her home as it was. She might need to come back here someday if she failed her husband and herself. She prayed she did not fail Levi and could always meet Bernard's demands.

Cecily wore a black blouse and skirt as she was in morning for her father, she had Clemmie pen on the broach that Levi had given to her at her throat and then had gone pale when Clemmie teasingly said, "Marry in black, wish yourself back." Clemmie saw Cecily go pale and made no other remarks in fun. She knew this wasn't the wedding that Cecily had dreamed of all of her life, it was not really even a wedding, it was just the exchanging of wedding vows, and it was really very sad, Clemmie thought because Cecily was grieving horribly for her father.

At the church, the Reverend Bidwell gave Cecily one of his hard stares and asked her if she knew her good fortune in having Levi Tucker marry her. She should be down on her knees thanking God that Levi would take her for his wife for the rest of his days, the Reverend Bidwell had further stated, and Clemmie burst into laughter, and even the Reverend's firm stare had no effect on Clemmie as she continued to smile.

Grant had worn his best suit and came inside the church before Levi. "He's fixing his tie," Grant explained to Cecily as she stared back at the door. "He says that he's not nervous, I know he is." Grant looked at Cecily's face and frowned, she was white as a ghost, and he then saw she was shaking all over, she could not deny her nerves as Levi had. She looked miserable on her wedding day; Grant thought and looked at Clemmie who was also staring at Cecily. "Don't look so worried," Grant spoke causing Cecily and Clemmie to both look at him at the same time. "Levi won't eat you for dinner," his comment was meant to bring a smile and some ease, but instead Cecily looked at him and stated very seriously,

"I should be so lucky that he would do so."

"Darling," Clemmie hugged her tight and tried to speak reassuringly to her best friend. "You'll be just fine. Honestly, old Reverend Bidwell is right, Levi will take wonderful care of you."

Levi came inside the church and took a moment for his eyes to adjust to the lightning. Then he saw Cecily waiting for him with Clemmie hugging her, and he smiled. His whole face lit up with the smile he gave to her. She was going to marry him, he thought, and he hurried to where she stood knowing that in just a few moments, she was going to be his wife. He couldn't help but see how pale she was, and how afraid, he would actually have had to have been blind to not notice her feelings as he took her cold hand into his own and turned to the Reverend Bidwell who had come into the church when he had. "I think we're ready now," he said and squeezed Cecily's hand tight.

She stood still beside Levi and listened as he pledged himself to her for better or worse and she prayed it would not be for the worse. He stated that he would take her for richer or for poorer and she prayed harder that she would not make him poor. And when he vowed until death parted them, she knew that she would rather die than have Levi see what Bernard had of her.

Levi slid the thick wedding band onto Cecily's slim finger before he bent his head and kissed her, his lips were soft as they brushed against her own and she trembled, not from desire, but from guilt. She felt her breath leave her body and she couldn't gasp for more air. She heard Levi say her name from somewhere far away and the Reverend Bidwell called out, "Levi, catch her quick!" and then the whole world seemed to be going black. Levi would be safe after all, came her last thoughts. She was dropping dead just like her father had. She was setting Levi free. She wasn't going to bring hurt and shame and pain and disgust upon him. She was dying, and in that death, her beloved Levi would be safe.

"My Lord," the good Reverend Bidwell said as Cecily slipped into her husband's arms and he lowered her to the floor in his embrace. "The child fainted, I wasn't expecting that."

Levi thought he wasn't expecting her to faint either as he touched her cheek and called her name in a soft voice. She lay still, so he took her shoulders and gave a gentle shake but still she didn't respond. All the excitement of marrying him and so soon after her father's death had been too much. He should have waited for her to deal with her grief and then he knew he would wait, he would give her time and he'd pay court to her as a gentleman should.

"Move, Levi," Clemmie gently said. She had a glass of water in her hand, and he just now realized she'd been gone a few moments while he stared at his new bride. He watched Clemmie splash water onto Cecily's face and then her blink and look up at him, reach for him and cry in a soft voice,

"Levi." Levi bent down and pushed past Clemmie.

"I'm right here, darlin'." He helped her to sit up and held her steady for a long few moments wanting to give her his strength; she was so hurt and so sad. Levi didn't want Cecily sad.

"I thought I was dying just like Daddy did," Cecily held tight to his hand. "Please, forgive me, Levi, I'm so sorry. I seem to ruin everything that I do." Levi reached for her and helped her to sit up as he placed a gentle kiss on her cool cheek.

"You didn't ruin anything, darlin'. And it should be me begging your forgiveness. You're not over your father's death yet. It was too soon. I won't allow you to rush anymore." He helped her to her feet, and Cecily clung to him for dear life. "You just need some rest and time. You'll be fine. I'm going to take good care of you from now on."

Cecily had been through too much in the past week, Levi thought. His kissing her in the field the day after her father died, he made love to her with his mouth on the way home from the funeral and again in front of his home. He was rushing her, and he knew that too. Even if she wasn't pure and had experience from Bernard, she was still grieving.

"Everything will be fine, Cecily. Let me get you home and some rest, and you'll be just fine." Cecily listened to Levi wishing that she was really and truly dead. He did not deserve what she was going to do to him. He did not deserve this; she cried inside. She was going to hell; she was in hell. She was Levi's hell.

The Reverend Bidwell, Grant, and Clemmie watched Levi take his new wife out of the church. They all saw how pale Cecily was and she looked scared out of her mind, sick with fear for anyone that cared to look could easily see. They all stood together frowning each wondering why Levi seemed so oblivious to his new wife's fear.

"Something is wrong with that girl," The Reverend Bidwell said looking from Grant to Clemmie. "She's more afraid than any new bride I've ever seen. And I've seen many new brides.'

"She really was scared," Grant agreed. "And half out of her mind."

"But she wasn't scared of Levi," Clemmie said and shook her head. Something was going on with her best friend, and she didn't know what it was. And she didn't know how to help.

"Something is wrong with her," The Reverend Bidwell said again. "And I don't believe that Levi Tucker knows there's something wrong with her. I think Levi is blind to everything but that girl's beauty and gentle, sweet nature. I wonder if she'll tell him what is troubling her now that she's his wife."

"I'm sure that if Levi doesn't know what's going on with Cecily, she'll tell him soon enough or he'll figure it out," Grant said. "He's spent a lot of time with her this past week. If she didn't tell him what's bothering her before, she will soon enough."

"Clemmie looked at Grant. She had known Cecily since they were babies in the cradle together and she didn't know what was the matter with her best friend, if she didn't know, then she was certain that Levi had no clue. Cecily had a secret that she was guarding well and with all of her heart. Clemmie wondered if it had something to do with the money that Cecily had said that she owed. After a few moments thought, Clemmie decided that it did have something to do with money. Cecily was in some sort of trouble, Clemmie was certain without any doubt. Cecily was in terrible trouble, and she wasn't going to let anyone help her. Not even Levi who was completely dumb to the fact that Cecily needed help.

Chapter Four

Cecily sat stiff beside Levi on the buggy ride home. She felt like she could not bear anything more. The burden of guilt was so heavy that her heart was hurting inside of her chest with a pain she did not want and could not take. And Levi, he sat beside her in total ignorance and believed that she loved him when she knew she could never allow herself to be totally in love with her husband. There was no way that he could ever understand her reason for marrying him, if he were to find out the truth, he would know that she had only married him for the protection his money offered her. What love she did feel for him would mean nothing. Bernard's threats were keeping her from Levi. Bernard's threats were making her hurt Levi.

Levi was not a dumb man regardless of the fact that he couldn't read and write and never had been able to learn to read. He knew how to make money well, he could add five digit figures in his head in a matter of seconds, and he knew the signs of pure, unadulterated fear. Cecily was in that fear. The only thing that he felt dumb about was that he could not figure out what had his Cecily torn up this way. What was so afraid of? He didn't want her to be afraid of him. He hoped she was not afraid of him.

Levi sat in the buggy on the ride home deep in thought. He searched his brain for what could be wrong with Cecily. She had been terrified out of her mind by Bernard Calhoun the other day, and now today she thought that she was dying like her father had died. He realized she was afraid of dying just as Daniel Walker had died and it brought her to this terrible state of mine. He tried to puzzle her out as he sat beside on the seat of the buggy. He was her husband now, she was his to protect for a lifetime, but he could find nothing to satisfy his mind of her fear. He knew of no way to help her, and he had to help her.

"I didn't mean to embarrass you, Levi," Cecily finally broke the silence that surrounded them when she spoke in a small strained voice. A frown covered Levi's face while he looked straight ahead.

"You didn't embarrass me, darlin'. You scared me near to death." He felt her eyes on him and stopped the buggy to look down into her eyes. "I don't know what's troubling you, Cecily. And I'd die if anything ever happened to you. I want to keep you safe; I want to help you. Won't you let me help you?" He saw Cecily stare hard into his eyes; her face had that tortured look on it that he was coming to hate. And then her head shook, and she looked away from him, and he knew that she wasn't going to tell him what was going on in her mind. "Cecily," he said her name softly and touched her chin forcing her to look up at his face. "I'm not blind. I can see you're fragile and hurt right now. And I also realize that if I were to touch you, you would break apart in my hands." Cecily gasped and looked away from him. Levi didn't force her to look back at him. "Talk to me, darlin'. Tell me what is wrong, and I swear by all I hold dear in this life, that I'll protect you and make it all right for you. Before God, I swear Cecily."

Her eyes went back to his face. If only she could tell him, Cecily thought. He did not deserve her silence, but silence was all she had to give him. He would not love her; he would not protect her; he would not stand by her if he knew what Bernard knew. She had nothing else that she could give to Levi, no matter his words. If she broke her vow of silence and told him everything he would never understand, not now. He would only know one thing were she to speak up now, and that was that she had married him for his money.

"So much has happened so fast, Levi. I feel overwhelmed," was all that Cecily could think to tell him. There was truth in her words to him now, too little truth.

Levi believed her words and accepted them for the truth and the fact that they were. He loved her; he could do no less than believe her. "What can I do to help you feel better?" he asked and put his long, lean arm around her slender shoulders wanting to take some of her burdens onto himself.

"Give me some time," Cecily said and looked up into his beautiful deep dark eyes. A blush covered her pale face for she knew that he would want her in his bed tonight. She wasn't ready for that; she could not be intimate with him; not with all the lies, she had told him. Guilt for what she had done to him today and for what she would be doing to him for the rest of their lives consumed her. And shame, the shame that she felt for her lies were more awful than her guilt ever could be, she would live with the shame always. "Give me some time to myself Levi. Please, I need some time to myself." Her voice almost broke, and she had to swallow hard to keep from breaking down completely and jumping from his buggy and running away to hide from him. She felt certain that he could see her shame and sin against him in her eyes.

"All right, darlin'. As of right now, you are free from all pressure and responsibility. You deal with your grief and whatever else there is you need to deal with." His eyes were serious, and Cecily wondered if he understood that she did not want to be in their marriage bed yet.

"Thank you, Levi. But you do understand what I'm asking you for?" Her eyes were as serious as his while she stared up at him wishing that she had not married him, yet knowing in her heart that she had no other choice. She had done what she had to do. She would always do what she had to do.

"The master bedroom is yours, Cecily and yours alone. Until you say for me to join you, I'll stay away." Levi reached for the reins and started the horses to walking home again. He wanted her so badly that his gut ached with his need, but he knew she was hurting, he would not add to her hurt. When he took her as his wife in their bed, she would want him there, and he would give her all of himself, she would take all of him and be ready for him, he would make her beg for him before he finally and at last joined her in that bed.

"I don't deserve you, Levi," she whispered, and he took a deep breath. "If I live to a thousand years old, I'll never deserve you."

Levi's frown deepened. Why would she think that she wasn't deserving of him? What was going on in her mind? And he knew beyond a shadow of a doubt that she was keeping something from him. He would give her the time that she had asked for, he would wait as he had been waiting for all these years, and he would watch her, every minute of the day and night that he could spare, he would watch out for her and over her.

Cecily laid her head on his shoulder, and Levi kept his eyes focused straight ahead of him on the clay dirt road that led the way home. He had done the right thing by her and for her. He just hoped that he still felt this way tonight in his lonely bed. He thought of the way that she had responded to his kisses, how she had kissed him back, how she had shattered in his arms. He knew inside his heart that whatever was going on with her wasn't about their love making; she was too willing to be in his arms. He felt secure in her love for him; he had no doubts. All these years she had been wanting him as he had wanted her, he had held himself away from her in fear of rejection. Cecily would never have rejected him, except now and only because of her grief. She was afraid of something; he thought again but had no idea what she feared. He would give her time, and she would tell him.

"Levi," Cecily said his name when he lifted her down from the buggy. "Would you mind terribly if I went to bed? I've not been sleeping much the last few nights," her eyes looked into his with a plea for understanding as his hands still held onto her tiny waist after he had her safely on the ground, her clear eyes locked with his own and he thought again of how much he loved her. He could see the dark circles under her eyes; those circles made darker because she was so pale. She did not look well; she looked like she might even be near to some illness. He had to let her alone. He had to give her time to get used to him and his home. He needed to court her as a lover. He had given his word he would not rush her and he would not, he was going to keep his word no matter how badly he ached to be inside of her. "I don't mind, darlin'. You just get some rest. Would you like me to have Ollie send you something to eat?" He let her go and backed away from her so that she could walk ahead of him into their home. Ollie had made a special meal for tonight, he wished that she had felt up to sharing that meal with him, but he completely understood that she was tired; it had been a long hard week for her. He pushed aside any disappointment that he might have felt aside and thought only of his wife as a good husband should do.

"I'm too tired to eat," Cecily said as she reached the doorway of her new home and gasped when Levi lifted her up into his arms. Tradition dictates that a husband carries his wife over the threshold of their new home and she knew that was what he was doing. His gentle, easy smile was on his face as he lowered her down to the floor inside the hall.

"Welcome home, Miss Tucker," he said softly and placed a gentle kiss on her cheek. "I love you," he said with ease and kissed her again.

Cecily stood stunned, she could not say those words back to him, she couldn't say anything to him, and she tried to not think of what kissing him did to her. "I'm so tired," she pleaded again.

"I can see that you're tired, darlin'. You don't have to say anything more." He went to the master bedroom door and led the way in for her. She put her handbag down on a chair by the door that led to the porch; the door was open to let in the cool air of the late day. "I had this added on to the house last year," Levi said as he opened a door to what Cecily thought was a closet.

"Levi, it's a bathroom, it's a real indoor bathroom," she said and walked inside the room, a shocked expression on her face. "I don't know anyone that has a real bathroom." Levi was smiling down at her, and she saw his beautiful smile.

"I had planned on moving into this room last year, but I wanted to wait until I was married, Cecily. Until I was married to you." He went and turned on the water and put her hand under the running water. "I had hot and cold water put in here. And Ollie hung all your clothes in the closet and put the rest in the drawers for you. I haven't moved my things in yet; I was waiting for you to be settled and rested." He hoped that it would not be long before his things were getting all mixed up with her things. He wanted her so much that he knew he would go down to the lake tonight and take a cold dip in the water to calm down his needs. He had to take a deep breath when he saw her go and sit down on the bed, that bed should be holding them both this very night.

"I can't thank you enough for what you're doing for me, Levi," Cecily spoke as she looked up into his handsome face. This was their wedding night. She wasn't blind to his desire for her; Levi's eyes hid nothing. First she had lied to him, Then she had deceived him into marrying her. She gave his money to Bernard Calhoun and now she was turning him away from his rightful place beside her in their bed and with him believing that she was an experienced woman, that she had been with Bernard the way a wife was with a husband. She could have him join her now, tonight and he would know the truth, that she was innocent. She sat on the bed thinking of letting him join her in this bed, but she knew the truth was she was far too tired, and she wasn't ready for this, not tonight and not now. When he did join her as he someday soon would, what would he do when he realized that he had had been wrong and that she had not set him right about her relationship with Bernard? She blushed red and felt horrified that Levi believed that she could have lain with any man without the bonds of matrimony. She needed time to think; she had to have time to set everything in her own mind right, or as right as she could set things that were nothing but lies.

"If you need anything, my room is just down the hall," Levi managed to say before he turned away from Cecily.

Cecily watched Levi leave her alone in the master bedroom. He was gone, and she had to let out a long deep breath that she had been holding when he pulled the door closed. Levi would let her alone, she thought again. He was going away, and she was letting him. She would have the time she needed to make everything right in her own mind so that she could accept this marriage that was based on lies. She knew that the threat of Bernard was going to make her life a living hell, it already had been, but if she were good and kind to Levi, she might be able to make up for what she was doing to him. She had to be good to Levi, he was giving her everything, and she knew that she was giving him nothing. She had to hold her heart from him along with the truth. She owed him her kindness at the very least. Her heart was her own, Levi must never touch her there, and yet inside she already knew, her heart wasn't her own, her heart had belonged to Levi and it always would. She was lost and without hope, even married she was alone, Bernard's threats had completely isolated her.

It was just getting dark outside when Cecily sank down into the hot water that filled the bathtub. She ached all over, and the water eased her body. She wondered how she could feel anything other than guilt after all the lies she'd told. She was heartless. Her body should be a hallow and empty shell. She had sold her soul to Bernard, and in so doing she had now involved a good and innocent man in her troubles. She covered her face with the damp washcloth and burst into tears. She had destroyed her father. Now she was going to take Levi down and all to save herself. If he ever found out, she fretted, and then thought, he must never, not ever, find out.

Levi attempted to eat the supper that Ollie had prepared for him and his new bride, and it was an excellent meal, but he couldn't choke down more than a few bites. He kept trying to force himself to eat, someone in this house should be happy tonight. He would try and make Ollie happy by eating the food she'd spent most of the day making. He tasted nothing, Levi thought as he forced himself to swallow each mouth full of the food he took. He longed for his wife. He longed to hold her, to kiss her, to touch her, to look into her crystal clear eyes and tell her he loved her. He was a man with a man's needs, and he had denied himself those needs for too long. He wanted Cecily, he had dreamed of Cecily and this night, and now here he sat married to her and eating alone in the dining room while she slept in their bed alone. She was keeping him from that bed, and he was letting her. He ground his teeth and prayed to God that his wife would let him join her soon. He had to make her completely and totally his.

"Where you going, Mister Levi?" Ollie asked as he walked through the kitchen and out the back door.

"I'm going to take a swim in the lake," he called back to her, and she watched him leave wishing he was where he was supposed to be on a night like tonight.

Levi stood down by the lake with his clothes hanging in the branches of a nearby tree. He lit a cigarette and tried to find some peace within himself. The crickets were using their mating call; their cries filled the night air. A night bird called out from the top of the tree, and he saw that the stars hung so low he felt he could reach out and touch them all at once. Even in the darkness, the whole world was awake and alive and beautiful, God's artwork, he thought. And here he stood in this darkness alone on his wedding night while his new bride slept in a huge bed meant for them both and filled with grief.

Today all of his dreams had come true; now he had to find a way to court his gentle wife and to show her his unending love and have the love with her that his parents had known. He wanted Cecily to be happy; he wanted to be happy. He reached his hand up and rubbed his stiff neck. He would honor her wishes, he would do as she asked, he would be tender and caring and she would see that there was no reason for this unexplained fear she had if that fear was of him. Her grief was hurting her, he hated her grief, but in time, that too would fade. They would be happy together.

Levi sat up straight, his eyes went wide, and he took a deep breath. Cecily had needed his money to pay off her father's debt. She had turned him down in the field that day when he had asked her to marry him and then she had come to him the next morning and told him of her need of money and accepted his proposal without him ever having courted her. And now she had put him from her bed. Cecily loved him, Levi thought as he tried to relax again. She would never marry him only for his money, she wasn't like that, and when he kissed her, she had melted over and over again in his arms. But something was wrong. She was afraid. She needed money. She closed the door on their being together as husband and wife. Something was wrong with his new wife, and he had no idea what it was, and he was more than certain that she wasn't going to tell him anything.

Levi closed his eyes and saw Cecily as a little girl clutching her old rag doll that he had known her to have with her since she was a baby, made for her by her mother. She had been a beautiful little girl, and he hoped one day they together would have a little girl just as she had been. And when she had turned fourteen years old, and he knew that he would wait for her to grow up, he had seen the woman inside of her that she would one day be. She would love him; she would be the mother of his children. Her soft and silent ways touched his heart and held his heart in the palm of his hand.

Cecily could never have married him for just his money. She was feeling lost and alone because her father had died so suddenly. Levi wished that he had been courting her all these many months past that he had put it off wanting to be sure she wanted him to pay her court. He had let the past two years slip by without allowing the bond that they had known all of their lives to remain close and bind them together. He had made a mistake; he had failed Cecily and himself in his own fear of rejection. He vowed to never fail her again. He would remain faithful and loving of her always. There was nothing in this world that would ever part them now; he loved her pure and true; she was his Cecily.

Levi hit the water and swam for what seemed like an hour, the moonlight was streaking across the ripples he had made of the water, and where the water ended, it appeared the moon began. A night bird cried out as he went back under the water thinking if he swam a long time he would be too tired to think any longer of his wife and his need. He swam for two hours and still, he thought of his wife and of his need.

Cecily woke up very late the following morning, she had never slept so late into the morning in her whole life, and she was surprised now that she had been so nervous the night before. She dressed with care hoping that Levi would be at his sawmill; she did not want to face him again until she had put her thoughts into some kind of order. And she had to tell him the truth about never having been with Bernard in that way; he had to know she had never lain with Bernard Calhoun.

Cecily went into the kitchen, and Ollie handed her a cup of coffee. They sat together at the table, and Ollie told her that all the cooking and cleaning of the house was done by Ollie and one of the stablemen's wives did their laundry each week. There was nothing for Cecily to do here. Levi's home did not need her, she thought. For the past two years in her father's house she had done everything, now she wondered what she was going to do with all the free time that she would have on her hands. Ollie smiled and told her to rest and get used to the place and settle in. Go visit her friends, take walks, read a book, enjoy herself. Cecily hadn't enjoyed herself in a long time.

She was at loose ends, Cecily thought. She did not want to be alone, yet she knew that she had to be alone to think. She didn't know what to do or where to go. She only knew that she was tired of being afraid; she was tired of the fear that ruled her. She wanted to live and feel alive again. She wanted a life free of troubles and worries. She wanted to love Levi without guilt, and she wanted him to have his rightful place beside her as her husband. She was doing him more wrong than she had ever dreamed that she would.

"I don't know what to do, Ollie," Cecily almost cried, and Ollie patted her back.

"Why don't you take a walk and have a look around. You haven't been here in a long time; Mister Levi has made some changes about the place. The stables are bigger and filled with horses; you always liked the horses when you were little. You might even want to take the buggy out and go over and see your friend, Clemmie. You girls are almost like sisters, growing up together like you did. And Mister Levi is down at the sawmill; maybe you could go down there and visit him, he won't be home until dinner time. You have time to do anything that you want to do."

Cecily stood after a few moments and moved out onto the wide porch. The yard was beautiful she thought as she looked around at the many towering oak trees above her head, their branches reached down everywhere offering shade from the bright sun. She saw many of the branches appeared to be grasping a hold of one another, like lovers on a dance floor as the wind blew through their branches, it was beautiful to stand and look up at this site, it was almost as if the trees were kissing, making love as she made love to Levi when he kissed her.

Cecily started walking with no destination in mind and thinking of what she was doing and what she might do to make things better. She had to handle Bernard by giving him every dime he asked for, and she knew his demand for money was endless. Always money was her concern. She thought over and over again of just telling Levi everything, living with his wrath, accepting his disgust of her, and now that they were married, hoping against hope he would forgive her and not put her from him. Divorce! The word was filthy. She had never even known anyone that was divorced. She gave a little cry of agony at the very thought. She remembered Bernard's nose and thought of Levi's anger over a comment about his hair at the age of five, what would his anger be were she to go to him now and just tell him everything? She might cry and get his pity; she might beg for mercy, shaking her head she thought she'd be better off to just drown herself in the lake.

She was making herself sick trying to find some way out of this mess. She had to accept this for all that it was. Her silence must not make any sound. She must keep everything within herself. She couldn't tell Levi anything, and she had to pray hard that he never found out. She came into this marriage with the knowledge of what she would do, and she couldn't change her mind now. What was done was done. She gave another cry out and shook her head knowing she now had to live with the choice. Better she had not married Levi. Better she had just let Bernard ruin her publically for good and all. But she couldn't go back, and if Bernard exposed her now, it wouldn't just be her alone that was ruined, she would take Levi with her in her ruination. It was too late. She was doomed. Another heartbreaking cry escaped her.

Levi came into the house a little after noon and let Ollie put a loan plate of food in front of him after he washed up. He had stayed away from the house for as long as he could to give Cecily time to adjust to being here as his wife; he could not wait one more moment longer than he already had. He looked down at his plate of food and wondered if she were still sleeping. He had known yesterday that she was tired, sleep was the best thing for her right now.

"I had to make Miss Cecily eat something before she left the house," Ollie said, and Levi swung around to face his maid. "She would only eat a piece of toast and that I almost forced onto her. We've got to get that girl to eat more. She's way too thin."

"Cecily's not here?" Levi asked while leaving his chair.

"Yes, sir," Ollie frowned at him as he stood up. "She left here nearly two hours ago. I thought maybe she would have come to see you at the sawmill or visit her friend Miss Clemmie."

"I'm not hungry," Levi said as he hurried from the house.

"Ain't no use in cooking for these folks," Ollie complained as she carried Levi's plate of food out to the backyard and gave it to an old dog that lived under the porch. "The only one around here that appreciates my cooking is you, old mut." The dog ate the food in silence.

Levi rode his horse over to Cecily's father's house and called out for her. When he got no answer, he hurriedly left his horse and searched the place. Cecily wasn't here. Levi climbed back onto his horse, knowing for sure that his wife had not come to the sawmill. He decided to ride over to Clemmie's house and see if Cecily were there. Clemmie wasn't home, Mr. Floyd told him that she and her mother had gone to Madison for the day and didn't plan on being back until late and he hadn't seen Cecily since her father's funeral. Levi thanked Mr. Floyd for the information and turned his horse toward Cherry Lake.

Levi had been married for less than twenty-four hours, he had not made his wife, his wife in the truest sense and now he had lost her. He tried to think of where she might have gone and of where else he could look for her, and then he knew just where to find his Cecily. He had been stupid not to realize where she would be. He felt like kicking himself for being so blind and dumb. He had always been dumb. In school as a child, he had been picked on for being dumb. He hated that he was dumb; he hated that he knew he was dumb.

Cecily sat beside her father's grave. She had spent the past hour pouring out her fears and feelings to the mound of earth that her father now lay under. Just speaking out loud of Bernard's demands that she marry Levi and Levi's total acceptance of her made her feel a little better and the situation seemed almost easier to handle. She ran a hand in the dirt and thought she needed to speak to Levi about getting a headstone made for her father's grave. She would need Levi's money to do that; she would always need Levi for his money. Flowers, she thought, she should plant flowers here. She had to stop thinking of Levi in terms of money. Guilt made her feel sick; she had to put this guilt away and try and live.

When Cecily stood, she went to Levi's parents grave and pulled the weeds from around their headstones. Ethan and Lilly had been a love story; they had married in eighteen sixty-five and lived happily together for more than thirty years, and they were now together forever in heaven. Forever. Cecily knew what Levi's parents now knew in their graves; there was no such thing as forever. Forever was only a word; forever was a lie.

Cecily wished that Levi would not love her as he did; she had cheated him when she married him yesterday. She could not think that way, she told herself firmly. She would find some way to make all of her wrongs, right. She felt her heart fall inside her chest, down into her stomach and knew that she would never make up to Levi for the lies, not if she really did live to be a thousand years old. She had cheated him when she married him yesterday. She hated herself.

Cecily moved to her mother's headstone beside her father now and pulled the weeds from that grave too. She missed her mother.

Every day she had been missing her mother. Amelia had died giving birth to Cecily's little brother, a brother that had been born pink and healthy and had died in the night for no reason. Her mother had been buried with that little boy in her arms in the same coffin, in the same grave.

"I miss you, Mama," she said softly and touched the headstone that held her mother's name. "If Daddy is with you, please tell him that I miss him, and I'm scared, and I'm sorry for everything that I did to cause him pain. I need him so much, Mama." Death was the end, Cecily thought. There was no forever here in this place filled with sadness. There was only a loss. Happily ever after couldn't be found here. There was nothing here for Cecily in this graveyard. This place was deserted for her, and she could find no help here. There was no help for her. She was lost, and she was alone, and she was scared. She was a liar; she was using Levi's love for her to get what she needed to be safe. Cold and harsh was her reality. Bernard owned her. She had nothing. She had nothing to give to anyone.

Levi sat on his horse and watched Cecily for a long while. She was cleaning up around her parents' grave as well as his own parents' graves. He should have done this for his own parents, they had been good to him, and he had loved them well. He just did not like the graveyard.

Even from a distance, Levi could see and almost feel his wife's grief. He had been right to give her time; he felt better even if he did want her in his bed so badly that he was ready to bust. She wasn't afraid of him; she wasn't afraid of anything. Cecily was just full of sorrow; he had been wrong to mistake her horrible grief for fear. He pulled on the reins of his horse and forced the animal to walk backward into the trees at the edge of the graveyard. Cecily could not see him watching her from here, he knew. He would stay hidden in the trees and watch her.

After a long while, Cecily stood up and brushed the grass and weeds from her black skirt, her hands stayed dirty, but she didn't care. More of her than her hands were soiled. She wrapped her arms around her slim waist and swayed. She was a long way from Levi's house, she thought. She was bone weary and knew that the walk home would seem longer than it actually was. She started to walk out of the graveyard but stumbled and then felt herself falling hard onto her hands and knees. And then she was crying, crying her heart out and calling for her dear darling Daddy. When she looked up and saw Levi running toward her, his was the name she started to cry over and over. Levi, he was all she had, the only person in the whole world that cared about her. He was the man that she would destroy if her secret were ever known. She was taking from him and would take more, and his only crime was in loving her. And here she kneeled on the ground crying out his name, needing him, wishing with all her heart that she was free to love him and that she had told him the whole truth right from the start. If only she could have trusted him.

She sobbed his name harder as she kneeled there on the ground not alone, Levi was there holding her in his arms and lifting her from the hard ground. "You're safe now, darlin'," Levi said as he held his beautiful wife in his arms and she wrapped her arms around his neck and held on to him tight. She was still saying his name over and over again as she buried her face in his neck and cried. "Don't cry, Cecily. I'll take you home, and you'll be just fine. Don't cry anymore."

"Levi," she moaned and gasped for breath. "I shouldn't have married you this way. I was so wrong. Please, please forgive me, Levi. You must." She sobbed against his neck, her tears soaking the collar of his shirt. Levi gently put her onto his horse and climbed on behind her while pulling her close against himself and putting his arm around her waist. "I'm so sorry, Levi," she kept crying over and over again.

"Hush, Cecily," Levi said as gently as he could. "I understand now. I know what's wrong with you and if you'll just give yourself some time, you'll be all right soon."

"I want my Daddy," she said pathetically. "I need him. You don't know how much I need my father." Cecily continued to cry as Levi held her and kissed her tear stained face.

"I'm here for you, darlin'. Just calm down, and I'll take care of you." Levi didn't know what else to say to her; he didn't know how to help her or even what he could do for her to ease her pain. All he knew was that he loved her and he would love her always.

"I'm your hell, Levi," Cecily cried and hid her face in her hands. "I'm your hell."

"You're my heaven, darlin' girl. I'll keep you safe, and we'll be happy. I promise; I'll take you to heaven every time I hold you in my arms.

There was no such thing as heaven, Cecily thought, just as there was no forever and no happily ever after. She would know none of those things, and she had cheated Levi out of knowing them now too. She was in trouble and trouble to Levi; she would know nothing but trouble. And Levi, he trusted her. "I'm your hell, Levi. The minute you married me I pulled you into hell. I shouldn't have married you."

Ollie helped Cecily to bed while Levi paced the parlor floor and worried about his wife. His horse still stood unattended in the front yard, and something was burning on the stove in the kitchen, but Levi didn't care. All that mattered to him was that Cecily was all right. He kept thinking of how he felt when his own parents had died. He had been sick with grief for days; his sister Sarah didn't stop crying for more than a week. And even today at the graveyard he had missed his parents still and felt a terrible ache deep in his belly. Time had made the loss of Ethan and Lilly more bearable for him. Cecily had to have time to get over her own father. She and Daniel had been close, closer even than he had been to his own parents. Daniel had been all that Cecily had since her mother's death more than seven years ago. And she had been Daniel's only child. All the other children Amelia Walker had given birth to died before the dawn of their birth and then Amelia had died with the last child, the only son to be born. Levi stopped his pacing of the floor and thought with a frown covering his handsome face. Cecily had called out for him in the graveyard. She had been calling out for her father, but once she had seen him running to her, it was his name she cried out. His eyes narrowed as he wondered what she could have meant when she told him she was his hell. Why in the name of God would she think that she could be anything to him other than a blessing? She was a gift from heaven; she was the answer to his prayers; she could never be his hell.

"I shouldn't have married you this way," Levi heard her words and thought that she was so full of grief from having lost her father that she knew she was not ready to love him as she could and did. He understood. He wanted her to know that he understood. And he would never be sorry that Cecily had married him. He had wanted her; she was now his. They loved one another, in a few weeks time she would be her old self again, and they would come together, and he would give her all of himself. She would own his body; he would gladly give it to her. Soon, Cecily would be his; her grief would fade and become bearable. Soon.

Levi sat down on the sofa and stared into the empty fireplace that filled up one whole wall of the room. When he had been seventeen years old a family had been passing through Cherry Lake on their way up north. They had a young daughter, and she took to Levi right away. He had been young and innocent, and the girl had loved him well with her body. He thought he knew something at that time that no one else knew and he had walked around with a smile on his face for days. The family had stayed and worked for his father for more than two months in which Levi had learned everything there was to know of the secrets of life. He had been happy, he had been fulfilled, he had learned well, and he didn't even mind when he found out that Grant was enjoying the girl as well.

After the family had left, Levi still had times to use his skills that the girl had taught to him when he went into Madison and visited a special house there just for men. Levi knew that he wasn't dumb in one way, and that was the way to please a woman. He would give Cecily pleasure; he would make her call out his name again, only the next time he heard his names called out by her, it would be from the pleasure that he gave to her body and her soul.

She's asleep," Ollie interrupted Levi's thoughts. "Oh, good Lord, I've gone and burned your supper, and you missed your dinner this afternoon." Ollie hurried from the parlor to the kitchen.

Levi went into Cecily's bedroom and stared at her beautiful face. She looked lost and small in the huge bed. He wished that he could share this bed with her, he ached to own her body, but he knew that she wasn't ready for him and he calmed himself down with a few deep breaths.

Cecily tossed and turned in her sleep and kicked the covers away. Levi reached down and pulled the sheet back up and over her, then smoothed her hair away from her face. She was crying in her sleep, he saw and reached down to wipe away a tear from her cheek. She turned onto her side and threw the covers off again. Levi didn't pull the sheet back up as he stood thinking of why she was crying in her sleep and of her grief. He had to find some way to make her happy. Levi wanted his Cecily happy.

"Where you going?" Ollie called after Levi as the back door slammed.

"Down to the lake for a swim!" he called back to her

"Never knew that boy to like the water that much," Ollie muttered to herself trying to salvage Levi's dinner.

It was pitch dark out and very late when Levi sat down in a rocking chair on the porch and lit a cigarette. He and Cecily had been man and wife in name only for more than a week now, and she still had him locked out of her room and for the most part, out of her life. She hadn't gone back to the graveyard; he knew because he had been watching her for days and she stayed close to home. He worked like the demons of hell were after him when he wasn't watching Cecily, he went to the lake every night and swam until he was worn out. All he could do was hope that soon Cecily would allow him into her bed and learn to be happy again.

"Levi," he heard his name being said and looked up into the darkness to see the shadow of Cecily standing nearby.

"It's late darlin'. You should be sleeping," he said, and she moved closer toward him. Levi felt the blood in his body run fast, and his heart pound hard in his chest. He wanted her too much. He wanted Cecily right now.

"I sleep all the time, Levi," Cecily said and stopped beside him as he tossed his cigarette into the yard. "I'm sorry I'm not being good to you," she said softly, and he reached out for her hand and pulled her down onto his lap.

"I understand, Cecily. We have a whole lifetime to be together. You just rest and get well; I'll still be here waiting for you."

"I'm not sick, Levi," Cecily said as she cuddled up close to her husband, she loved being in his arms, she loved the clean smell of him, he was fresh, and he smelled secure. She was his hell, but he was her heaven.

"When my own folks died, I felt like I had died too. I know what you're going through right now, Cecily." Dear God in heaven, Levi prayed to himself; she was killing him by sitting on his lap this way. He could feel himself growing hard and firm and prayed that she would not notice. What could he have been thinking to have pulled her down onto his lap like this? It was torture. He was losing his mind in his need of her.

"I'm sorry I'm being such a problem right now," Cecily said and kissed his chin in the darkness. Levi's lips found Cecily's mouth, and he moaned as he covered her mouth with his own, his tongue touched hers and begged hers to touch his. Cecily moved closer to him; her firm breasts were pushed against this chest as he held her tightly and close. Levi felt he was losing himself within his wife. He wanted to pick her up and carry her into their bedroom and make love to her all night long. He longed to show her that he could make her body want his body and that his body needed hers.

Cecily had been sitting on Levi's lap, and the kiss just happened, somehow, she didn't know how, maybe he did something, or maybe it was all her, but she was now straddling his lap in the chair. Cecily wasn't stupid when it came to knowing what went on between a man and a woman even if she were still a virgin. Her father had sat her down after Bernard had tried to touch her once and explained why men wanted women. Daniel had threatened Bernard's life if he ever laid a hand on Cecily again.

Cecily felt Levi's hardness against her, felt him pull her nightgown up and the rocking chair rocked as they kissed. His hands were on her breast, and she realized that what he was doing felt good and she didn't want him to stop, but then she didn't want this with him. If she did this with him, there might be a baby, if he learned of what Bernard had on her. Cecily went stone cold; if she had a baby and Levi divorced her because of what Bernard had on her, she would lose her child. No judge in this land would give a child to a mother that had done what she had done.

Levi unbuttoned her nightgown and went to take her soft firm breast into his mouth; he knew he wasn't going to last long with Cecily sitting on him this way and rocking against him, he had to give her pleasure before it was too late.

"Stop, Levi," Cecily begged as his mouth covered her breast. "We have to stop," she sounded frantic and was crying.

It took every ounce of strength Levi had to pull away from his wife, and she stood up, and he watched in the darkness as she buttoned up her nightgown. He knew it didn't matter now; he'd had his own release, he was sad he hadn't fulfilled her as she had him. "You're my wife, Cecily," he said in a broken voice. "I want you. I want to be with you. We can't go on like this forever." Cecily heard the hurt in his voice; she knew she was hurting him and hated herself. She was also denying him what he had a right too and what they both wanted. But the reality of making a baby with Bernard's hold on her, she could lose more than Levi's love.

"I can't do this Levi," her voice was as broken as his own had been. If he found out what Bernard had, he would leave her, he would hate her if they had children; she would lose those children. She couldn't believe that she was standing here actually praying silently to God for Bernard's death so that she could have a life. "I'm not ready for this," she said again, and Levi watched her shadowed figure run into the room they both should be sharing.

She may not be aware of the fact, Levi thought, but Cecily was more than ready for him. He had never had a full release without being inside of a woman before tonight. He'd never known pleasure like this that she gave him just by kissing. Next time they got lost in the kiss, he would see she found what she had just given to him.

Levi stood up to go back into his own room and change his pants and ready for bed. His body was throbbing with what had happened; he felt calmer and that he could carry on for a time while Cecily got over her pain and loss and grief. When the time came, and they did come together, he knew it would be beyond anything he had ever known. If he could have this happen without being inside of his wife, what would it be like when he was inside of her? He knew he had to wait to find out, and he knew it would be worth the wait.

Cecily lay down in her bed thinking that Levi caught her on fire with his very touch. And he had no idea that she was innocent of ever having been with a man. She wanted to be with him, she wanted him now, to just go to his room. But reality came crashing in on her, and she remembered a bedtime story her mother used to read to her of a woman that had promised her baby to a man that spun straw into gold for her. If she had Levi's baby and Bernard exposed her secret, Levi would divorce her, and she would lose her child. She couldn't have a baby. And she knew the act between a man and a woman often produced a baby.

How long could she and Levi go on like this? She rolled onto her side and held perfectly still as she knew if she didn't find some way to stop this making love, it was going to go too far, and she would have a baby. Would Levi stay married to her if she denied him her body and his rights to her body? She felt a sob escape and knew; no man could live that way with his wife. It was more trouble she had to figure out a way around. And she knew, there was no way around this.

Cecily woke up early the next morning and met Levi over breakfast, every time she made eye contact with him her cheeks felt like they were on fire and he had an easy smile on his face, as though what happened in the night had a good ending. She didn't know that for him, it had. "I'm going to Brooks County to check on the property I bought there a few weeks ago, Cecily. I won't be home before dark." He left his chair, placing his napkin by his plate and came to where she sat and kneeled beside her. "Thank you for last night," his eyes were looking into her eyes, and she was confused. "I love you, Cecily. I love you so much that it hurts." Without any warning to her, Levi covered her mouth with his own and plunged past her lips with his tongue, his hand going to her breast. He wasn't surprised when she pushed against him and moaned. He knew she wanted him, but something was holding her back, and he couldn't figure out what. As he had given no warning to the start of this, he gave no warning when he pulled away and put an end to it. Cecily was breathing hard and fast as she saw him stand up, his hand touched her cheek and his voice husky when he spoke, "I'll be back later tonight or in the morning, darlin'." He then gave her one of his easy smiles before turning to leave the room.

Cecily didn't have any time to try and think about what she was going to do about Levi and their lovemaking. Bernard had sent her a note, delivered by a boy in town, to meet him at her father's farm before two in the afternoon.

Cecily knew she was in serious trouble. She didn't have any cash, all her money that Levi had given to her was in the bank in Madison, and she couldn't get to the money by early afternoon and back here. What could Bernard want with her so soon, she worried. She had just given him two thousand dollars that Levi had paid her for the farm, Bernard couldn't be back for more so soon.

At one that afternoon, Cecily left the house from her bedroom door and slipped into the woods beyond the house. She was sweating and shaking when she looked back to make sure that no one was following her or had seen her leave. After a few moments, when she knew that she was safe, Cecily broke into a run, her heart pounding in her chest and in her ears. She didn't stop running until she was standing in her father's front yard. She was standing still in the very place where her father had dropped dead.

"You're early," Bernard said from behind her and Cecily whirled around still breathing hard from her run here. She screamed loud when Bernard stepped closer to her, and she fell back and away from him. "You really have no reason to fear me, Cecily," Bernard said, giving her his mean grin. He looked terrible with his nose all crooked and bent and even smashed in. He had once been a handsome man; the nose ruined his good looks. "You give me what I want, and I leave you in peace, this is how the game we are playing works. You know that you've known that for years."

Cecily shook her head and stared at Bernard. He would never leave her in peace, she knew what he wanted, and she worried about how to give it to him all the time. And what he wanted from her gave her no peace because she knew that she didn't have enough for him. Bernard was her nightmare in the daylight. "I just gave you all the money I got for the farm from Levi," she said and took another step back and away from him.

"It's gone, Cecily and I need more," Bernard said as he reached out and took a hold of a lock of her hair that had fallen free of the knot on top of her head from her run here.

"I don't have any more money to give to you. Not yet; it's too soon." Cecily hated the tears that fell onto her face; she hated Bernard Calhoun more than her tears.

"Maybe you have something else that you can give to me." Bernard let his hand leave her hair and touched her long slim neck. Cecily went still all over. "Maybe you can show me what Levi has taught you," he grinned an even more evil grin, "in bed."

"No," Cecily gasped and jumped back as far as she could away from Bernard. She was terrified now. Bernard might touch her; she could not stand for Bernard to touch her.

"Don't you like going to bed with your husband, Cecily?" She shook her head hard, and all the color drained from her face. "The poor bastard," Bernard laughed out loud. "You're keeping him from your bed." Cecily kept backing away as Bernard came toward her until her back hit the porch ledge and she was forced to stop and stand still.

"Please, Bernard," she whispered when he reached out and touched her breast; she was cold all over with fear and shame. There was no one to protect her from this. She didn't have the strength to stop what Bernard was doing, and she hoped that he would do nothing more than this to her.

"Poor Levi," Bernard laughed again softly. "I could almost feel sorry for him." He let go of Cecily's breast, and she sagged in relief when he took a step back away from her.

"I'm telling you the truth, Bernard. I don't have any money right now," she hated the sound of her own voice; it was filled with her weakness for Bernard to hear.

"Maybe I'll just go and show your new husband what I have. I bet you he'll pay me not to let what I have become public. He would look like the fool he is if I displayed for this community what I have on you." Cecily gasped.

"No. Don't do that," Cecily pleaded and felt that Bernard was enjoying this torture far too much, he was making her want to die in shame.

"What do you have of value that you can give to me to keep me quiet, Cecily?" Bernard looked hard into Cecily's eyes as she thought. There was nothing left for him in her father's house; she had nothing. "Make it good, Cecily. I need some money real quick."

"I don't know!" she cried out and bit her bottom lip so hard that she tasted blood.

"Then I guess I need to go and see Levi and have him give me the money I need." Cecily shook her head and clasped her hands in fear. Levi must never know what Bernard had on her. No matter what she had to keep the ugly truth from her husband. Levi would hate her. And then suddenly she knew, she did have something she could give to Bernard that would make him leave her alone for a little while longer.

"Here, take these," she said as she pulled off Levi's mother's rings from her left-hand finger and handed them to Bernard.

"This is good, Cecily," he said taking her rings from her. "I think they'll do, until the next time I need money."

"I think they're worth a lot of money, Bernard. Please, leave me alone. I'm begging you. I need time to get to my money in the bank in Madison. I'll give all I have when I do; I swear I will."

"I bet Levi would give me more money than you ever would, Cecily," Bernard threatened her. He knew that he would never go to Levi Tucker for money. Levi would kill him and ask why he wanted the money after he was long dead. Levi could be mean. He remembered when they were in school together. Bernard had made a comment on Levi being dumb because Levi couldn't read and Levi had gone mad and beat him up. It had taken two teachers to pull Levi off of him. Everyone said that Levi was laid back and easy going, but Bernard knew the truth, if he had any doubts they were gone after Levi messed up his nose, Levi could hurt someone in anger, he was a dangerous man. You never wanted to make Levi mad or cross him if you could help it, and Bernard could get what he wanted from Cecily with threats and leave Levi out of this.

"Levi would divorce me before he gave you anything, Bernard," Cecily said in fear.

"He should divorce you for keeping him from your bed," Bernard said followed by an ugly cruel laugh. "You look beautiful in black, by the way, Cecily. Your skin is so pale it's almost white. If you were mine, you would not ever keep me from your bed." Cecily said nothing more to Bernard, but he called out to her after he had mounted his horse, "thanks for the rings. Until next time."

Bernard watched Cecily run from the yard. As long as he had what he had on her, she would pay him. She would do anything to keep him from telling on her. Levi Tucker would have paid a small fortune; it was a shame that Levi has such a nasty temper, Bernard could have been rich in no time, as it was he would have to bleed Cecily dry a little at the time of Levi's money. Bernard didn't really mind; he would get his money one way or another.

Cecily fell to her knees in the woods halfway between her father's home and Levi's home and threw up what little breakfast she had eaten that morning. She would die if Levi saw what Bernard had on her. Levi would kill her if he ever saw what Bernard had on her. She had to find some way to keep paying Bernard. She always had to pay.

She stayed on her hands and knees for a long while and shook all over in her weakness and fear of Bernard. He had tricked her, he had used her, and he had been blackmailing her for two long years because of her stupidity. She had no way out except to pay and pay she would.

She had her broach left, she thought. That would keep her safe until she could find some way to Madison and get her money from the bank. Maybe Levi kept money in the house; she thought and then hated herself for such a thought. But she remembered the strong arm box on the mantel in the parlor and thought she knew where Levi kept the key; she would search in that box as soon as she could.

Dear God, she was going to steal from her own husband. Deep wracking dry heaves forced her to stay still before she began to sob. She would rob Levi blind to protect herself if she had too. She could not let anyone see what Bernard had. She must keep Bernard quiet and her secret safe from everyone for the rest of her life. She would do anything that she had to do. Anything.

Cecily saw Clemmie's buggy in the front yard, and Grant was standing on the front porch with Levi when she left the woods. Levi was home really early, and she knew only one thing, she could not let him see her this way. She went around the house and thought to enter through the kitchen door in hopes that no one would see her until she had a chance to get cleaned up. She had no luck at all; Clemmie was in the kitchen with Ollie talking when she entered the house.

"My goodness," Clemmie all but cried out when she saw Cecily. "What in the world happened to you? You look awful."

Cecily went to the sink and filled a glass of water and rinsed out her mouth before she washed her face, then turned back to Clemmie and Ollie. Both those women were staring at her as if she had grown two heads since last they had seen her. She could not imagine what they were thinking of her; she knew she must look awful. There was dirt on her skirt where she had fallen in the dirt when she had been sick, and her hair was falling down around her shoulders and back. She wished that she were alone so that she could get cleaned up and not have to explain anything to anyone.

She felt tired again. She was tired all the time; sleep was her escape from her fear. Sleep kept her safe from the nightmare of her life.

"I thought Levi was going to Brooks County to check on his land," she said in an almost panicked voice.

"He changed his mind when one of the blades needed fixing at the sawmill," Clemmie said still staring at Cecily and wondering what had happened to her friend.

"I can't let Levi see me like this," Cecily said and almost panicked when she thought her husband and Grant were coming into the kitchen from the porch at any moment and he would find her this way. Levi would wonder at the mess she was in if he found her looking as she looked right this minute. She had to hurry and get cleaned up.

"Don't worry," Clemmie said. "He's talking to Grant on the front porch. Let's get you to your room and cleaned up."

"I'll fix you a cup of strong black coffee," Ollie offered as Clemmie took Cecily from the kitchen to her bedroom.

"What's going on with you, Cecily?" Clemmie asked in a way that only a sister can ask that sort of question, and there was a demanding to know in her voice that Cecily couldn't ignore.

"Nothing," Cecily whispered and went to the bathroom to wash up while Clemmie paced the bedroom floor. Something was going on with Cecily, Clemmie knew her friend, and this was more than grief over having lost her father. She had been afraid at church on the day that she had married Levi and she was still afraid. Clemmie could see the fear in her best friend's eyes, and she was afraid for Cecily.

Ollie slipped into the room with the coffee and interrupted Clemmie's thoughts as she took the coffee from the maid and put it down on the vanity. "Thank you, Ollie, you're a good soul," Clemmie said and turned to see Cecily sitting in her petticoat and corset at her vanity looking small and weak. Her waist length hair was so beautiful, thick and straight and heavy. When Clemmie saw

Cecily start to cry, she went and picked up the hairbrush and gently started brushing out her friend's hair. "Are you that unhappy being married to Levi?" Cecily shook her head.

"This has nothing to do with Levi. I can't talk about this with anyone, Clemmie. Not even you. Please, don't ask me; just understand I can say nothing." Clemmie put the brush down and gave Cecily a quick hug, her cheek next to Cecily's as they both looked at one another in the mirror of the vanity.

"I've known something was wrong for a long time, and since your father died, you've been really looking scared Cecily. If you can't tell me, and I won't beg you too, I'll try to understand, but you can't go on like you are. You have to talk to someone. Levi is your husband now; he can help you, he loves you, Cecily. Go to him, go to Levi and tell him what's got you so afraid. He will help you; I'm certain he will."

"I can never tell Levi about this problem, Clemmie," Cecily said urgently.

"I don't know how to help you," Clemmie said and wiped the tears off of Cecily's face with a handkerchief.

"You can't help me, and I'm not asking you too. Just help me to dress. Levi mustn't see me this way; he would never understand."

"And you think I do?" Clemmie asked as she returned to fixing Cecily's hair.

"Don't hate me, Clemmie. Just be my friend. Please." Cecily reached for her hair and pulled it up so that Clemmie could put the pins in to secure it on top of her head.

"You're like my very own sister Cecily. I could never hate you." Cecily pulled on a clean skirt while Clemmie stared at her. She was pale, the circles under her eyes were dark and deep, and her lips had less color than her face. She was sick, Clemmie throught and felt shocked by this discovery. And then Clemmie knew the truth, Cecily was worried sick, and she wouldn't let anyone help her. Clemmie didn't know what to do.

Levi stood on the porch with his best friend and smoked a cigarette. He knew that Grant wasn't blind to the fact that something was bothering him, he could not hide his emotions from Grant, they had been too close for too many years, they had always known each other, only a year separated them in age, and they had grown up together.

"It's Cecily," Levi finally said.

"I kind of figured that out for myself. You haven't looked like the happy groom these past couple of weeks. She's still sick about her father's death?" Levi nodded his head. "I know how she feels, Levi. I'm not over my father's death either. I'm struggling with the grief."

"I'm really sorry, Grant. I know it hasn't been that long since your own father died." Grant looked up at Levi and nodded his head.

"Life has been kind of hard for me. I loved my Pa, he was a good man, and he died in his sleep at the age of forty-eight. I never once told him how I felt about him. We just got along and were close; the telling of my feelings never seemed important until it was too late to do so." Grant tossed his cigarette into the yard and leaned back against the porch post.

"Cecily's taking her father's death real hard also. She'll be fine in a few more weeks, I hope." Levi went and sat down on the top step of the porch.

"She's not sick, at least not like a doctor can cure her. Be good to her Levi, and wait. She'll learn to live with the loss in time. After a while, it gets more bearable." Grant offered this advice to his friend.

Levi saw Cecily and Clemmie before Grant did and he stood up and gave his wife one of his beautiful and easy smiles. "Well, what do you think?" he asked Cecily as she came to him and he took her hand. Cecily gave him a confused look while Clemmie answered his question.

"I forgot to tell her," Clemmie said and held out her hand to Cecily. "Grant asked me to marry him. And I said yes.

"You forgot to tell her?" Grant laughed and grabbed Clemmie around the waist, and she leaned back against his chest.

"We were busy," Clemmie said and gave Cecily a look filled with concern. Cecily stared at Clemmie's left-hand ring finger and thought of her own rings. Levi's mother's rings. They were gone now, lost to her. She hid her hand in the folds of her skirt.

Levi saw the concerned look that Clemmie was giving to his wife and looked down at Cecily's face. She was too pale, and she had been sleeping all the time. When she was awake, she looked like she had just finished crying or that she might start crying again at any given moment. He didn't know how to make her happy. She shut him out with her silence. There was no room in her life for him, and her silence was telling him so louder than any words that she might ever say to him. He was losing her, and he had never had her. Two days ago he had taken her for a buggy ride and other than comment on the weather which had been sunny and fine, she had sat beside him, alone in her own world, a world that she was seeing afforded him no place beyond what had happened on the porch in the rocking chair last night. Cecily was filled with sorrow and silence and was lonely and making him lonely.

Cecily saw Levi watching her and looked quickly away from him. He should hate her, but she only saw deep concern for her that filled his eyes. She had given the rings that he gave to her in love and honor away to Bernard Calhoun. She was going to steal from him if she had too in order to protect herself. Cecily was more afraid than ever. If she could not satisfy Bernard, the hateful man would go to Levi and show him everything and Levi would divorce her as well as hate her for what she had done. She would lose her husband. She was without hope. Right now, it was only a matter of time before Levi learned the truth about her, every minute was a minute that her past would come to haunt her and it would cost her everything. There was no way to save herself for long, and there was no savior in the world she was living in. And what hurt the most, she was going to lose Levi.

Grant and Clemmie stayed for supper at Levi's invitation. Cecily tried to join in and be a part of them as she used to in the old days, but she couldn't keep from thinking and worrying about Bernard. She was an outsider looking in at her friends as they shared the afternoon meal. Cecily struggled to eat and smiled only a little and then only when she had too. And Levi, she looked up several times and saw his eyes on her face. He loved her; he was a fool for loving her; one day he might know just how big a fool she was making of him. She was going to lose him, and she gasped and drew a deep breath. She was living in the moment; soon this life would come to an end. There was really no such thing as forever; she thought as she stared at her handsome husband who would one day too soon hate her.

As dusk was coming on Clemmie asked Cecily to take a walk with her while Grant and Levi went down to the sawmill to close up for the night. Cecily thought of sharing her problem with Clemmie, she knew that Clemmie wouldn't hate her, but Clemmie would tell Grant and Grant would tell Levi. Cecily knew there was no one to trust. Even with her best friend, Cecily knew she was alone.

As she walked arm in arm with Clemmie down the clay dirt road, Cecily thought of what would happen if she told someone the truth. Her story was too impossible to even begin to be believed. She knew she needed help; she knew she had needed help for a long time. In church on Sunday and every night she prayed on her knees to God to help her, she begged him to show her what to do to be free of Bernard's hold on her, God never gave a sign that He heard her. She felt as though God had abandoned her. Even God, who knew the truth, did not believe her or feel her worthy to be saved. There was no help for her and telling anyone what happened and what was being done to her wasn't an answer to her problem.

"I'm so blessed, Cecily," Clemmie said and pulled her friend close. The night birds were singing in the trees; the sun was sinking causing clouds in the west to turn pink and orange and even a dusky shade of blue. "Levi and Grant are best friends, just like you and I are. We will always be close. Our children will be best friends too," Clemmie almost sang the last few words.

"I don't want children," Cecily almost whispered.

"Don't want children? Cecily, how can you say something like that?"

Cecily pinched her lips together and stayed silent. She and she alone knew if she had a child it would become a victim of her past, she would lose her child, she would lose Levi, it was enough living day in and day out with the knowledge that at any moment, in order to get more money than she could give, that Bernard might take what he has to Levi. "Are you afraid to have a baby because of your mother dying?" Clemmie saw the play of emotions on Cecily's face and thought it was fear of dying in childbirth as her mother had was the reason she wanted no children.

"I'm not afraid to die," Cecily said simply, dying would see that Bernard's evil game came to an end for her.

"Are you afraid that your children might be like Levi?" Clemmie stopped walking and turned to look at Cecily's face if only her friend were chatty and happy like she use to be.

"I would be honored to have children like Levi," Cecily said seriously and started to walk again with Clemmie falling in beside her.

"That's good," Clemmie nodded her head, and Cecily hoped that this conversation would change, she did not want to talk about having a baby, she couldn't even think of that right now. "But it would be sad if your children had to struggle as Levi had too."

"What in the world are you talking about Clemmie? Levi never had to struggle a day in his life." Cecily stopped walking, and Clemmie stopped with her, they were now facing one another.

"Well, you know." Cecily shook her head in total confusion. "About Levi never being able to learn to read. Grant told me how hard Levi tried in school and just always failed. Grant does all the reading and writing for Levi at the mill. Levi can do figuring, he is good at that sort of thing, but he can't read." Clemmie noticed Cecily's confused look as they stared one another in the eye. "I thought you knew."

"Levi is a very smart man," Cecily said firmly almost feeling sorry for her husband that he had such a hard time learning in school. She would be lost if she couldn't read. But it certainly wasn't the end of the world, and it wasn't like her secret. Grant reads for him; she could read for him if he needed her too. "I never would have guessed he couldn't read, he's so smart," Cecily finally spoke and started walking back toward the house.

"Levi is smart because his mother read to him," Clemmie said as she returned to walking arm in arm with Cecily. "She read Shakespeare to him and Grant when they were boys, Levi understood every word his mother read to him Grant told me, but he can't make out the letters to read. Grant says that Levi loves to be read too and his parents read him anything and everything. He learned all he could by listening. Even Sara read to him. Levi's not a dumb man; he just never could understand letters."

"And Grant told you all of this?" Cecily asked as the sun fell away and darkness took over. They were almost back to the house.

"Yes, Grant said that Levi always believed that he was dumb because he couldn't learn to read, but Levi's not dumb. The teacher in school said that Levi was the dumbest boy that she ever knew and the smartest boy she had ever met. He always got into a lot of fights when he was younger because the children would pick on him for not being able to learn to read. But when he got older, he learned to control his anger over his inability. I'm surprised that Levi hasn't told you all of this, Cecily."

"I guess we all have our own secrets," Cecily said before she and Clemmie both fell into a comfortable silence. She wasn't the only one in this marriage that had a secret, she thought. Levi had a secret too. And he was ashamed; he might understand something of what she was going through. Shame, secrets and sin, this marriage wasn't on any kind of solid ground. The sand was shifting fast. If Bernard carried out his threat and went to Levi, the sand would swallow her up, and she might as well be dead. And Levi had a secret too.

Before Grant and Clemmie left, Cecily hurried to her room and closed the door; she didn't want to face Levi tonight. Maybe he would go to Brooks County and check on his land tomorrow, and she'd be alone to go to Madison and get the money for Bernard. As she lay down on her lonely bed with her aching heart, she wondered if tomorrow Bernard would go to her husband with what he had. She fell asleep afraid and certain that soon Levi, the man she loved, her husband, the only thing in the world she had, would soon hate her forever.

Levi watched Cecily across from him at the breakfast table; he wished he could read her beautiful mind. He wished she would talk to him and trust him with all of her troubles. He felt so shut out of her life. "Levi," she said his name, and he gave her one of his easy smiles, he did not know that when he gave her one of those smiles she thought he was the most beautiful man in the world. "May I ask you a question?" Her soft voice sounded so serious to her husband that he decided to be playful with her.

"You may ask me anything," he tapped her on the nose with his fork trying his best to get a smile from her.

"How much money do you have?" Levi had not expected this question, and he frowned. After a moment he put the tips of his fingers together and tapped them wondering why she would ask him such a question and why she should wonder what he was worth. "I just was curious," Cecily said in a very soft voice as she saw the change in her husband's face. "I don't ever want to worry about money again, Levi. Daddy and I really struggled a lot, and well, Daddy worried so much of the time." Cecily squeezed her eyes shut tight for saying what she had, but it was the only thing she could think to say, and there was truth to her words, she and her father worried over money night and day because of Bernard.

"Well," Levi sat back and stared at his wife. "I have enough money to buy you the moon, darlin'." He was back trying to tease her out of being so serious. He also didn't want her to worry about money; he had enough to support her in style. He saw her frown and knew that his answer was not sufficient; she was still afraid of being poor. "I have a quarter of a million in cash in the bank, Cecily," he said and heard his wife gasp. "I probably have twice that tied up in land and cattle. And another couple of hundred thousand in bonds. My father wasn't a poor man when he came south, Cecily. And we lived frugally. Every cent added up over the years, and now I'm pretty well off. Plus I work hard. I always have." He saw his words did not cause his wife to relax if anything she appeared to be even more upset.

Levi was rich, Cecily thought. No, Levi was filthy rich. He would never miss what she took from him to pay Bernard. He could keep her safe. And he would never know the truth; he would never see what Bernard had on her. And maybe, maybe she could get enough money to buy what Bernard has if Bernard was willing to sell. The only problem was how she was going to get the money from Levi without him knowing that she was taking his money.

"I'm glad that you didn't know," Levi said while smiling at Cecily's shocked and worried face. "I never liked the fact that my mother married my father for his money. Everything worked out for my parents, and I know their story well, I was raised on their story, but I wanted love from the start, Cecily. I wanted you to love me, money or no money." Cecily felt a fire in her face as guilt consumed her. "I know you love me, darlin'. And I love you too. This is just a bad time for you right now. You'll feel better soon, grief takes time, and I'm willing to wait for you. You're worth the wait."

"You must be a very smart man, Levi," Cecily said looking down at her hands folded in her lap and wondering how she could get the money she needed to pay Bernard.

"I'm smart at what I do well," Levi said and touched her chin, forcing her eyes to look back up into his own. "There are things that I can't do."

"There are things that I can't do too," Cecily muttered thinking of how she couldn't get the money from him to pay Bernard, and she had to have that money. It was eating her alive, it was all she could think about and now knowing that they were rich, she could keep paying Bernard, she could be safe, it was all in her grasp, but she had no way to get at the money she needed.

"All I have in this world, Cecily," Levi whispered as she stared at him, "I gladly would give to you." He saw her eyes fall back down to her hands in her lap.

I don't need or want all he has in this world; Cecily thought desperately, I just need money to pay Bernard so I can have my life back. We can be married for real, and I could have children, and no one would ever know about my past, I could be safe. Her mind was racing with these thoughts as she stared at her folded hands in her lap.

"Levi," she said his name in her soft voice again and looked back up into his eyes, his beautiful dark blue eyes that saw only goodness in her when there was no goodness in her.

Levi could not stand for her to be sad and he left his chair and reached down for his wife pulling her into his arms. She felt so right in his arms; he wanted her here in his arms all the time; he wanted to make her safe and keep her safe and love her always.

Cecily looked up at her husband, tall and strong and holding her gently. If only she could trust him with what Bernard was doing, she thought for the millionth time, and her head ached with the thought. And then she saw him move, his mouth coming closer to hers and heard him tell her he loved her. He covered her mouth, and she cried out into his as he pulled her close. His knee was between her legs, and he was pushing up while she was pushing down, he couldn't believe how fast she'd opened up to him and still kept him from his bed and his room with her. "God forgive me, darlin'. I have to have you." He picked her up into his arms and carried her to their room laying her on the bed.

"No, Levi," she whimpered, and he put a finger over her mouth.

"I only want to kiss you; only kiss." He lay down next to her and pulled her into his arms coming up over her as he kissed her mouth and her ear and her cheek, his leg between her legs rubbing her and feeling her ride his knee. "I love you," he breathed into her mouth and saw her head go back, the pins had fallen from her hair, and it was down and surrounded her. He kissed her eyelids and her neck, his hand found her breast, and she gave a cry right before she turned into liquid fire and burned up in her husband's arms.

"We're so good together, Cecily," he whispered into her ear as she trembled in his arms from the after-effects of his lovemaking. "Don't shut me out any longer, I beg you."

"I can't do this right now Levi," she said, and he watched her pull away. "I don't know if I can ever be a real wife to you," she all but whispered.

"What are you saying, Cecily?" Levi choked on his words; he had just brought his wife pleasure, they had made love in their bed; they were each on fire for the other.

"I'm saying I never should have married you," she cried out. "I can't let you touch me like this or any other way again." If she let him touch her like this and she couldn't find a way to pay Bernard, she would lose more than anyone could imagine.

"Why?" Levi asked as he took a deep breath looking down at his wife. Cecily didn't want him, his wife didn't want him, yet she'd just exploded in his arms. "We're in love darlin'; this is grief talking. We're perfect together; we just showed one another that right here on this bed. I want you to have my children. I want to grow old with you. I want to love you throughout time."

Unless she had money to pay Bernard, she could never have his child. And she heard his words, love him throughout time, grow old together; she wanted that more than anything in the world and a whole house full of children that looked just like Levi. But that would not happen for her, not now, she didn't have a normal life any longer, she couldn't lead a normal life.

"I could never have your child," Cecily whimpered. "I can never give you a baby."

"You don't want to have my baby?" Levi asked in stunned disbelief.

"No," was the only answer that she gave to him.

"Do you love me Cecily?" he saw her shake her head. "Are you saying you don't love me?" he watched her hang her head in shame and didn't understand her. "You'll never let me in this bed as your husband?" Again she shook her head; she was denying him his place in her life as his wife. This was more than grief and sorrow, Cecily was turning him away and saying she didn't love him.

Levi closed his eyes and waited for Cecily to speak. Fear raced through his blood that she did not love him, that he had been wrong and made a mistake in believing that she wanted him and not just his money to pay her father's debt.

Levi fell back onto the bed and looked up at the ceiling feeling as though he might break down and cry. And then she threw herself at him, her arms going around him and her lips finding his. What was going on with her? His mind screamed in confusion. Was she losing her mind in grief? Was this grief? He wished that he could climb inside of her head so that he could understand what was going on with her and find out what she was feeling for him.

"Forgive me, Levi. Please, forgive me. I'm so sorry," Cecily said as she kissed his ear the way he had kissed hers. "I don't know what I'm doing. I don't know what I'm saying. I'm so sorry."

Levi squeezed his eyes shut tight and let his wife kiss him, her hand on his chest as he had held her breast only moments before. "Do you love me Cecily?" he begged of her and held his breath waiting for her answer.

"Yes, yes, yes," Cecily said kissing him with each yes and he released his breath.

"God," he said in a prayer-like fashion, "you're killing me." He rolled her over and started kissing her, pushing his body on her as he'd pushed his knee on to her earlier. "I want you," he cried out before he lost control and fell next to her breathing hard. He had never known lovemaking could be this way.

Another week passed, and if it were possible, Cecily pulled more inside of herself and away from Levi. And Levi existed in the world that she had created for them. A world in which she kept to herself and seemed to be worried and fearful all the day, or clung to him and allowed him to make love to her with his mouth only. He was alone as she was alone beyond their lovemaking and he could do nothing but wait and watch his wife and wonder what was going to happen next.

There was no one to talk too, Levi thought as he watched Cecily. She had trapped him with her in her silence. He was silent with her. He could not take her on a picnic, he could not take her for a ride, she did not want to be with him in the day time, and he was ashamed for anyone to know the true state of their marriage. He had thought of taking her down to Madison to visit his sister, but he knew they would have to share a bed and he could not put himself through that kind of torture. He could not lie next to her all the night long and not bury himself deep within her body. Life had become a hell in that way already, he could only touch and pet her and go so far and then he had to stop when he never wanted to stop.

Whatever was wrong with Cecily wasn't just grief, Levi decided after some thought, and he went to watching her every move. He never went to the sawmill; he stayed close to home and saw her sleep and barely eat and avoid him. And then he noticed her wedding rings were gone and he went cold all over. Her left ring finger was empty, and there wasn't even a mark where the rings had been. If she had lost them, why hadn't she told him? He wondered, and he worried about her missing rings. Maybe the rings weren't lost at all; maybe she had removed them because she really didn't want to be married to him. Dear God, she was killing him a little more with each passing day, he thought. She was breaking his heart, and she didn't care. She didn't care about anything, but herself and whatever was going on in that silent world in which she now lived, and he was helpless to her and to himself. She didn't want him, and yet she did want him. He was confused, she had him tied up in knots, and he couldn't tell anyone what was happing to them and to their marriage.

Levi heard the front door open and close and looked out the parlor doors in time to see Cecily race across the yard and into the woods. He saw her worried face as she glanced back at the house and yard and he sucked in a deep breath. Cecily had looked terrified out of her mind. The strain and fear he had seen on her face were all telling; she needed no words for him to understand her. He had never seen Cecily look like that ever.

"Ollie!" Levi called out for his maid as he left the parlor and met Ollie in the hall. "Do you know where Cecily was going?" Ollie looked puzzled as he did and shook her head.

"No, sir. A letter came for her a few minutes ago from her friend, she said. I think it must have been Miss Clemmie as that's her only friend that I know of. Maybe she's gone to meet with Miss Clemmie."

Levi didn't believe that his wife was going to meet Clemmie Floyd. Cecily had looked frightened out of her mind; she would never be afraid of Clemmie. He went past Ollie and into his wife's bedroom. Her jewelry case was open, and on her bed empty, a piece of paper was crumpled up beside the case. Levi picked up the paper and smoothed it out before he looked down at the paper with letters on it that made no sense to him. He wished that he could read; he had always wished that he could read. He felt more than dumb at times like these. Dumb and helpless.

"What does it say, Ollie?" He handed the maid the paper and Ollie squinted her eyes as she looked at the words before her.

"You know I don't read so well, Mister Levi," she said while trying to make out the words to herself before reading the paper to him.

"Meet me now," Ollie read. "Bring val u ables." Ollie looked at Levi. "What does that mean?"

"I don't know, Ollie. Is it signed?" Levi leaned forward and tried to make out the name on the bottom of the paper.

"Be-nar-d," Ollie sounded out the name slowly.

"Oh my God," Levi said as his eyes met Ollie's.

"Who is this Be-nar-d? And what does this word val u ables mean?" Levi took the note from Ollie and crumpled it up worse than it had been.

"Ollie, don't you say one word about this to anyone, ever. Do you hear me, Ollie?" The maid nodded her head. Levi didn't see her nod; he was running out the door.

Bernard was doing something to Cecily, Levi thought as he ran through the woods. And Bernard wanted her to bring valuables. Blackmail! Levi thought and stopped to stand still. Bernard had some kind of stranglehold on his Cecily and was scaring her. He started running again to the only place that he could think to go in search of his wife — Daniel Walker's farm.

Cecily's fear, Levi thought as he ran, his stomach in a knot of pain for what his wife had been going through. She had never been suffering from grief as he had thought; all along she had been afraid. She had been afraid and was afraid of Bernard Calhoun. Her missing rings, he fought to breathe as he saw in his minds eyes her empty left-hand finger. Her rings were given to Bernard in fear. What else had she given to that no good stinking bastard? Levi asked himself as he ran faster. Her father's debt! There was no debt, and there never had been. The money he gave to Cecily for the farm went to Bernard. But why? Had her father done something wrong and bad and Bernard found out about it, and now Cecily was paying to keep what her father had done a secret?

Levi stopped in the woods and saw his wife pacing in her father's yard. She was alone, and for one brief moment, he thought that he would go to her and demand an answer as to why Bernard was blackmailing her and why in the world was she paying that blackmail. Then he saw Bernard ride into the yard and held still. Cecily was still now too, Levi saw.

Cecily faced Bernard, she had just given him her rings not that long ago, and he was already back for more. He knew what she had just found out a week ago. He knew that Levi was a very rich man and he would be back often, too often. She had to find some way to stop him for good and all; this could not go on.

"Do you have money?" Bernard asked as he stepped down from his horse and came toward her. Cecily shook her head. "What do you have?"

"Please, Bernard, I just gave you my rings," Cecily hated the weakness in her voice when she spoke to him, but she was scared, she was so scared all the time.

"I wasn't able to sell the rings. Too many people know those rings belonged to Lilly Tucker. Why haven't you been to the bank?" He stepped too close to her as he spoke.

"There hasn't been any time to go." She squeezed her eyes closed tight when he reached out and grabbed her breast. Cecily pinched her lips together tightly to keep from crying out when Bernard fondled her breast. He was humiliating her; his touch made her sick.

"What can you give me, Cecily?" Bernard squeezed her breast tight before he let her go and took a step back from her. "Don't worry, if I had wanted only your body, I would have taken you a long time ago. I know you have something for me; you might as well give it to me."

Levi watched his wife and Bernard from the woods. He saw Bernard touch Cecily's breast and felt like killing them both. It took all of his strength not to go forward and break Bernard's ass for having touched Cecily, his self-control was near to the breaking point. She gave Bernard money, her rings, what else had his wife given to the man? Levi watched as the sun hit the object that Cecily was handing over to Bernard and whatever it was, it sparkled bright in the afternoon sunshine. The broach, he thought. She had just given Bernard the broach that he had given to her before their marriage.

Levi watched as Bernard got back onto his horse and left. Cecily started for home with her head hung down and looking like she had looked these past few weeks. Tortured. Bernard Calhoun had been torturing her, and she hadn't trusted Levi to stop the slimy little worm from hurting her. She had just given Bernard everything that she had of any value; she gave to Bernard Stinking Calhoun.

Levi forced himself to stay still as he tried to think. For one brief second he thought of going to Cecily, he would shake the story from her silent lips if he had too. "No," he said out loud and only to himself. No, he thought, he would not torture Cecily as Bernard was. He would leave her be; she had not trusted him with this problem she had, she wouldn't trust him now if he shook her to death. He would go right to the source of the problem. He would go to Bernard Calhoun. First thing tomorrow morning he was going to Madison, and he was going to see Bernard, and he wouldn't leave the bastard until he knew what Bernard had on Cecily that was causing her to live in fear as she had been all this time.

After a long while, Levi started the walk home. All around him birds sang happily in the trees, the wind blew the leaves of the tree, and that haunting sound of the leaves in the wind joined the chirping of the birds, but Levi heard nothing. Once, not too long ago, Cecily's father had been well off, the farm and the horses had made a good living for them. When Daniel Walker died, the man had been broke. Daniel Walker had given everything to Bernard to keep Bernard quiet, Levi felt certain of this. And now Cecily was giving Levi's money to Bernard. What could Bernard be using against her? He racked his brain in wonder. And why hadn't Cecily told him what Bernard was doing to her? Levi thought so hard that his head was killing him. He could find no answers.

Cecily had let Bernard touch her, Levi swallowed hard and felt almost sick. He had been jealous of Bernard for a long time; now he was even more jealous as he thought that she let Bernard touch her, but not him. Cecily had pushed him away; she had not let him be with her as her husband, not in the truest sense. She had stood still and allowed Bernard to touch her. Levi felt hot with rage, hot with jealousy and furious in his anger. She was his wife, and that scum Bernard had touched her.

Levi stopped and stood still, the chirping birds were getting on his nerves, and his head ached even worse. Cecily loved him. After a few seconds, he started the walk home again. Tomorrow he would go to Bernard. Tomorrow Bernard would tell him what he needed to know. And then Levi would deal with Bernard and Cecily would be safe. He would see that she was free of Bernard's blackmail. They could then live; they could have a life, at last, a life without fear and silence. And he would make sure that Cecily knew that she could have trusted him, that she should have trusted him. He loved her.

Why hadn't she trusted him? He wondered. This question would haunt him.

Chapter Five

Cecily walked home slowly and wondered what she was going to do about Bernard. He would be back again and soon. She had to get to the bank in Madison, she had to have money, and she had found none in Levi's strong arm box. Her beautiful broach was gone like Levi's mother's wedding rings. They were all gone, and she would never have them back again. Everything that her father had was long gone even her own mother's jewelry. She had nothing left except the two thousand dollars that Levi had put in the bank for her in Madison. Soon that would also be gone. She would then be in very real trouble when there was nothing left to give Bernard.

She entered the house and didn't notice the look that Ollie gave to her as she walked by her and went into the bedroom. She locked the door, and no one bothered her about eating. She was alone. She climbed into bed and thought of Levi. He was innocent of all of this. She could not use him or his money. She would not use him to protect herself. He deserved the truth from her. If he hated her, if he divorced her, well that was what she deserved. She had lied to him. She had deceived him. She was not worthy of him or his love for her.

Cecily had no other choice but to tell Levi everything. She could find no other way out of this mess that she had made. She would throw herself on him and plead for mercy. She could not go on the way things were. She had to put a stop to Bernard, once and for all. And if in stopping Bernard she lost everything, at least his reign of terror would be done. Levi might even help her, one time her father felt they should go to Levi and enlist his aid in solving this situation.

Cecily prayed that Levi would not stay mad at her forever and that he would believe her when she told him what really happened. She loved Levi. She wanted a life with him. She had no one in the world except for Levi. She could not lose him, not now, not ever. She would make him see that she had only done what she had done because she was afraid of losing him and he would understand, he would love her still. Levi was her savior.

The next morning dawned cloudy, the sky was dark with the threat of rain, but no rain fell. Cecily looked up at the dark sky and asked God to be with her; she had asked God to be with her many times. He never had been. She turned and went to her closet where she dressed quickly and hurried from her bedroom. She had to see Levi; she had to tell him everything before her determination to do so failed her. She could not keep this silent vow she had made any longer. She knew now that she never should have kept silent. She should have trusted Levi right from the start. She had been wrong not to trust him. She stopped in the hall and said a quick prayer that he would believe her, that her husband would forgive her this mistake and the other and they could start again. Levi had to keep her, he couldn't throw her away, she would be nothing without him, she had wanted him her whole life long, he was the man of her dreams.

Ollie greeted Cecily with her usual breakfast of toast and coffee, but Cecily didn't sit down to eat. Instead, she went right up to Ollie. "I need to see Levi right away, and he isn't in his room. Has he gone to the sawmill already?"

"He left, Miss Cecily."

"Left? Where did he go?" Levi had to be back soon; she had to tell him, she couldn't wait any longer. She had already waited too long.

"He went to Madison before the sun came up. He said that he would be back by early this afternoon," Ollie said as she stared hard at Cecily.

Cecily groaned out loud in frustration. "I need him, Ollie. I need Levi right now; I can't wait."

Ollie shook her head. She knew that Miss Cecily hadn't needed Levi once since their marriage. The girl had kept him from her bed; Cecily was breaking Levi's heart and didn't care one lick that he was in love with her so much so that he was dying inside for what she was doing to him.

"He'll be back soon. You just gotta wait on him," Ollie said and handed Cecily a cup of coffee.

"Oh, Ollie," Cecily moaned, "I've been such a stupid fool," she paced the kitchen floor, coffee spilled on her hand, but she didn't seem to notice or care. "The Lord threw me into Levi's lap. Levi was the answer to a long said prayer, and I didn't see. I've been blind and dumb. God gave me Levi, and I need him. I need him right now."

Bernard Calhoun looked up when Levi Tucker entered his shop. Bernard wasn't a stupid man, he could see with one glance at Levi's face that Levi was out for blood, his blood. That stupid Grant Whittaker, he thought. Grant probably went straight to Levi and told what he had done, and Levi was here on Grant's behalf. Or had Cecily gotten suddenly brave and told on him. He wondered for a long few seconds. He couldn't believe that Cecily would ever tell Levi what he was doing to her, but she had been scared of him yesterday, she was always scared of him, and you could never tell what Cecily might do, she kept everything inside of herself.

"We have to talk," Levi said in a deadly voice, and Bernard knew, Cecily had told him everything and probably so had Grant

Whittaker. Bernard didn't want to see his own blood today. He knew what he would have to do to keep Levi from hurting him again.

"I figured my game was up when you walked in here," Bernard said and took a box from his file cabinet. "I guess you might want these." He threw the box at Levi and Levi caught it with both hands.

"What's in here?" Levi asked with a deep frown and heard Bernard swear under his breath.

So Levi didn't know, after all, Bernard thought and smiled. He would take great pleasure in the telling of this. "You must have been born yesterday, Levi. I always knew you were nothing but a big dumb bastard, but you're dumber than even I thought you were." Levi looked ready to kill him, but Bernard didn't care. He was fixing to have a laugh at Levi Tucker, and he would put the idiotic man in his place. 'You didn't really think that Cecily married you because she loved you? She married you for one reason and one reason only. Because she needed money to pay me for what is in that box in your hands, she was under the impression that I might make what's in that box public."

"You've been blackmailing her," Levi said, and Bernard laughed.

"Maybe I have. She posed so nicely for those pictures. You really should take a look at them." Levi opened the box in his hands and lost his breath. They were pictures of Cecily. His wife was stretched out on a bed, her long hair hanging down beside her and her head resting on a pillow, all throughout her beautiful hair were roses, and that was all there was on her, no clothes. His first reaction was complete shock, then he thought how beautiful his Cecily was, and then he felt sick. Cecily had given more to Bernard Calhoun than Levi had known. Cecily had given Bernard everything of herself.

"Her friend Clemmie liked Cecily's pictures so much that she came to me and I took some of her for Grant. I heard that Grant wasn't too happy about Clemmie posing for me nude. I think he might have broken off their engagement."

"Cecily and Clemmie let you take these pictures?" Levi asked in a low husky voice. He could not believe what he was seeing of his wife. There were half dozen photos of Cecily that he had looked at already and more still in the box.

"Yes. Cecily wanted me to capture her that way forever. She loved me, you know. She would have done anything for me. She didn't love me after I asked her father for money for those pictures. She didn't even like me much, but that didn't matter to me. I needed the money to open this place up, and her father gave me the money I needed. And since Daniel Walker died, I've been using your money." Bernard liked the look on Levi's face, he had hated the man since they had been children and now he hated Levi more for his ruined nose. "I've liked thinking of you trying to touch your wife and her turning you away; she told me that your touch made her sick. When you did touch her, she had to think of me in order to stand being with you. I told you she had beautiful breasts too, didn't I?" Bernard saw Levi still staring at the pictures. "I knew what her breasts looked like, you never have known, until right now, and you're her husband." Bernard laughed when Levi looked up from the pictures. "Yes, she told me that living with you was like living with a big dumb ox. She didn't want anything to do with you. Cecily even laughed at you for believing that she wanted to marry you, she turned you down, she told me so. You big dummy."

"Shut up," Levi said in a warning tone of voice.

"Why? Can't you take the truth? The only reason Cecily married you was because I told her too, I told her to marry you and get the money I needed, or I'd make the pictures public. She doesn't love you, Levi; you're nothing but the money she needs. She made a fool out of you, and you let her with your silly notions of love."

Levi could barely breathe. He stared hard at Bernard Calhoun and hated the man and his wife. "Say one more word, and I'll kill you where you stand," Levi said closing the distance that separated him and Bernard as he walked across the room.

"Go home to your whore wife, Levi. The plates are in there along with all the photos. I won't bother her for money anymore. And Clemmie's photos and plates are beneath hers. You might want to give Grant what Clemmie wanted him to have. Clemmie's not as good as Cecily, but she did well. Grant should marry her; she knows what to do in bed. Just like I taught your pretty Cecily, I taught Clemmie a few things too."

"You are a stinking no good worm," Levi hissed.

"Better that than a dumb son of a bitch like you, Levi. And I'm not married to a woman that can't stand me either." Bernard laughed in Levi's face.

"One more word," Levi warned Bernard.

"Your wife knows tricks to making a man happy. I bet she could teach you how to do it, Levi. If she ever lets you in her bed which I doubt she will." Bernard didn't say another word; Levi had a hold of his throat.

Levi climbed onto his horse fighting mad; it wasn't good enough that he had just broken Bernard's nose again and very probably the man's jaw. No, Levi wanted to hurt someone else. He wanted to kill Cecily. "She married me for my damn money!!" Levi screamed once he was well out of town and alone in the woods headed home. He even growled like a monster deep in his chest as he cried out again, "She married me for my money!" She had told Bernard that she couldn't stand his touch, all these weeks he had believed that she was making love with him with her kissing him and he had believed she loved him. She had said she didn't want his child; he remembered and almost burst into tears. She had told him over and over she shouldn't have married him and now he knew, she couldn't stand to be with him. She had only married him for his money that she gave to Bernard.

Levi hung his head and fought to keep from screaming again. Cecily had turned him away from her bed. She had never meant to allow him his rights as her husband. She didn't want him. All that she had wanted was his money for Bernard. She had been laughing at him for loving her. She had known how dumb he was and she'd used him and tricked him. She had ruined her own father by posing for these photos, and she had married him knowing she would ruin him as well because Bernard was blackmailing her and had been. Why had she posed for these photos? And he knew, because she loved Bernard at the time, she had no idea that one day in the future he would use the photos against her. He groaned out loud and opened the box with the photos and plates inside. He lost his breath looking upon them. Cecily was more beautiful than he had ever imagined. He felt his heart ache so bad that he thought he'd die. The photos were beautiful beyond words, and at the same time, they had ruined his life. What kind of woman would pose nude, surrounded by flowers, her hair long and loose and flowing about her? And Clemmie had done so as well; they were cut from the same cloth, he thought and tried not to cry out again.

Cecily had never loved him, Levi now realized. He closed the box and turned his horse toward home. Cecily didn't want the world that he had wanted to give her. She hadn't wanted anything at all from him except for his money. These past weeks he had been a fool trying to seduce her and give her pleasure and all the worrying over her fragile state he'd done, and why? Because he loved her with all of his heart, deep and true. And all along she had been laughing at him and allowing Bernard to touch her and give him money. He wondered what else she had given to Bernard besides his money and jewelry these past weeks.

He thought of the look on her face yesterday as she'd left the house. She wasn't afraid of Bernard; she was afraid that he would find out about the photos he now held in his hands. He remembered her calling out his name in the graveyard; he remembered her hurt and tortured look. Tortured because she was married to him and didn't want to be married to him, she had only wanted his money.

"I'm your hell," she had said to him once. She may be his hell, but he was fixing to take her to hell with him.

Cecily paced all throughout the house and wished that Levi would come home. The sun finally came out, and it never had rained. She felt like he had to be home soon, it was late afternoon. When she heard a horse trot up into the yard, Cecily nearly tore the door off of its hinges getting outside.

'Cecily!" Clemmie cried out her name, and Cecily rushed to her best friend as Clemmie jumped off of her horse and ran to Cecily. "I'm in terrible trouble. I don't know what to do."

"Calm down, Clemmie," Cecily said while grabbing a hold of her and they both nearly fell to the ground. "What's happened? What's wrong?"

"I went to Madison with mama a couple of weeks ago while she was shopping and I had my photo taken for Grant. Bernard took my photo then he offered me a glass of tea. Oh, Cecily, I fell asleep, and yesterday Bernard came to Daddy," Clemmie fell silent sobbing with no control. Cecily held her tight as her own eyes grew wide with shock. Bitter tea, having her photo made for her father, Cecily knew just what was happening to Clemmie.

"No," Cecily whispered before closing her eyes. What had happened to her two long years ago had just been done to her friend Clemmie.

"He had, Bernard had, oh Cecily, it's awful. He had photos of me without my, Oh Cecily! They were terrible photos of me."

"Oh, Clemmie," Cecily felt sick inside.

"I didn't have any clothes on, Cecily. Bernard offered to sell them to Daddy; Daddy refused to pay any money to Bernard ever. Bernard then took them to Grant and today, Grant came and asked me to give him his ring back. Bernard told Grant that I wanted to pose for those photos, he told Grant that I had fun and that I, oh Cecily he told Grant the worst thing you can tell a fiancé."

"Is Grant going to pay Bernard the money for the pictures?" Cecily asked as she stood still in the yard almost holding her breath.

"No. Grant said that he told Bernard to go to hell." Cecily gasped. "Then Grant told me to go to hell with Bernard." Clemmie cried harder.

Cecily hung her head and fought to breathe. This was all her fault. Every second of this could have been avoided if she had only told Clemmie what had happened to her two years ago. Clemmie would never have gone to Bernard and had her picture made. She should have told, Cecily thought. She had made so many mistakes.

"Daddy put me out of the house this afternoon. He said that I made him sick to look at, that I had ruined myself and shamed our family name. Mama just stared at me like I had grown two heads or worse; she hadn't spoken to me since yesterday when Bernard left our house going to find Grant."

"Oh Clemmie, forgive me, forgive me please," Cecily said and hugged her friend closer. "Bernard has been blackmailing me for over two years with the same kind of photos. Daddy paid everything we had to keep me safe, and I've never been safe."

"Cecily," Clemmie said her name and looked at the pain on her face. "Your secret," she whispered, and Cecily nodded her head. "That's why you needed money after your father died?" Again Cecily nodded her head. "And Levi, does he know?"

"I plan on telling him right away," Cecily said in a firm voice.

"Bernard said that he is going to make my photos public. I have nowhere to go. Cecily, I don't know what to do. Grant hates me now; I've lost everything."

"Let's go to Daddy's house. You can stay there for now." Cecily took the reins of Clemmie's horse and started walking. "The tea that Bernard gave me was bitter; I didn't know he took the photos of me either until he came to Daddy."

"When I was drinking it, Cecily, I honestly thought that Bernard couldn't make a decent pot of tea. And when I woke up, I was lying on a bed in his studio, but I was fully dressed. Only my hair was down, and my top button of my shirtwaist was undone." Cecily nodded.

"Me too. Daddy kept saying how much like Mama I looked, and he had no likeness of Mama, so I went into Madison and had Bernard take my photo for Daddy, I still have it, it's on the mantle above the fireplace at my house. And shortly thereafter, Bernard came with the photos of me without my clothes on."

"At least your father paid Bernard. I'm ruined. Daddy won't pay anything ever; he said he wouldn't. And Bernard said that he would leave those pictures of me all over town for my friends to find." Clemmie let out a soft cry of horror. "I've lost Grant; I'll never be able to show my face anywhere ever again. And my father, Cecily, he was so mad at me, he said he'll never forgive me, and I'm no daughter to him as of this day, that's what he said to me. I've lost everything; I am completely ruined."

"I'll tell Levi. I'll tell him everything the minute he gets home. I have to trust he'll help us, Clemmie. He loves me; I know he does. I should have told him from the start; I was just so afraid of losing him."

"He'll just hate you, Cecily. The same way that Grant hates me. He won't listen to you any more than Daddy would listen to me. Don't tell. Pay, don't ever tell anyone and just keep paying Bernard."

"You don't know Levi; I didn't either until yesterday. He loves me; he honestly loves me," Cecily said in a certain voice. "Levi knows Bernard, he'll believe me. He has to believe me; I love him so much." Cecily hoped that she spoke the truth. She couldn't lose Levi, not ever; he was the love of her life. She was the love of his life; he would believe her.

"He won't believe you, Cecily. You'll be ruining yourself if you tell him. You have to stay silent about this. Isn't it bad enough that one of us can't ever have a normal life again because of Bernard? I don't want you hurt like I am. Please, I'm begging you, don't tell Levi anything."

"But Levi can help us, Clemmie. I know he can." Clemmie just shook her head at Cecily's words. "No one can help me now. Bernard has taken my whole life away from me."

"Don't say that, Clemmie," Cecily begged as they reached her father's house. "You stay here; you'll be safe here. And I'll go home and tell Levi what Bernard has been doing to me and has done to you. I should have told Levi before I married him, I should have trusted him. I was stupid not to have told him. I'm going to now though and pray it's not too late."

"No, Cecily, please don't do this thing, I don't want you ruined," Clemmie tried to convince her not to tell her husband one last time, Cecily didn't listen to her.

"I'm taking your horse; I'll bring it back to you later. Try and rest. I'll see you soon." She hugged Clemmie at the door of her old home. "I promise you, Clemmie; I won't let this destroy you. I'll fix everything. Trust me."

"Cecily, you haven't been able to save yourself for two years; how do you plan on saving me?"

"Levi," Cecily said firmly. "I'm going to get Levi; he can fix this for us both." She mounted Clemmie's horse and said again only this time her voice was firm and certain, no doubts or fears. "Levi will save us."

Cecily saw Levi's horse grazing in the front yard when she returned home, and she jumped down fast from Clemmie's horse and hurried inside the house. She looked for him in the parlor, the kitchen, every room, but she couldn't find him. Finally, she hurried to her own bedroom as it was the only place in the house she hadn't looked for her husband. She stopped in the doorway when she saw him standing by the door leading out onto the porch looking outside and away from her. He was here; she sagged in relief. He could help her. He could save her.

"Levi," she breathed his name, and he turned to face her. She gasped and took a step back when she saw his face. Cecily had never seen Levi look like this before. His face was nearly red, his eyes were narrowed, and she knew, he was angry, he was angry with her.

"Do you need more of my money, Cecily?" he asked as he came toward her and she shook her head hard and fast. "No? Why not? After all, we both know my money is the only reason you married me.

He knew, her heartbeat inside of her chest and loud in her ears over and over, he knows! "Levi," she said his name and started to move toward him. "Please, Levi. Just give me a chance to explain." Cecily begged her husband.

"Oh, I think I have all the explanation that I need, Cecily. These explain everything very well." He threw the photos of her onto the bed. Cecily closed her eyes; she had seen those photos one time in her life, the one time had been enough, she never wanted to see them again. "The plates are here also. Your lover gave them over to me really very easy."

"Lover?" Cecily breathed the word with her hand over her heart.

"Bernard told me everything that's been going on between you two for a long time. I didn't even have to hurt him to get these from him." Levi walked toward her, the anger in his eyes made Cecily fall back a step, but he followed her. "Everything that you ever said to me was a damn lie," Levi screamed only inches from her face seconds before he threw the plates at her feet and they shattered all over the floor. The only thing left of what she had done was the photos in the box on the bed.

"Levi, I'm so sorry, if," she reached out her hand to her husband as she spoke and he slapped her hand away causing her to fall silent.

"I just bet you're sorry, Cecily. Kind of like the fox in the hen house with a mouth full of feathers and a gun pointing at him sorry!" Cecily shook her head no. "Caught! You're sorry because I found out that you married me for my money!" Levi hung his head, and she thought that he might be so mad at her that he would hit her and she fell back away from him further. But when he looked back up at her, Cecily saw the most awful look of hurt in his eyes that she had ever seen in her life. Her husband wasn't just mad at her; he was devastated and in agony over her having married him for his money. "I loved you. I loved you and the whole time we've been married you've been laughing at me behind one hand for being dumb and giving Bernard Stinking Calhoun my money with the other hand."

"No, Levi! You're so wrong," Cecily tried again to reach out to him, Levi moved from her shaking his head and looking even more hurt than he had before. The hurt in his eyes she could not stand.

"Don't lie to me; damn you!" Levi screamed at her, and she screamed in fear and jumped back another step. "You married me for my money and for no other reason. You never had any intentions to love me or let me love you. I was never anything to you until you needed my money to keep Bernard from showing the world what a whore you really are. I wasn't ever anything to you." Cecily heard the pain in his voice and felt like crying; she then realized that he had been crying, his eyes were swollen and red-rimmed. "I loved you," Levi said while holding her eyes with his own. "I loved you so much; I would have done anything for you. But the Cecily I loved wasn't even real."

Cecily gasped when she realized that he had said he had loved her, he didn't love her anymore. To tell him now that she did love him and had wanted him always would only make things worse, he wouldn't believe her, not like this. She thought of falling to her knees and begging him to forgive her for being stupid, but the look that he was giving her was enough to make her stand still and not move, much less speak. If she did move or say one word, she felt certain that he would hit her and maybe with what she had done to him, she deserved to be hit.

"I could divorce you for these, Cecily," Levi said as he reached and picked up a handful of the photos. "Do you want that? Do you want a divorce?"

"No, Levi. If you'll just give me a –,"

"Shut up!" he screamed at her, and she closed her mouth while he turned his back toward her and ran a hand through his thick hair. "Why?" he asked in the most tortured voice that Cecily had ever heard in her life. She had done this to him, she had hurt him like this, and she had done this thing with the full knowledge that if he one day learned the truth he would hate her. She had let this happen by not telling him the truth right from the start. She had told him none of the truth. She had only given him lies. And when she realized that she could trust him, that she should have trusted him from the start, it was too late, he knew everything, and he hated her as she feared he would.

Levi turned back around and faced Cecily. "You could have told me what Bernard was doing to you. I would have gotten these pictures for you as well as the plates and a piece of Bernard. I loved you, Cecily. I would have done anything for you. I loved you so much I would have died for you. You were everything I ever wanted." He closed his eyes and shook his head. "And I was nothing to you; I didn't matter to you at all in any way, shape, form or fashion."

"Levi, I was afraid," Cecily gave him the only excuse that she had to give and it was the truth, something truthful coming from her at last, she thought. "I was afraid you would hate me if you knew."

"And you think now I don't? My God, Cecily. I could have forgiven you anything; I loved you that much. But to marry me only for my money that I can never forgive you for. Not ever."

"It's not like you're thinking, Levi. If you'll just let me explain how everything was," Cecily pleaded with her husband for understanding.

"Yes, do explain Cecily. Explain why you could give yourself to a man like Bernard, but not to me, your own husband. Explain how you can take off your clothes for photos like these and pose for your lover, but hide your beautiful body from me, the man you pledged your life to. There is no way to explain, Cecily. I wouldn't believe one word that you said to me now or ever even if you could explain."

Cecily watched as Levi went to her dresser with the wooden box and took out more photos. "Here, take these to your whoring friend. Tell her I was a gentleman and didn't look. Grant's well rid of her, I think. But you, you're not rid of me Cecily. As God is in heaven, you will pay for everything that you've done to me and then some. You're still my wife."

Cecily took the box he held out to her, her fingers touched his, and he jerked his hand away almost spilling the contents of the box onto the floor. She knew it would do her no good to try and tell him the truth right now. He was hurt; she had hurt him as she knew she would. He was also furious with her, and he had reason to be furious. She had made a mess of everything, and it was too late right now to fix it, it would take time to fix.

"Everything you've done to me, Cecily." Levi whispered, "I will do to you. You are my wife; I own you. You have to come back here after you deliver those pictures, and when you do, I'll be your hell." Cecily heard his voice break, she saw his hands shaking, and she knew that she had hurt his heart. He felt betrayed; he had been betrayed and by her. He had loved her true and with all of his heart, and she had used that love against him. She would come home, and she would tell him the truth when he was calm enough to listen. She loved him; she wanted him, she would fix this when she came home.

"Levi," she reached out her hand and gently touched his face. She saw stars when his hand punched her in the face so hard that she fell to the floor. Cecily put her fingers to her lips, and when she pulled them away, she saw blood, she tasted blood. Levi had hit her. When she looked up at him, she saw he wanted to hit her again; his hands were fists at his side; she couldn't believe that he had hit her.

"You lying no good whore," Levi stared down at his wife. She was crying, but he didn't care, she had made him cry and hadn't cared. "Tell me the truth, Cecily, if you are capable of telling the truth. Was it just my money? Only my money that you married me for?"

Cecily stood up slowly and backed away from Levi. He had hit her, and he might hit her again. He wouldn't believe her if she told him the truth; he might hit her again if she told him she loved him. She backed away from him, the box held close. "Yes," she said what he wanted to hear, the only word he would believe of her right now. And then she was running, running from Levi, running from her truth and from the lies he'd been told with blood dripping from the side of her mouth and nose.

"Damn you!" Levi's anguished cry followed his wife out the front door as he fell on the bed knowing without doubt that he was what he'd been labeled as a child, a dummy.

Clemmie's horse was still standing in the yard, and Cecily got on it and kicked the animal hard, her skirt was pulled up well past her knees, and the box that Levi had given to her was under her arm. She had ruined everything by not telling Levi what Bernard was doing to her before she married him. Her lack of trust had wrecked her marriage, her life, and Levi's life. Because of her silence, she had pulled them both into hell, and she rode the horse fast in an effort to escape the flames that meant to burn her alive. God was damning her for all her lies.

Cecily held on to the horse and fought the pain in her heart. How had Levi found out? And why hadn't she told him everything last night? Why had she waited, waited until it was too late? She had ruined everything by not being honest with her husband before he was her husband. He was right when he had said that he would have gotten the pictures for her, she knew he would have, he would have done anything or her, he loved her. He never would have hated her if she had just told him the truth. He had been her Levi; he had always been her Levi. All along he could have saved her if she had only trusted him as he trusted her. She was one big huge mistake. Everything she had done had been wrong. She had trusted Bernard long ago to make a picture of her and instead he had drugged her, removed her clothing and taken pictures of her that had ruined her life two long hard years ago. If she had told Clemmie what was happening to her the same thing never would have happened to Clemmie. Her silence had destroyed everyone she loved today, her silence had killed Levi's love for her, and it had killed her father. Her father was in an early grave because of those photos, and her father had wanted to go to Levi, he had wanted her to tell Levi and get his help.

Cecily thought of Levi and how mad he was with her. No, mad was too simple a word to describe what Levi was feeling for her. At long last, she was safe from Bernard and the threats of exposure, but she was not safe from her husband's anger. Levi had said that she would pay for what she had done to him and she believed him. Levi never lied. She lied. And God help her, she loved her husband, she had always loved him, and she had brought him to this, this horrible pain and awful humiliation. He had hit her in his pain and anger; he had hurt her, punched her in the face. She deserved what he had done and worse. She had never told him that he was everything to her; she had treated him like he was the nothing that he had said she thought he was. The pain in his voice when he had said that he was nothing to her would haunt her until she set things right between them. She had to set thing things right with Levi; she had to take the pain she had put on him away from him. She would start fixing this as soon as she got home.

God had thrown her into his lap, he was the answer to her prayers, all along Levi could have saved her and her fear had made her blind, her fear had hurt Levi and herself. She heard him damning her and with his words she had heard his pain and his crying. She was damned. She should be damned. She had hurt her Levi, and she knew that she would.

"Grant!" Cecily screamed at the top of her lungs as she pulled the horse to a stop in front of Grant's home. She may have messed up her own life, and it was surely all her own fault, but there was no reason for Clemmie to suffer the same fate as she. The truth had to save someone in this horrible situation that she had made. "Grant!" she screamed again.

"Go away, Cecily," Grant said as he came out onto his front porch.

"No, you listen to me!" She screamed in near hysteria. "Bernard drugged us with something in a glass of tea. He drugged us, and he removed our clothes, and he took our pictures. We didn't know! We didn't know Grant!" Cecily was crying so hard that she didn't see Grant had moved and was saddling his own horse in the yard. "We didn't do anything wrong, Grant," she said pathetically. "He's been blackmailing me and Daddy for years, and I didn't do anything but drink a glass of sweet tea he offered to me. Please, you have to believe me. Look at the photos; we're sleeping; look at the photos."

"Calm down, Cecily. You're going to make yourself sick," Grant said and pulled his horse next to her horse.

"If I had told Clemmie what Bernard was doing to me, she wouldn't have gone to have her photo made by him; he never would have done the same thing to her. Bernard is evil. And I didn't tell Clemmie, and I didn't tell Levi. I didn't tell anyone Grant; I didn't tell."

"Cecily," he said gently and put a hand onto her hand. "I believe you. Stop crying and tell me where Clemmie is." He handed her his handkerchief, and she wiped the tears from her face before she wiped the blood from her chin. She felt her lip and knew that it was swollen; it felt huge. She still could not believe that Levi had hit her.

"Clemmie is at my father's house,' Cecily said to Grant as he looked at her touch her bloody swollen lip, she would have a bad bruise tomorrow he thought.

"Are you all right?" he asked as they turned their horses to ride to her old home.

"Yes, I fell down," Cecily said, the lie tasted bitter after she had seen what the other lies had done to her life. "I'm sorry, Grant, I should have told Clemmie about Bernard," she was speaking in a much calmer voice.

"You did what you thought you had to do, Cecily. You were scared, and you had to protect yourself. I'm not your God; I won't sit in judgment of what you've done. And I know Bernard, what you say he did to you; I believe he did to you."

Cecily hung her head and said a quick prayer that Levi would forgive her so easily. She shuttered when she remembered how he had punched her hard and so fast, without any warning that he was going too. She didn't think that Levi was going to be in a forgiving mood for some time to come. She had done him wrong, and he had hit her for the wrong. She prayed that he would not hit her again.

Levi stayed on the bed for a long time after Cecily ran from the house, his shaking hands he put over his face and gasped for every breath that he took. He had hit his wife; he had punched his Cecily in the face. After a few long moments, he reached and picked up the photos of her that he had thrown on the bed earlier and he looked again at his wife's nude body. She was more beautiful than he had ever dreamed she would be. He stared at her breasts knowing he'd never seen them in the light of day. He wanted her as his wife; he craved to be with her. And she didn't want him; she had never wanted him for her lover. All the making love to her, hearing her moan in his mouth, feeling her mold her body into his, shaking apart in his arms, it had all been with another man in her thoughts, another man besides him she wanted. She wasn't making love with him, nor even to him, for her was it an act she was carrying out, she wasn't seeing him.

Levi groaned in a physical agony as he remembered the night on the porch in the rocking chair. He couldn't think of that, he cried inside and closed his eyes. A few moments later he stood up on unsteady legs and went to his strong arm box where he locked the pictures of her up for safe keeping. He would not destroy them; Bernard had given them to him. He now owed these pictures, just as he owned Cecily. He had hit her; he thought again and hated himself for that act. He was a gentleman; he knew not to ever hit a lady. Cecily wasn't a lady, Cecily had been with Bernard, she had been Bernard's whore. Now she would be his. He would take what he could from her and satisfy this burning desire he had in his gut for her. And she would pay for the pain that he was in. The pain she had put him in.

Levi went into the kitchen for the broom and dustpan before he went and cleaned up the mess that he had made when he had shattered the plates at his wife's feet. She would come back here. She was his wife, and she would come back to him. When she did, he would be ready and waiting for her. He had waited too long for her; his wait was near to an end.

Levi closed his eyes again as he thought that he had hit her. He had never struck any woman in his life; he wanted to hit her again. He wanted to hurt her as he had hurt Bernard. There were other ways that he could make Cecily pay for what she had done to him. Ways that would not hurt her, but would tie her to him, tie her tightly to him when she didn't want him. The rest of her life she would pay for having married him, he would see to that. He would hold her with his body and his need. Levi wouldn't be done with her until one of them were both dead. "Till death do us part, Cecily," he said softly to himself. "Death won't take you from me for a long time. I own you." His words and thoughts didn't make him feel any better. His heart still hurt. Levi knew that his heart would always hurt.

After Cecily left her, Clemmie paced the floor of the kitchen and worried. Levi could no more help her than Grant would. There was no help for her. If only she hadn't drunk that glass of tea Bernard had offered to her. If only she could live that one moment all over again and have her Mama come with her to the photography studio while her photo was being made. She grieved that she didn't leave the minute Bernard had finished taking her picture. But she couldn't go back and fix what she had done now, she had lost Grant, and her family had put her out. She had nothing left. Bernard Calhoun had destroyed her life.

Clemmie sat down at the kitchen table and wrote Grant a letter. She explained everything in great detail; she told him that she loved him and only him and always him and she had been faithful to their love. She couldn't live without him; she didn't want to live without him. All of her thoughts and feelings and fears were put to paper, her tears streaking down her face.

She knew that Bernard would make good his threat; he would make her look like a whore to everyone in Cherry Lake. Clemmie lay her head on the table and cried harder, thick hot tears fell from her face into her lap, and her whole body shook with her crying. She didn't want to live in this shame. She didn't want to live shunned and hated by everyone she knew and loved. She could not live her life this way. She cried harder as she finished her letter to Grant and folded it up, leaving it on the table.

"Clemmie!" Cecily screamed her best friends name as she slid off the horse in the yard. "Clemmie we're here, I brought Grant!" she called out as she rushed through the kitchen door.

"Are you sure she's here, Cecily? Maybe she went home," Grant said as he left his own horse in the yard and followed Cecily into the house.

"I left her right here about an hour ago. She said that her father had put her out of the house and she had nowhere to go," Cecily spoke in a rush as she went into the kitchen.

Clemmie had laid down on the bed in Cecily's old room; she had rolled up the sleeve of her shirtwaist, laid her wrist bare and wondered at how pale her skin was. She had taken the sharpest knife she was able to find in the kitchen and made a clean cut on her wrist, it hadn't even hurt that much. And then she waited, waited for all of her troubles to be at an end. Bernard couldn't hurt her now.

Cecily saw the letter on the table and picked it up before glancing back at Grant. "She left a note," Cecily read the first few lines and knew, she threw the letter down on the table and screamed as she ran to her bedroom. Grant followed after her and grabbed her hand while she stood screaming in the doorway. Clemmie was lying on the bed, blood was everywhere, and she was almost white. "No, Clemmie," Cecily cried as she ran to her friend.

"Oh God, Clemmie, no," Grant cried out as he followed Cecily to the bed.

"Grant, hurry. Go for the doctor," Cecily pushed on him to go back to the door as she bound Clemmie's wrist tight with the handkerchief Grant had given to her earlier.

"Is she dead, Cecily?" he asked in a horrible voice. He had never seen so much blood in his whole life. And it was Clemmie's blood.

"She's still alive Grant," Cecily saw the horror on his face and felt that way herself. "Go for the doctor, hurry." Grant stood unmoving staring at the blood. Cecily left Clemmie and went over to Grant, she slapped his face, not hard, she didn't want to hurt him, she only wanted to get his attention off of the blood so he could do what needed to be done to save Clemmie's life. "Grant," she said when his eyes cleared and focused onto her, "go for the doctor now, as fast as you can." She saw his head nod, and then he turned and ran from the room, she saw his horse fly by the window and knew help would be here soon.

Cecily hurried back to Clemmie; she was scared out of her mind, blood was everywhere. She applied pressure, and the bleeding finally stopped, the handkerchief was tied so tight that it stopped the gushing blood.

Clemmie lay in her old bed looking white as her sheet and too small. There were dark circles under her eyes that were almost purple; she looked like she was dying right before Cecily's eyes. Clemmie wouldn't have been brought to this if Cecily had told her the truth a long time ago. And she could have trusted Clemmie, Clemmie, who was more than a sister to her, true sisters couldn't have been closer than they were.

Her father was dead, Cecily thought. The stress from Bernard's constant threats had just been too much for her father's heart, and in one second it had stopped beating, and he died. And Levi, Levi was hurt, she had broken his heart, and she had to find some way to make him see how sorry she is and that she always has loved him. And Grant, poor Grant that she had just slapped and ridden away from here in fear for the woman he loves, and Clemmie's parents had hurt their innocent daughter by believing Bernard's lies. Silence, Cecily thought, her silence had done so much harm. Too much harm and to those that she loved most in this world. She vowed right here and right now to never be silent again. If only she had known that it would come to this. But she hadn't known. And it was too late to correct all the mistakes her silence had brought about. The silence makes no sound, she thought, the silence is isolating. She would never be silent again.

After the bleeding was stopped completely, Cecily stood and went back to the kitchen. Clemmie had to live she prayed and begged of God. And no one must ever know what really happened here today. This was an accident. No one could know that Clemmie had deliberately hurt herself. She picked up Clemmie's letter to Grant and put it up the sleeve of her shirtwaist.

"How is she?" Grant almost begged to know as he rushed inside the house with the doctor on his heels.

"She's alive," Cecily said gently while touching his hand. "She's resting peacefully." Cecily led the doctor to her old room, and he quickly examined her.

"How did this happen?" the doctor asked as he threaded a needle. Grant looked at Cecily, and she looked at him.

"An accident," they both answered at the same time.

"I don't think so," the doctor said and began sewing the cut Clemmie had made on her wrist. "Try again," the doctor suggested. Grant still looked at Cecily; she didn't know what to say any more than he did, but she knew that she was the liar in the room and she should think of something.

"Grant," Clemmie called out softly for the man that she loved, and he rushed to her side.

"I'm right here, sweetheart. I'll always be right here." Grant took a hold of the wrist that his fiancé had not damaged and held it close to his heart. "I made a mistake, Clemmie. I was wrong. You can't ever do anything like this to yourself again. Don't ever do this again. I love you; I don't want to live without you." Clemmie started to cry.

"You don't hate me anymore?" she pleaded to know, and Grant kissed her pale cheek.

"I can't ever hate you, you're going to be my wife," he said firmly.

"Well, I can see what's gone on here," the doctor said as he finished with Clemmie's wrist. "I trust that you'll not let a lovers' quarrel go so far again young man," the doctor spoke sternly to Grant.

"We will never quarrel again," Grant said to both Clemmie and the doctor.

"We can hope," the doctor said in a dry voice while still looking sternly at Grant. "Keep her in bed for a few days, feed her well and lots of fluids. If she starts to bleed again, tie off the wrist and come for me right away."

"Yes, sir," Grant said as the doctor walked up to Cecily.

"What happened to your face, young lady? Did you get between those two when they were quarreling and get punched?" Cecily shook her head and touched her face; it hurt bad to touch.

"No, I fell," she said softly, and the doctor gave a bitter disbelieving laugh.

"About as truthful as her 'accident,'" he pointed back to Clemmie. "It doesn't look like any teeth were broken, but whatever hit you, see it doesn't do so again." Cecily watched the doctor leave and touched her lip again.

"We'll stay here if it's all right with you Cecily," Grant said to both Clemmie and Cecily. "The second you can stand up and ride Clemmie, we'll go see the Reverend Bidwell."

Cecily left them alone and went into the kitchen. She started a fire in the stove and opened the damper all the way. When the flames were high, she picked up the box that Levi had given to her with Clemmie's photo inside and put it in the stove. Clemmie's troubles were now all over.

"Grant," Cecily said softly from the doorway of the room where she stood. "I burned the pictures, and Levi broke the plates, and here," she pulled Clemmie's letter to him from her sleeve. "This is yours. I hid it because I didn't want the doctor to see it."

"How can I ever thank you, Cecily?" Grant asked as he folded up the letter and put it into his pocket.

"This was all my fault; you shouldn't be thanking me. Take care of Clemmie. There are some jarred foods in the pantry and a ham in the smokehouse still. You won't need to worry about food for a few days."

"Cecily," Clemmie called her name, and she went to the bed. "How did you get the pictures?"

"Levi got them from Bernard. He got mine too." Cecily touched her swollen lip and flinched. She had to go home to her angry husband. She had to make him hear her as Grant had heard her. Once she explained everything, Levi would forgive her.

"Thank God for Levi," Clemmie whispered. "How did he know?"

"I don't know, Clemmie," Cecily said and wished that she did know. "Levi didn't have time to tell me before I went to get Grant and then came here to you. And it doesn't really matter how he knew, all that matters is that you're safe."

"You're safe too," Clemmie whispered and closed her eyes. "You were right earlier today when you said Levi would help us. Thank you, Jesus, for Levi," Clemmie prayed.

"Get some rest so you can get well, sweetie," Cecily kissed Clemmie's pale cheek. She wondered what Levi would do to her when she got home. He had been furious with her. And she had to go and tell him that she had only married him for his money, she groaned out loud thinking of having done that. Why hadn't she told him that she loved him? That she always has loved him. The worst lie of all was the last one when she had said she only married him for his money and she felt like crying.

"Tell Levi that I thank him too," Grant said as he went back to Clemmie's side and Cecily moved to the door. Cecily could only nod her head as she wondered if Levi would let her explain everything to him.

"Levi was very angry with me," Cecily said to Grant and bit her bottom lip in worry.

"Don't worry, Cecily. Levi never allows himself to get mad; he hasn't since we were kids. He knows if he gets mad he can't get over it; he's been that way his whole life. He's probably just mad at Bernard anyway; he could never get mad at you." Cecily knew that Grant was wrong. Grant didn't know what she had done to Levi. Only Levi knew how she had hurt him; only Levi knew what Bernard had said about her. She knew that her husband believed that she had lain with Bernard, she should have told him the truth about that weeks ago, and she could have, but she hadn't, another mistake that she had to add up with all the others.

"Tell Clemmie that I'm sorry when she wakes up again," Cecily said to Grant and moved out of the room.

"Thank you," Clemmie's weak voice stopped her from leaving the house.

"Don't thank me, Clemmie; I feel awful that I didn't trust you years ago and tell you about Bernard. I'm so sorry." Cecily turned and ran from the house and down the road, it was almost dark, and she had to go home, she had to face Levi. She touched her swollen face and mouth as she hurried, the sun was falling away fast, the sky was almost a dark pink, and the clouds were getting dark. She wanted to pray, she wanted to plead with God to help her reach her angry husband with the truth and that he would believe her despite her lies. But she couldn't pray, she couldn't plead. All she could do was hear her heart beating fast in her chest, the pounding sounding like the words over and over again, "home to Levi, home to Levi, home to Levi…"

Chapter Six

Cecily came into the back door and saw that the kitchen was nearly dark and empty. The house was too quiet; she didn't like the sound of the silence anymore. She walked through the dining room to her bedroom thinking that she had to have a bath. She would deal with Levi later.

"I wondered if you would come back," Levi said from where he reclined on her bed and Cecily startled and stopped to stand still. "Aren't you glad to see your husband, Cecily? Or do you have a problem with my being in your bedroom?"

"No. I mean yes. I mean, I don't know what I mean," Cecily stumbled over her words and thoughts while trying to breathe. "Levi, I need to talk to you."

"No, you don't," Levi said in a low and deadly tone of voice, his eyes narrowed as he stared hard at her. "You will shut up and listen to what I tell you." Cecily didn't like the sound of his voice any more than she liked his words. Levi was unreasonable when he was mad; she was fast coming to realize. She thought of the little boy that had been angry over someone's comment on his hair before she listened closely to what he was telling her. "Here are the rules from now on. We live my way. You speak only when I tell you to speak, and you do everything I say when I say. Do you understand?" She nodded her head slowly while staring into those narrowed dark eyes. "Good. Simple instructions, follow them and we won't have any problems."

Well, he won't listen to her right now, Cecily thought. He was still mad with her, but he would get over his anger in a day or two, and she would explain everything to him, and they would be happy together at last just as Clemmie and Grant were happy now. Her dreams would come true; she just needed time. Besides, you can't take a caring man like Levi and expect him to be angry for too long, she thought. Levi was good and understanding and kind. Cecily believed that he still loved her; he couldn't just stop loving her for the mistakes she had made. He would forgive her; she would make him forgive her, Cecily thought again and again while staring into his narrowed eyes. She had to believe what she was thinking or she would break down and cry forever, her life would be nothing if Levi were to stay mad at her for too long and he just couldn't stay mad, he loved her.

"I want you to go and take a bath. And then you will join me here," he patted her bed, and Cecily shook her head. "You will do just as I say when I say. That's the rule. Besides, I've given you enough time to prepare yourself for our wedding night. Tonight will be that night. Better late than never. Now go get your bath."

Cecily hurried into the bathroom and closed the door. She pulled off her clothes and wondered just what Levi would do to her. She scrubbed herself hard and shook all over and tried to take all the time that she could, afraid to face her husband. He had hurt her, he had hit her, and now he wanted her in his bed. And he thought she'd been with Bernard; he wouldn't know to be gentle with her. As she left the tub and dried off she realized that Levi wasn't really a violent man, he had hit her because he was hurt because she had hurt him. He would never hit her again, he had loved her yesterday, he still had to love her today, you just can't stop loving someone, she knew. She remembered when he had broken Bernard's nose, how he had beaten Bernard up and she took a deep breath; he would never do anything like that to her. Anger didn't lead to pain, and he was just angry. She pulled on her robe and tried to convince herself that she was safe at last, from Bernard and from Levi.

Levi sat on her bed with several pillows behind his back. He had removed his shirt and shoes and only wore his trousers. She looked at his shoes on the floor and not his bare chest. "Come here," Levi ordered, and Cecily went to him, too afraid not to do as he said. She had never seen her husband this way; he was frightening her. She wished for her old Levi back, this new one she could not like. He was hard, and he was cold, and he sounded cruel. "I've lived in hell these past weeks wanting you and not being able to have you," he said, and Cecily knew that he spoke the truth by the way he looked at her body. "Take off the robe." Cecily's mouth fell open, and she shook her head.

"Not this way, Levi," she cried out softly, and Levi left the bed.

"Do not speak!" he ordered, and she closed her mouth and swallowed hard. "I told you to take off your robe. Take it off, or I'll tear it off of you."

Cecily was shocked. Her gentle, caring, loving Levi had turned mean in his anger with her. She slowly let her robe fall to the floor and knew, as of right now she was free of Bernard Calhoun, but evil had a new face. The face of evil now was her husband. She stood before him and shivered despite the fact that the room was not cold, she was frightened, she was frightened of Levi.

Levi stood before his wife and stared at her beautiful body. Cecily felt herself turning to fire at his stare and tried to look away from him. "Bernard said that you had beautiful breasts," Levi said and reached out to touch her naked breast, the very breast that he had seen Bernard touch the day before. "I broke his nose for saying your breasts were beautiful. Do you remember?" Cecily nodded her head. So that was why Levi had beat Bernard up the day of her father's funeral, she thought again and wished she had told him the truth before he had found out on his own. "On the dresser is a bottle of oil, go and get it." He took his hand from her breast and Cecily left him to do as he had asked of her feeling raw and uncomfortable, she wasn't use to walking around without clothing. Levi had pulled off his trousers, and when Cecily turned back to him, she gasped. "Here, give the oil to me and hold out your hand." Cecily did as he said; she was too confused to think of not obeying him; she had never seen a man without his clothes on. Levi poured the oil into the palm of Cecily's hand and rubbed it around with his own hands. Her eyes were locked with his eyes as she was afraid to look anywhere else at him. She had no idea what he meant to do to her and thought there was no way that he was going to fit inside of her, he would tear her apart; he was too big.

Levi held her hand, and as he forced her to touch him, she gasped, he did as well. Cecily could not believe where she was touching Levi and felt a fire spread throughout her whole body. She would have continued looking into Levi's eyes, but his head was thrown back, and he was breathing hard. She closed her own eyes and let him use her hand on his hardness as he would. She didn't understand any of this, but he seemed to like what he was having her do to him, so she stood still and waited to see what he would do next.

Levi guided his wife's small hand over the thickness of himself. It had been too long since he had had a woman and he had spent the past weeks in pure frustration wanting her and being denied her. After a few long moments he pushed Cecily's hand away and taking a deep breath, he reached out and touched her breast. "I want you," he said in his husky voice, and Cecily looked up at the hard look in his dark eyes. He touched her swollen lip and cheek; the look on his face changed to one of agony. "I don't want to see your face," he almost whispered, and she couldn't mistake the hurt that was now in his eyes, the hard look faded away. He bent and blew out the bedside lantern, the full moon shone in through the door and window, bright on Cecily's face and Levi fought to breathe. He could not look at her when he took her, not knowing that she had given herself to Bernard while keeping him away not while believing that she had to think of Bernard in order to bear his touch.

"What?" Cecily asked when Levi told her to get onto the bed on her hands and knees.

"Do like I say and don't talk," his voice was rough and hard again Cecily obeyed. She knew that he was going to join his body to hers, but didn't understand how.

Levi knelt on the bed and not very gently entered his wife. Cecily cried out, and he knew that she hadn't been ready for him. He reached for the bottle of oil and while within her only a half of an inch, he poured oil onto his hand and reached down to fondle her while pulling her back and up against him, his lips moving to her ear, his tongue diving in and out of the hollowness of her ear as he moved gently now within her. She was starting to relax, Levi felt and moved a tiny bit faster, his hot breath inside of her ear, he had to loosen her up, or he would hurt her, he really didn't want to hurt her.

Cecily felt Levi's fingers stroking her; he was making her burn inside, his hot breath in her ear was making her lose her own breath. He was inside her, and at first, he had hurt her, now he wasn't hurting her so much. He was making her feel what she felt when he held and kissed her. She heard herself moan, his hand fondling her was making her feel like liquid fire, and she was fighting to breathe. Her husband shoved himself deep within her, and she cried out and went stiff again, but Levi didn't stop what he was doing to her. He was plunging within her, and she knew that he was tearing her apart and she couldn't stop him.

"You're so tight," Levi cried out as he picked up the pace and moved harder and faster into Cecily. He knew that she wasn't ready for him; he couldn't stop himself; he had to have her. "You're so tight," he said again and reached his fulfillment far too soon.

Cecily felt Levi pull out of her; the moon touched her face as he fell down beside her and looked up at her kneeling still on the bed. What he had just done to her had been awful. He was too big down there; he couldn't fit inside of her, she was too small. Oh God, he had hurt her, she realized and lay down on her stomach. She was throbbing in pure agony. No one had ever hurt her like this before. For a few moments it had felt good, for a few moments it had felt like when he kissed her, but now, afterward, she felt like she was burning up inside.

"Regardless of what you may believe at this moment, I didn't mean to hurt you," Levi said. "The next time I'll make you ready for me." There would be a next time, Cecily thought and prayed that he wouldn't do this again to her anytime soon. "I wanted you too badly, and I wasn't as gentle as I should have been," Levi stared at the ceiling and wondered if she had been dry and tight for Bernard. Or had she welcomed Bernard with moisture and love? Levi knew that she had and felt sick. He would make her want him the next time he took her; he would make her cry out his name. He would make her body want him. He would die if he failed in gaining her desire.

The darkness was relieved only by the full moon falling into the room through the sheer curtains of the window and the porch door. Levi felt Cecily roll onto her back, and he turned on his side to look at her. She was a fire in his blood, a fire that only her body could put out and he had to have her. It didn't matter to him that she didn't love him, he didn't care that she didn't want him, or he tried not to care. He would make her want his body and to hell with love. He would make her beg for his body.

Cecily knew that Levi was watching her and closed her eyes tight; she could not look at him and not think of what he had done to her. She had hurt him, and now he had hurt her. As she thought this, her husband's hand touched her stomach, and his mouth touched the nipple of her breast, she tried to push him away from her, he wouldn't let go. "No," she cried and squeezed her thighs together. His mouth attacked her breast, he was licking and sucking and kissing her naked breast, and she felt herself relax against her will. He wasn't hurting her, she thought and let him have his way. She could only hope that he would be done with her soon.

Levi forced his hand between her legs, but he couldn't go far, she wouldn't let him. "Open up your legs, damn you," he ordered as his mouth came up to her mouth, his lips touching her battered and sore lip and face causing her to cry out in pain. Levi pulled away from her, and she saw in the moonlight, his fist drawback and away and knew he was going to punch her again. He punched the pillow beside her head instead.

"My mouth," Cecily cried out, "you punched me earlier today, my mouth hurt when you kissed me," she whimpered in fear he'd punch her again. She deserved any pain that he would give her, she had hurt him worse, and she knew that too.

Levi took a deep calming breath and went back to her breast, his hand still forcing her legs apart. He touched her gently with his fingers; he played with her breast with his mouth, he rubbed her until there was no pain. This didn't hurt at all; Cecily thought as she relaxed even more and leaned into the pads of his fingers that were caressing her. His mouth made her breast ache for more and his fingers on her were making her tense all over, she couldn't get enough, she wanted more. "That's it, Cecily. Feel me," Levi said in a hoarse voice against her breast before he took it into his mouth again. Cecily cried out, her whole body shaking apart as her thighs squeezed together on his hand. "We won't need the oil this time," Levi said as he came up over her in the darkness.

"No, you're too big, you won't fit," Cecily cried as she pushed against his chest with her small hands.

Yes, Cecily, I'll fit; you'll let me." He put his tongue back on the nipple of her breast and circled it, Cecily felt herself relaxing again, he breathed his hot breath onto her breast, he rubbed that large hard part of himself against her then sucked on the nipple of her breast again. "You want me," he said in a broken voice, and Cecily knew at that moment that she would let him do anything he wanted to her. The hurt in his voice broke her heart. "Oh, God," Levi breathed as he entered her. She was hot and moist; he had made her ready for him; he had made her want him. He began to pump himself within her; he was saying her name over and over as he moved. "I can't believe how tight you are. I've never had a woman so tight before." Levi was losing himself within his wife; he wanted to stay lost within her forevermore.

He wasn't hurting her, Cecily thought and gasped, if he was hurting her, it was a good hurt. She felt as though she were climbing higher and higher as she pushed against him and held on to his arms. She was shaking apart again; she felt Levi shake with her seconds before he fell forward onto her and covered her body with his own.

Levi lay within his wife for only a second before he pulled from her and fell on his back beside her. He didn't know that Cecily was feeling empty and alone, he didn't know that she wished that he would hold her in his arms, that she needed to always be held in his arms.

"Bernard was right; you are good in bed." Cecily bit her lip to keep from crying out. Bernard had led Levi to believe the worst of her and Levi did believe the worst of her. And she had every chance to tell him the truth and never once did she take that chance. She had made too many mistakes, and now Levi hadn't even realized she was untouched before him, he had taken her virgin body rough believing Bernard's lies, but then, he had believed her lies as well.

"Go to sleep, Cecily," Levi ordered her when he rolled over and saw the moonlight on her face. "I think I'm done in for a while." He put his hand on her breast and didn't let her go.

Cecily closed her eyes, but still felt the throbbing between her thighs. Levi had forced her to take his body into hers and then he had forced her to want his body within hers. She deserved what he had done to her, she deserved worse from him, and she knew that too. This would never have happened if he had been home this morning. She had brought all of this onto them both with her silence. Too much silence. And now Levi was demanding more silence from her.

Levi lay still for a long time thinking of what he had just done to Cecily. He had more than rushed her the first time; he had wanted her so badly that he hadn't thought or cared to prepare her for him. But he made it up to her the second time from what he hadn't done the first time. She was so beautiful; she made him hard just to look at her. All these years he had wanted nothing more than to join his body with hers. After all this time of waiting for her and wanting her, he knew that he would never let her go. He would do everything in his power to make her body want his body as much as he wanted her. He would make her beg for him to make love to her. He would give her everything he knew to give her of his own body, and she would take everything that he gave to her as she had been planning on taking his money all these weeks. Levi could and would love her body well, even if he did hate her. Hating her had not killed one ounce of his desire for her. Nothing she could do would ever make him not want her. And now, she was his, and he wasn't going to let her go.

Levi woke late the next morning and left the bed. He was dressed when Cecily got up and pulled on her nightgown and robe trying not to notice that her husband was watching her every move. She reached back to pull up the covers on the bed and gasped, Levi's eyes followed her eyes to the bed, and he frowned. She had been moist and ready for him last night; he had been so certain that she had wanted him and that he had given her pleasure the second time that he had taken her. Now, looking at the bed with her, he wasn't so sure of himself.

"Your monthly time has come," Levi said, and Cecily looked confused. "Well, you're free of me for a few days at the least." Cecily shook her head as she stared down at her own blood on the bed.

"Oh, no. It's —."

"You do not speak unless I say so," he ordered her to be silent, and Cecily closed her mouth. "Go to the bathroom and clean up," Cecily hurried to the bathroom her face on fire and gave out a sharp cry before closing the door.

Levi was so certain that she had slept with Bernard that he had mistaken her virgin blood for her monthly time, Cecily realized as she filled the tub with hot water. She sank down in the tub and began to scrub all over, the soap and washcloth were turning her skin a bright red. He would leave her alone. He thought that she having her curse, he wouldn't touch her. He would have time to cool down, and she could tell him how she really felt once he was calm. And he would believe what she told him and everything would be all right. She started to cry and couldn't stop. She stayed in the tub for over an hour.

Levi stormed out of the house. Cecily hadn't wanted him last night; she would want him the next time that he took her, he would see that she did. He would teach Cecily to crave his body if it was the very last thing that he ever did. He would drive her mad with her own need of him and satisfy his own need of her by doing so. Damn her if she was comparing his lovemaking skills to Bernard Calhoun. Damn her to the hell she had put him in.

Cecily drank a cup of coffee and didn't say one word to Ollie. When Ollie had taken her soiled bed linen and seen her bruised lower lip Cecily had seen the maid's eyebrows raise. Ollie knew that Levi was mad as fire. Ollie had been sent home yesterday afternoon and could now see that Cecily wasn't happy this morning. But then, Cecily had not been happy since she had come to live here as Levi's wife.

"Just where the hell do you think you're going?" Levi's words stopped Cecily in the yard.

"Clemmie had an accident at my father's house yesterday afternoon, and I thought that I would go over and check on her this morning," Cecily hated the meek voice that she used, but Levi looked so angry that she was afraid to speak any firmer and besides, he's allowed her to talk so there was hope that she might explain soon everything to him.

"No," Levi stared at his wife. "You are not to have anything further to do with that woman, are we clear in this?"

"Why?" Cecily asked, then she began to back up as Levi was coming toward her with that angry look on his face. He reached her and held on to her wrist in a death grip, he was bruising her, and she was scared he would hit her again. She turned her head away, and he could clearly see her swollen lip and bruised face.

"You do as I say," his voice wasn't so harsh, she didn't know that seeing the damage that he had done to her face the day before nearly brought him to his knees. He wanted to control her and hurt her as she had hurt him, not destroy her. "The rules, you do as say." He saw Cecily try and nod her head. "I trusted you, Cecily. I loved you. And you did nothing but make a fool of me. You were so silent before when I was dying to hear you speak to me. Now I don't want to hear anything that you have to say, ever." He heard her gasp and put her free hand that he didn't hold over her mouth. "And if you don't obey me always, I will hit you again. Do you want me to hit you again?" Even as he said this, Levi knew he wouldn't hit her; he just wanted her to live as she'd been forcing him to live, to know the same kind of pain. She was his wife, and it was going to stay that way, every single day he would wake with the certain knowledge that she married him only for his money.

Cecily felt herself go weak all over; she could not believe that her tender Levi was saying these things to her. No matter how mad he was with her, she would never have believed that the Levi she had known all her life would threaten her with physical violence.

"I swear if you don't follow my rules Cecily, I will hit you so hard that the punch I gave you yesterday will feel like a kiss in comparison," he groaned when he said this to her and saw the horrified look on her face. "I loved you," he said next, and she saw that hurt look in his eyes. She had hurt him first, and now he was hurting her.

"Levi, if you'll," Cecily cried out as he twisted her arm around behind her back and pulled her body into his from behind, his hot breath on her neck as he held her firmly and close and knew he wasn't hurting her arm.

"Quiet, you stay quiet like you were before. No more lies." He let her go, and she stumbled away from him breathing hard, he again saw her swollen face and groaned.

"I've never hit a woman in my life, Cecily," he sounded like he was crying. "I've never wanted to hit or hurt anyone like I want to hurt you," his voice broke, and she saw his eyes bright with tears. "You betrayed me, you lied to me," he put his hand over his eyes, and she knew, without doubt, he was on the verge of crying. She had done this to him; she had hurt him far more than he had hurt her. And he wasn't going to listen to her, not today. And she was afraid. She was afraid of her husband's anger. "As long as you obey me, I'll not hurt you," Levi's voice softened, and he removed his hand. "Don't make me ever hurt you again, Cecily." He sounded like he was begging her. Cecily looked back up into his eyes and saw his tears, they had fallen, and he was hurriedly wiping them away. She almost went to her knees in sorrow; she had hurt her husband too much when she never wanted to hurt him at all.

Levi was trying to get away from her; she had unmanned him; he was crying like he did when he was a little boy. He had backed away from her and then she was there with her arms around his waist and holding him tight, he tried to push her away, but she wouldn't let him. "Kiss me, Levi," she pleaded and turned her face up to his. "My lip doesn't hurt today," she lied. "Please, kiss me."

Levi looked at her knowing he wanted to kiss her more than anything, but she would close her eyes in the kiss and think of Bernard, all of her responses to his kisses were from her memories of what she had done with Bernard.

"No," he almost cried out and forced her arms from his waist. "No," he said again, and she watched him leave her.

Why had she lied to him? Cecily cried as she went back up onto the porch and into the house. She was sobbing within a second and laying on their bed, her knees drawn up feeling still as she'd felt since Bernard first started making demands, her life was without hope. She was in complete and utter despair.

"I don't like your hair up like that," Levi said when he came into the house for dinner. Cecily didn't understand his words, she had always worn her hair up this way, or at least she had since she was sixteen years old. "From now on, when we are home alone together, I want you to wear your hair down." Cecily could only give him a nod of her head. "Go and take your hair down. I can't eat and look at you across the table from me." She hurried from the dining room, and Levi finished his meal thinking that he was hurting her with his words and was unable to stop himself. She had spent weeks hurting him with her silence.

When Cecily came back into the dining room, Levi was gone so she finished her meal alone praying that the man that she loved would soon come back to her and this anger filled Levi would leave. He had told her once that he had a bad temper; she hadn't believed him, she believed him now.

"Levi never gets angry, he knows he can't get over being mad," Cecily heard Grant's word to her from the day before. She had known Levi all of her life, and she had never known him to treat anyone as he was treating her now. He was mad with her; he wasn't going to get over being mad with her today. She had to wait and give him time. He would become reasonable soon; he couldn't stay mad at her forever. He loved her, and she loved him.

Later that afternoon, Cecily sat sewing a tear in one of her skirts in the parlor. She gave a loud cry when Levi grabbed her from behind and pulled on her long braid hanging down her back. "What did I tell you?" he asked her and Cecily fought the tears that formed in her eyes from him pulling on her hair.

"You told me to wear my hair down," she almost whispered. "It's down, Levi." He nearly snatched her baldheaded undoing the long braid, her hair soon loose and flowing around her and down her back.

"Now your hair is down, Cecily." He touched the softness of her hair, it was so beautiful, he thought and remembered how it was in the photos, he could get lost in her hair. He saw her looking at him, and he pulled away and let her hair go. "I want you to put another sheet on the bed. You don't share well, and I was cold last night." Cecily dropped her mending in the chair and rushed to do as Levi said, the memory of the look on his face as he held her hair in his hand is what she took with her. Soon, he would soften and get past his anger, and she could reach him, she could get him to listen to her.

Levi left the house and leaned against the porch rail. He felt sick. He hurt all over, and he still wanted his wife even knowing she only wanted him for his money. She married him because he was dumb enough to believe she loved him. He gave a small cry of agony at this thought. He was dumb to have loved her; he was dumb now for wanting her still. Having had her once only made him want her again and again. And he wanted her to know the pain that she had caused him. He wanted her to pay for the hurt he was in because he loved her. She would never feel his pain; he knew beyond doubt, because she did not love him. Another soft cry of agony escaped him.

Levi lit a cigarette and sat down on the porch swing. He knew he never got mad because he had a hard time getting over being mad. He found it almost impossible to forget and forgiving never came easy for him. He could feel his anger burning inside his gut every time he thought of Cecily marrying him for his money, marrying him because he was dumb. And he had thought that she loved him

His anger was going to destroy him, or his anger was going to destroy Cecily. He couldn't stop what he was doing. She was the one woman that he loved, the only woman that he had ever truly loved, and she was the only woman he had ever hit in his life. He didn't want to hit her now, he was sorry he had hit her yesterday, more than sorry. Violence wasn't going to make her see what she had done to him; violence wasn't the answer to making Cecily pay for what she had done to him. Hitting her would only make her hate him more than she already did.

Levi threw the cigarette out into the yard and covered his face with his hands. Cecily hated him, she couldn't stand his touch, she married him for his money, all these thoughts hurt him clear down to his bones. He still loved her, Levi knew and hated himself as much as she hated him.

"Levi," he heard Grant say his name and looked up to his friend on his horse at the porch railing. "I've come to ask you if you'll stand up with me tomorrow when I marry Clemmie?" Levi looked at his best friend in disbelief. After what Clemmie had done with Bernard, Grant was going to marry her? "And Clemmie wants Cecily to stand by her," Grant added not seeing the expression on Levi's face.

"No," Levi said and stood up from the swing. "If you marry Clemmie Floyd, you're fired."

"Levi," Grant leaned forward in the saddle baffled and confused. "What's going on?"

"Nothing. I'm telling you right now if you marry Clemmie Floyd, you are not to ever set foot on my place again."

"Well, I am marrying Clemmie tomorrow, Levi. So I guess I'm not just fired, but I'm no longer welcome here either. When you feel ready to tell me what's wrong with you, you know where I live."

"I just forgot, Grant," Levi said firmly staring hard at his friend.

Grant sat straight in the saddle with a frown covering his face, "where's Cecily?" he asked.

"In hell," Levi answered him.

Grant looked beyond Levi and saw Cecily standing in the doorway, she motioned for him to meet her out back in two minutes and he nodded his head. "Look, Levi, I don't know what's happened or what you think has happened, but I want you to know, I'll always be your friend."

"No, you won't, not with her as your wife." Grant watched as Levi went into the house and slammed the door.

After circling around through the stand of trees in the side yard Grant came to a stop seeing Cecily leaning on a tree and breathing hard, she kept looking behind her. "Cecily," he called her name, and she shook her head at him and put her finger over her lips.

"Levi will be mad if he finds me talking to you, Grant," Cecily spoke in a soft voice as she held on to his horse to keep it quiet as well.

"What is going on here?" Grant demanded to know in a low voice.

"I told you yesterday that Levi is mad at me. Bernard told him," she blushed not wanting to say that Bernard had led Levi to believe they were intimate. "Well, Bernard told him something awful about me, and Levi believes it and Grant," she looked away from him, "I did lie to him, and he thinks I married him for his money only. It's not true Grant, I swear it's not, yes I needed money, but I've always loved him, always Grant, I swear."

"Well just tell him, he'll listen to you, Cecily. What's the holdup? Go tell him now," Grant urged.

"He has ordered me not to talk, ever. He's just so mad."

"Cecily, did he hurt you?" Grant reached down and touched her bruised face; he felt cold all over with the knowledge that his best friend that he loved like a brother had hit this small innocent woman that was almost like a kid sister to him.

"You have to go Grant. I just wanted you to know, I need time to," her words were cut off by her husband,

"You have five seconds to get off my land, or I'll shoot you." Grant stared hard at Levi.

"Then shoot me, better than beating on your wife, at least I'm not defenseless," Grant said sitting up taller in the saddle.

"Please, Grant, do like he asks. I'll be all right, honest. It's Levi," she looked at her husband with pleading eyes and then grabbed a deep breath and did the only thing she could think to do to diffuse the situation. She went to her husband and put her arms around him and smiled up at him before turning to Grant. "It's Levi, and he won't hurt me."

"You harm one hair on her head with your anger, Levi," Grant pointed a finger at him, and Levi narrowed his eyes.

"She's my wife."

"By the grace of God," Grant shot back. "You may not know it right this minute because you're hurting and mad but Cecily is the best thing that ever happened to you."

"If that's the case, I'd hate to see the worst thing that ever happened to me," Levi shot back.

"Cecily, if you need Clemmie and me, you know where to find us." Cecily felt her husband stiffen beside her at these words.

"Thank you, Grant, but honestly, I won't need you. Levi won't hurt me," she took a deep breath and hoped her words were true.

Levi watched Grant ride away beyond the trees and then looked down at his wife. "What a pretty little liar you are Cecily."

"I didn't lie, Levi," she tried to say.

"I told you to be silent, and I meant it," he saw her arms still wrapped around him, and he pulled away before ordering her back to the house.

Cecily walked back to the house slowly knowing that Levi was watching her. He wasn't going to hit her again; she felt certain of that because if he were, he would have hit her for meeting Grant just now. He was using his words to hurt her, and he was doing a good job. She had to give him time and in giving him that time she had to show him how she really felt for him.

"You can go home, Ollie. Cecily will clean up the kitchen after supper from now on," Levi said when he came in the back door of the house and met Ollie in the kitchen. Ollie hurried and left not wanting to get between the feuding couple.

Cecily looked at Levi from the kitchen doorway as he washed up at the sink and wondered what he had planned for her tonight. The last three days he had been nearly unbearable, dealing with his anger and his silence or worse, his finding fault with her was like living in a nightmare. Last night she had tried to speak to him, and he had sent her to bed without supper like a naughty child. She didn't know what he would do. Next, she felt like she was standing on the edge of the roof and he would at any given moment, push her off.

"Is supper on the table?" Levi asked her while turning from the sink with a dry towel in his hands. Cecily nodded her head, her clear crystal eyes locked and held by his dark pools of blue. "Good," Levi said in his deep husky voice, she didn't hear any hurt in that one word, nor any anger, he almost sounded like her old Levi. "Take off your clothes."

"What?" Cecily asked stupidly and wished that he would send her to bed again tonight for having spoken when he had not given her permission to do so.

"I said, take off your clothes," Levi spoke slowly, Cecily didn't move, she could only stand still and stare at her husband's face. "You have one of two choices here, Cecily. Take off your clothes like I asked you to do, or I can take them off for you. Which will it be?"

Cecily gritted her teeth and did as Levi told her to do. "Levi," she tried to speak when her clothes were on the floor in a pile at her feet, but the look in Levi's eyes made her fall silent. She had never seen him look as he was now looking at her and she didn't know what to expect next.

"The rules, Cecily. You speak when I say. Simple rules, don't forget them again." Levi tried to ignore the tears that burned bright in her eyes, but his wife was getting to him with those hurt eyes and her sad face. He kept having to remind himself that she did not deserve his pity. She had done him wrong. She had used him; she would have given everything he had to Bernard Calhoun. She had loved Bernard and never loved him. His touch made her sick; she had to think of Bernard when he touched her. She didn't even want to have a child by him. She didn't want him and now this madness that consumed him, this madness not to hurt her, but to have her want him with the same passion as he wanted her.

Levi was bound and determined to keep her silent, Cecily now knew. Why had she lied to him? Her heart cried out. Why had she hurt him so badly that he believed Bernard's lies and wouldn't allow her to even speak? She'd lied to him; she knew that. Had he lied to her, would she believe what he said when he was caught in the lie? No one would. She could only do as he asked, show him the kindness he was not affording her and hope that soon he would forgive her and know it was always him that she loved.

Standing without her clothes before her husband, Cecily fought not to blush. She would give him all of herself. Levi would know that she wanted him, only him. She prayed it wouldn't hurt when he entered her again, but if it did, she would bear the pain gladly to earn his love, trust, and forgiveness.

Cecily watched Levi walk toward her, his hand touched her breast, and she touched his cheek and held his eyes wanting him to see she loved him. He released her eyes and put his mouth on her breast, and she gasped. Levi lifted her up in his arms and sat her down on the dining room table, his mouth teasing the nipple of her breast.

"Bernard told me that you tasted of milk and honey," Levi said, and Cecily gasped in horror that Bernard would tell him such a horrible lie. "I'm going to find out if that's true. Spread your legs for me." Cecily almost shook her head, she didn't know what he planned to do, but she felt certain she did not want this. "You gave to Bernard, but you would deny me, your own husband?" she heard the hurt in his voice and hurt along with him that he believed she'd been with Bernard as she was with him. Levi was right in his way, she had denied him, those first weeks of marriage she'd kept him from his rightful place, and now he believed she'd been with Bernard and gladly when that wasn't true at all. "Spread your legs," he said again.

She opened her legs for him and waited, her heart was slamming in her chest at what he meant to do to her, she had no idea, and he didn't realize just how innocent of this act of love his wife really was.

Levi touched her with his mouth, and Cecily nearly cried out. He gripped her thighs and buried his face between her legs, and she grabbed two fists full of his hair, his beautiful dark hair was held tightly as she fought to breathe. He was killing her; he had to stop what he was doing. If he stopped now, she would surely die, Cecily thought as she tried again and again to breathe and couldn't. She had to make him stop; she was gasping for air, he was killing her, of that she was certain. Cecily let out a soft cry, shook all over and went over the edge of sanity while she fell backward on to the dining room table trembling all over and the dishes clattered loud, and a fork fell to the floor.

"Well, if I were to describe your taste," Levi said and felt like he had won a battle, "I'd say you were spicy." Cecily had wanted him, he had just given her the ultimate joy a man could give to a woman, and she was ready for him. Let her compare his lovemaking to Bernard's now. He sat down in the chair and put his finger inside her, she moaned and arched her back upward, and he smiled. She was aching for him. She may not love him, but her body was craving his.

After a few moments, Levi reached for her hand and pulled her up, Cecily could only stare at him as he helped her to stand on the floor. She wondered if he would send her away now. He didn't look angry, and the hurt that had been in his eyes for the last few days was gone as well. He looked hot, Cecily thought; she knew that she was hot. "Now it's your turn," he said in a deep husky voice which seemed deeper to Cecily. Her eyes grew wide while watching him remove himself from his pants.

"Please, I," she started to speak but Levi shook his head, and she backed up against the table. He was huge and swollen and hard, and she was afraid of him.

"Touch me, Cecily, please," he begged, and she looked at him with wide crystal clear eyes. "Don't deny me anymore, Cecily," he said with a frown, his eyes filled with that hurt she'd brought to him. She caused all of this because she'd lied to him, it was up to her to fix their marriage, she couldn't do that by turning him away. But she didn't know what he wanted of her either, this was all new to her, and she was unsure what he meant for her to do now. When she took him in her hand, he was throbbing and rock hard; he gasped just because she was holding him.

Levi saw that she was truly innocent of what he wanted her to do, he would be her first, in this, there would be no jealousy over Bernard Calhoun.

"Go on your knees, darlin'," Cecily heard him use his pet name for her, he'd not used that in days and she did as he told her. She would do what he wanted and in so doing, show him her love for him.

Levi held Cecily's eyes with his own. With her hand on him, he felt no insecurities. He knew that he had been blessed with more than most men, Cecily held his blessing within her hand. Even without passion raging through his body and blood, he was still a big man. "Take me into your mouth," he pleaded, and Cecily fought not to shake her head and run from the room and him. "Do it," he begged and sucked in his breath when she did put him in her mouth. He reached down and took each side of her head and guided, allowing her to fill her mouth one second and let him go with the next.

Cecily saw that her husband liked what she was doing to him; she tried to do just as he wanted her too. If he saw that she was willing, he would see that she didn't mind, that she wanted to please him and be his wife in every way. Bernard wouldn't stand between them, Bernard's words wouldn't hurt Levi anymore, and he would listen to her and know the truth. She could win him back by doing what he wanted. She remembered his mouth on her breast and how he gently sucked on her and did that to him. Levi lost his breath and cried out when she sucked him into her mouth.

"You have to stop, darlin'," Levi used his pet name for her again, and she almost smiled. He pushed her away knowing if he didn't it would be too late. He watched as Cecily stood on unsteady legs and clung to him when he lifted her up into his arms and sat her again on the table. He reached for her and found that she was still ready for him. He thanked God that she wanted him and he entered her slow and easy making sure he wasn't hurting her in any way.

Levi filled her so full that she thought she was going to bust. There was no pain tonight. It was heaven, and it was hell when he moved she moved with him and clung to his wrists, his hands supporting himself on the table top. She was holding on for dear life. And then he shouted her name and flung his head back and made her see stars on the dining room ceiling.

Cecily watched Levi leave her and push himself back into his pants. He didn't look at her but instead turned away, his head lowered. "Go get your robe on," he told her, and she heard the hurt again in his voice, he sounded more hurt now than he ever had before and she frowned wondering what she had done wrong. She had tried to please him. She had tried to show him her love for him; he hadn't seen that love. She wished that he would call her darlin' again, he didn't say anything more to her, so she climbed down from the dining room table and went to get her robe as he had told her to do.

Cecily wished for her old Levi back, the one filled with love and concern. Not this Levi with his anger and hurt – hurt that she had caused him, anger that she had forced him too with her lies. She had turned him away for weeks; she had denied them both even this pleasure they had just shared, because of her fear of Bernard. But she would make everything right. She would give him everything. She would do anything to take the hurt from him his voice and his eyes and his heart. And he would see the love she has for him. She would have her old Levi back, and he would be calling her darlin' all the time again because she would be darling again to him.

Cecily hurried fast and pulled on her robe, she came to the dining room door and saw him with his back to her bent forward and his shoulders shaking. Putting her fingers to her forehead, she backed out and into the hall where she stood silent and watched her husband cry. She had done this to him; she closed her eyes and felt the tears fall down her face. She had brought them both to this because she wouldn't trust him. If she had told him, he would have believed her, just like Grant believed Clemmie. But Bernard had told him things that weren't true, and because of her silence and lies, he believed Bernard. And now all she could do was wait for him to know her feelings by her actions.

Levi sat up straight knowing Cecily would be back any second. He wiped his face and felt less of a man. He had always prided himself on how strong he was, and he wasn't strong at all, he was weak, Cecily was his weakness. He looked up and saw her standing across from him; he didn't know she was still lightheaded from what he had done to her, he didn't know she wanted him to do more to her.

"Fill a plate and go eat in the kitchen," he said softly, and Cecily did as he told her to do, she would do everything he told her to do, she would win his love again. And there was no anger in his voice. Soon he would forgive her. Soon he would listen to her. And soon he would love her again and know she had always loved him.

She was beautiful, Levi thought as he picked at his food. He had wanted her too much and for too long and she had kept him shut out of her life. She wouldn't shut him out again; he would not let her. And he would keep her filled up with himself until she needed him as much as he needed her. Her body would be one with his, Cecily would become his, all his. She had liked what he had done to her body tonight; her body had been more than ready for him and was begging for him.

Levi put down his fork and thought of what Bernard had told him. Cecily could teach him, Cecily knew all the tricks. She had sucked on him and nearly made him lose himself with her mouth; she was as skilled as Bernard had said. He gave up all pretense of eating as he thought of Cecily. He wanted to tell her that he loved her. How could he love her when she had not even wanted to be his wife? He was not just dumb; he was a fool. And still, he wanted to hold her in his arms and be good to her. He wanted to give her the sun, the moon and the stars all at once. He had wanted a life filled with happiness and children and a home that knew only joy and laughter.

Levi gave a bitter laugh and leaned his arms on the table at the elbows before he put his face into his hands. He was a fool. He had always been a dummy, now Cecily had made him a fool as well. She had lied to him, and he believed her lies. She had told him that she loved him when she lied. She had deceived him by marrying him in the name of love only to want what he could give to keep her safe from Bernard. She had no desire for him before tonight and any desire that she felt for him now, he was forcing onto her. And worst of all, she had not trusted him. She had no faith in him or his love for her; she didn't want his love for her and never had. And now he had to bury his love that he felt for her deep within himself and hide it from her so that she could not hurt him again. He would not let her make a fool of him twice.

Grown men did not cry, Levi thought as he swallowed hard and knew he was going to cry again. All of his hopes, all of his dreams were gone. He was filled with anger, humiliated by the one woman he had loved forever, there was no one with whom to share this burden of his wrecked heart with, his father who advised him well was long dead. Cecily had forced him to live in her isolated and lonely world. Cecily's world was one filled with silence.

To Cecily their marriage meant nothing, it never had, Levi thought as he took a deep breath. He would make their marriage mean something to her. He would show her that he was ten times the man that Bernard Calhoun had ever thought of being. He would infect her soul with his own, and in the end, he would own her as she had always owned him. And he would never be a dummy again. He would force her to live his way; he would make her see that she could not get away with using him. He would get everything from her; he would give no love, his love for her, she must not ever see again.

Levi sat back up and looked down at his plate of food lost in his thoughts. Cecily. He could not quit thinking of her. He was so angry with her that his gut burned just thinking of how she had tricked him into believing that she loved him. Thinking like this was the worst. Thinking made him remember Bernard's words to him of how Cecily couldn't stand his touch, and she had to think of Bernard when he touched her. Dear God, he thought he was dying of a broken heart, she couldn't stand him, and he was forcing himself onto her. And then he wondered if Cecily wished she were dead right now instead of married to him.

Levi covered his face again and felt like he could hate Cecily. But how could he hate the woman he loved so much. His heart no longer made any sense to him. And he wanted to hurt her; he wanted Cecily to feel his pain. He thought again that grown men did not cry and blinked back the tears that burned his eyes.

After a long while, Levi stood and took his dishes from the table and into the kitchen. Cecily was at the sink washing up the dishes and his gut burned from something other than hate, it burned with his need of her. The tears filled his eyes again and he fought against the ache they caused him. He wanted her. His body craved for hers more than any child ever craved for sweets. She was in his blood; she made his blood pound in his veins for her.

Levi took his dishes to the sink and put them in the hot water. Cecily bent forward to pick up his plate, and her robe fell open. He could see her small, perfect firm breast begging for him to touch. He reached his hand into her parted robe and took the nipple of her breast between the pads of his thumb and index finger; his breathing became hard and uneven, so did hers.

"I can't believe that I want you again," he said, and Cecily turned to look up at him, her crystal clear blue eyes were bright and glowing in the soft lamplight.

Cecily thought that she knew the way to finding her old Levi, she could get past his pain and anger and she would be loving him while doing so. She reached down and untied the belt that held her robe closed and saw Levi breathing harder when she pushed it from her shoulders. The robe fell to the floor in a silken pool at her feet. He would see that she wanted him, that she needed him, that she loved him. He would feel her love for him when he touched her body and found her ready for him to join his to hers. He would know that she had lied when she had said that she only married him for his money.

"Do you want me?" Levi asked, and Cecily nodded her head. He touched her and found her ready for him, and he almost busted through his pants with his own need of her. "I don't know what you're doing to me," he said softly as he pulled off his shirt. She helped him with his pants, and that only made his need for her worse. He had to suck in his breath when she touched him and then he had to fight to breathe as she used her hand on him.

Cecily let Levi push her hand away from him before he lifted her up in his arms and sat her down on himself. She moaned out loud, and he told her to wrap her legs around his waist and hold on. She did as she was told, her face buried in his neck as he held on to her.

"I'm touching your heart, darlin'. Do you feel me? I'm touching your heart," Levi said as he carried her through the house and into their bedroom lost deep inside of his wife. Cecily had never dreamed of doing something like this with Levi, she would dream of doing something just like this with Levi from now on. He pushed her down onto their bed and looked down into her crystal clear blue eyes as he lay above her. "Do you hate me, Cecily," he asked in a broken voice as he moved in and out of her. Cecily saw the tears in his eyes by the light of the lantern. He started to move faster, and she shook her head. She could never hate her Levi; she had loved him almost all her whole life. "Do you still only want me for my money," he begged to know as he picked up the pace of his lovemaking. Cecily couldn't answer him; she was lost and shattering to pieces all around him. "I hate you, Cecily," he said in a low tormented voice near her ear. "I hate you!" he cried out and went stiff before he fell onto her. Cecily screamed and squeezed her hips tight with her legs around his waist the instant that he fell on her.

Levi pulled out of her body and Cecily watched him roll away from her to the far side of the bed. He lay still and silent with his back to her, except for her labored breathing there was no sound in the room; she was as silent as he was. Cecily looked away from Levi's back and stared up at the ceiling; a tear slid down her face and into her ear. She had known that the truth would hurt him; she had known that he would hate her with the truth. She let her tears fall and felt the pain that Levi was feeling. How could she have let this happen? He had loved her, she had known that he loved her, and she had used that love that he gave to her freely to be safe. She had been selfish and thought only of herself, and in so doing, she really had destroyed the man that she loved. He was lost among the anger and the pain she had gifted to him

"Get up and clean the kitchen," Levi finally broke the silence to say in a hard and cold voice. "And bring our clothes in here when you come back to bed. I don't want Ollie to find them in the morning."

Cecily left the bed and the room. She had to keep swallowing hard so that the tears that burned her eyes and throat would not fall. Levi wasn't going to let her talk to him; he wasn't going to give her a chance to explain. And he hated her; he said that he hated her. She had to right the wrong that she had done to him. For him and for herself. She had to make things right again. She hung her head and fought harder against the tears that threatened to fall from her eyes. Levi hated her, and she had known that he would.

Chapter Seven

They didn't go to church, Cecily was never allowed out of the house. If Levi left, she was watched by one of the men from the stables, and if Levi was there, he watched her every move. In the daytime he was cold to her and distant; sometimes he was even mean to her. He had told her not to wear black anymore, and when she had asked him why he had stated that she had killed her father by her relationship with Bernard Calhoun. She had no right to mourn for Daniel Walker he had told her when she was probably the very reason Daniel had dropped dead. Her heartless ways killed her father. Cecily had cried at his words; she knew that there was some truth to what her husband said.

Cecily often saw anger fill her husband's deep dark eyes, the anger she could bear, but when she would turn and see the hurt in those eyes, guilt would consume her. She would rather have his anger than his hurt.

Cecily could do nothing to please her husband in the light of day. If she reached for his hand to hold his hand, he would pull his hand away from her. If she gave him a smile, he would turn and leave her where she stood. And she kept remembering the many easy smiles that he gave to her before he learned of her lies and now, he never smiled at her or anyone else. Now he had one of two looks on his face at almost all times, a look of anger or a look of hurt. One night he had sent her from the dining room and had since refused to eat with her, he had told her that looking at her ruined his appetite.

Cecily stood in the parlor looking up at the portrait of Levi at sixteen with a much younger Sarah. He was beautiful; he was still beautiful. She closed her eyes and held his image on her lids. They could have been so happy; they could have really lived happily ever after except for Bernard, he had ruined her life without exposing those horrible photos to the town as he had threatened so often to do. Tears began to flow, and she bowed her head watching them slide down her nose and make a puddle on the floor.

Levi stopped in the parlor doorway and watched his wife staring up at his picture and then close her eyes. He looked away from her wondering what she was thinking and then he saw the tears fall. He took a step into the room, and she heard his footfall and turned, and their eyes met. He said nothing; she wasn't allowed to say anything. And then she was in his arms, and hers were around his neck pulling his face to her own, only an inch away. They were going to find their way back to what they had lost; she knew it in her heart. Standing in her father's field and kissing, in the buggy the day of the funeral that they ran off the road, kissing on the porch in the rocking chair, the love was going to come back for them and the agony of the past weeks would be gone. She could tell him everything, and he would listen and know the truth.

"God save me," he breathed before his mouth covered her mouth; it was just like before; they were melting into one another. He pulled away, and she cried, trying to pull him back. "It's too hot. I'm too hot," he breathed and took her hand pulling her behind him.

"Where are we going, Levi?" she begged to know, and he gave her a stern look better than the Reverend Bidwell could. She didn't want to ruin whatever was happening between them, she wanted to be with him without pain and anger, and she wanted him to feel her love for him.

"You should have trusted me," he said as they reached the lake and she nodded her head. "We could have been happy. Picnics on the lake, swimming, rowing in my rowboat. Our children could have been playing here." He let go of her hand. "If only you had trusted me."

"I'm so," his hand covered her mouth and stopped her words

"Let us have this," he breathed and removed his hand to go to the buttons of her blouse. "I don't want to be hot," he breathed, and she reached to help him with the buttons. She had never gone into the lake without clothes and felt sinful for doing so, if the good Reverend Bidwell knew she was doing this, she would be barred from ever attending church again.

Levi held his wife in his arms and went out into the water; she was facing him and had a smile on her face. Today he would pretend, today she loved him, and he loved her, and she had never lied to him. He went under the water, and she turned looking for him, he was under a long time, and then something had her leg, and she was snatched under the water. She came up in Levi's arms laughing; it felt good to laugh. She couldn't see a thing; her long thick hair was covering her face and eyes.

Levi heard her laughter and smiled; relieved that she couldn't see the smile because of all her hair. She was beautiful, her laughter unchanged from when he first realized he was in love with her. He dove again and grabbed her leg and pulled her under, this time he came up facing her, holding her in his arms and pushed her hair back from her face, her nose only an inch from his own.

Cecily gasped when she saw his face; he looked like her old Levi. She wrapped her arms around his neck and laughed, "Levi, oh Levi, I've missed you so much." She saw his face change in that instant, and he shoved her away.

"We can't go back to the way we were Cecily. I thought we could, but we can't. If I can't have you for my wife, I don't want you for my friend." Cecily watched him leave the water and start putting on his clothes. What had just happened? They were playing like they used too when they were young. She went underwater wishing she could drown and free this poor man from her presence. He was never going to give her a chance. And he was mean. This new Levi was mean, and she wanted to get away from him.

One minute Cecily was thinking these things and the next she realized she was tied up in the weeds and couldn't get back to the surface. She was fighting trying to free her legs; she didn't want to die; she wanted to win Levi's love again. She couldn't go like this and leave him behind so unaware of her love for him. She wanted his baby; she wanted to grow old with him. She wanted her Levi back.

She heard her name being called from far away; it sounded like Levi calling for her and then she was spitting and coughing and throwing up lake water. There was soft grass beneath her, she wasn't tangled in the weeds at the bottom of the lake any longer and she could breathe.

Levi was staring down at his wife; he was shaking all over in the fear he'd felt when he turned around after pulling on his clothes and shoes and found her gone. It had only taken a couple of dives under the water to get her, she had been trapped by some weeds around her left leg, and the weeds were still there, he'd snatched them by the roots to get her free. "Lay still and catch your breath, Cecily," he ordered in a gentle voice, his bangs wet and dripping water in her eyes as she tried to move and kept coughing and choking.

Cecily coughed for what felt like forever when she was able to sit up, she saw the weeds, roots and all around her leg. She'd had one foot in heaven; she knew that. There was so much wrong here that she had to make right; she couldn't leave here yet; she wasn't ready to die. "Levi," she cried his name; he was still sitting on his heels looking down at her. "Love me, Levi. Please, please, love me, Levi." She saw him close his eyes and take a deep breath before she grabbed him, her arms around his neck pulling him down onto her, her mouth seeking and finding him and moaning into the depths of his mouth to love her.

He had almost lost her; the water had almost taken her from him. Would his pain have been any less if she were gone? Would his anger end? He didn't know, but he wanted this, he wanted her to want him as badly as he wanted her and he gave her what she wanted, the warm summer soft grass their bed and the world beautiful around them.

Levi made love to his Cecily slow and playfully, she begged for him, she reached out to him and pleaded for him to take her as he took his time using his mouth to arouse her, to tempt her, to make her want him. And then he'd slowly, for more than an hour, made love to her causing her to lose control and shatter on him time and time again. Then he pulled her back into the water, safe in his arms and they washed one another, and he listened to her laugh, and she couldn't see in the darkness beyond the shadows of his face that he couldn't smile. His heart was breaking that it couldn't always be this way. But reality kept crashing down, and about him, she had married him only for his money, she didn't love him.

Cecily pulled on her dress and poked at Levi's stomach as he dressed, "Ollie's dinner for us is probably cold Levi, hurry up and let's get to the house." He pulled on his shoes and saw her run, she looked back at him over her shoulder, and the moonlight touched her face, and he saw the wide smile and heard her laughter. Her long hair flowing out behind and around her as she turned back and looked at him as she did all those years ago when she was only a girl, and he had first fallen in love with her. She was racing him, and he knew he had to catch her. When his arms grabbed her from behind at the waist, he twirled her around, and she giggled hard.

"The race isn't over, we aren't home yet," she teased. He put her down, and she ran ahead. Home, his home was home. He wanted that. Their home; a family, laughter, and joy. He saw her look back at him and then stop in the yard and wait for him.

"The rules," he said firmly. "no talking." He went past her, and she watched him, the hurt back in his eyes. She didn't wonder that something she said might have hurt him; she just knew that she had hurt him and it would be a long time before he knew how sorry she was. One summer day at the lake making love wasn't going to make up for her lies, she was realizing that now.

Levi saw the sadness on Cecily's face as she stared out into the yard from the porch swing; he tossed his cigarette away and lit another while he watched her swinging. He loved her in spite of his anger. He had been a fool, a bigger fool than she had made of him because he should have seen the truth; it had been staring him in the face those first weeks of their marriage. He had wanted her so badly that he had ignored the truth. Cecily could have had any man that she wanted; she was beyond beautiful. She could have had a man that owned a house in town and worked at the bank or owned his own store like his sister's husband, Franklin. She would never have wanted him; he had known that deep down inside of himself for years, it was why he had stayed away from her; that was the real reason he hadn't courted her. To Cecily, he was a childhood playmate, the older big brother that watched out for the little ones. He was dumb, he couldn't read, all he had was a bunch of money, and that was all she found appealing about him.

What was he doing to her? He asked himself. Every night and even in the day, he was seducing her. He was using what he knew to make her want him; it was all they had. It was all they would ever have. There would be no love story like his parents; there would be no intimacy beyond the bed. She would never adore him, and he could no longer adore her. She was his whether she wanted to be his or not; it was too late to change what was. She was his wife, and he intended to keep her. He walked across the yard and up onto the porch and didn't stop until he was standing before her. Cecily looked up at him with those crystal clear eyes, and he held out his hand to her. She took his hand, and he pulled her up from the swing and led her to their bedroom.

Cecily stared up at Levi as he reached and undid the buttons of her blouse; his fingers touched her neck as he pushed the shirtwaist from her. He was making love to her with his eyes, Cecily thought as Levi brushed her hair back away from her face. She stood on the tip of her toes and touched her mouth with his, Levi groaned and pulled her close.

"You said that you would," Cecily started to speak, but Levi covered her mouth with his own to silence her.

After a long few moments, Levi lifted his mouth from hers. "Don't say anything, darlin'," he whispered while removing his hand from her mouth. He lifted her up into his arms and carried her to the bed. "I can't take your words, Cecily. Everything you ever said to me tore me apart. All I want to hear from you is your body needing mine."

Cecily stared up into her husband's eyes as he stared down into her eyes. She had wanted to tell him to take her to heaven. He had once told her that he would take her to heaven every time that he held her in his arms. He would not even let her say something as simple as that to him. He had forced her into the silent world she had brought to him when she first married him, and she wanted out of that world and him out of it with her. She had to find some way to save them from this place they were trapped in. When they had been down at the lake, they had so much fun, playing like children, laughing and him chasing after her. She wanted forever with him; she wanted her happy Levi back.

"I know the truth, Cecily," he said in a broken way, and she looked up at him trying to see into his mind by way of the windows to his soul, but his eyes revealed nothing beyond a horrible pain.

"Bernard told me that you couldn't stand my touch. All the time you kept me from your bed when you kissed me, it was him you were thinking of kissing." His hand went over her mouth; he could see she was going to say something. "Please, spare me the denial; I already know you only married me for my money. And I saw him, the day you gave him the broach I gave you for a wedding gift, you let him touch you, you didn't pull away." Her head was shaking back and forth; his hand stayed in place. "You may not love me, you may not even like me or be able to stand my touch, but you're my wife, and you're going to stay my wife no matter what. And no other man can have you." He took away his hand and covered her mouth with his own, he was so lost in his passion and desperation to keep her that he didn't notice it was her arms pulling him down to her, it was her deepening the kiss, and within minutes, it was her helping to remove his clothes.

Cecily tore at his shirt, ripping it along the seam, thinking that if this were all he would allow for her to speak, then her lovemaking with him would be her words. Now that she knew how wonderful this was between them, she wanted him all the time, and all he had to do was touch her, and she melted in his arms. She had been so stupid to have kept him from their bed; she should have never have put him away. If she had it to do all over again, she would have pulled him into bed that first night and not let him leave her for a week. Bernard had played her and her father, then he had played her with his threats and now her Levi, poor Levi had thought that she was Bernard's lover when that was never true. Bernard had taken the photos, and his first move at blackmail had been her allowing him to court her. She came from a fine upstanding family, he didn't care about her, only that he could show the world he was with her, and she never wanted to be with him, it would better his station in life to have courted her. Bernard was more evil than she had known; he had tricked Levi into believing his lies and not seeing her truth. All the kisses they had shared, the way he had made her feel before she even knew of the bedroom side of making love, none of that was made up on her part; it was all too real because she loved Levi, she always had.

She felt him pick her up into his arms and carry her to their bed and she thought of speaking, but she knew, he wouldn't believe her words. Let this speak for me, she thought and pulled him down with her, her nose touching his, her hands firm on his chest, his bangs on her forehead. Let this be her voice; she declared to no one other than herself. She reached down and took him in her hand and guided him into her body. Let this be her words, she thought and lifted her hips up to meet him.

Levi felt his wife's hips moving up to meet him and then falling away, he was holding still above her, she was taking him in and out of her body and then she was moving with him, he was taking her to heaven, and she gasped and cried out. When he fell onto her, she didn't know; Cecily had gone so high that she had fallen too fast and she had fainted in her husband's arms. She didn't hear him cry out that he loved her; she didn't know that he held her and sobbed quietly, his face buried in her hair.

Levi left Cecily and got control of himself before she woke. He sat on the side of the bed with his elbows propped on his knees, his face in his hands. He lived a tortured life for loving Cecily. And he knew that he could not make her love him. He was hurting her. He shook his head and looked up and out the doors that led to the porch and the outside world. Cecily may not love him; he may not be a smart man, but she liked what he did to her with his body. He prayed to God that she was not dreaming of Bernard while he held her in his arms.

Cecily reached out her hand and touched Levi's shoulder; she saw him flinch as well as felt him flinch before he stood his back to her. "Levi, please, let me talk," she begged, but he did not turn to face her or give his permission for her to speak. She spoke anyway. "I made a mistake."

"God, please make this woman be silent," Levi said as he went to pick up his pants from the floor. He knew that she had made a mistake. Her mistake was marrying him.

"Listen to me!" Cecily shouted at him, and Levi turned to face her. She had never seen such a tortured look on his face before. She had never seen such a tortured look like this on anyone's face before.

"Don't you understand, Cecily? I can't let you go. I don't care that you are thinking you are with Bernard when I make love to you. I don't care that you married me for my money." He didn't see his wife's eyes grow wide at his words; he didn't see the shocked look on her face. "My heart is bleeding for what you've done to me, Cecily. You would have been kinder to stab me with one of the kitchen knives right here," he motioned on his chest where his heart was. "Your thoughtless ways have broken me, darlin', there's nothing left of me. You have all of me, and you don't have the power to give me back any more than I have the power to take myself back. I only know I'd go down on my knees and beg you not to say another word to me for as long as you live. You've got me all torn up inside; I can't take your words. I don't want your version of the truth."

Cecily saw him hurriedly pull on his pants and shirt. She couldn't let him think that she thought of Bernard while in his arms. He had to know that it was him that she wanted in her arms. "Levi, I want —,"

"No!" he shouted at her. He knew what she wanted; she wanted a divorce. He would not give her one. "No," he said more softly and headed for the door. "You are mine, Cecily," Levi said without turning around. "I keep what is mine."

Cecily sat still on the bed after Levi left the room. The pain in his voice had shaken her as much as his words had. He wasn't hurting her because he wanted too. Levi was hurting her because he didn't know what she felt for him; he didn't know that she loved him and had for a long time. Levi only knew what Bernard told him and Bernard was believable because she hadn't told him anything but a lie. She pulled her knees up to her chin while she thought. She had to make him see. She had to let him know she wanted him. She shook her head because she couldn't think what to do to make her husband see the truth. He was failing to see her desire for him; he was failing to notice that it was she making love to him, not him making love to her. She was failing him; she wasn't making what she had done to hurt him not hurt him anymore. He wasn't going to let her talk. She looked up when she realized that he was afraid of what she would say to him. Levi just wasn't angry and hurt, Levi was afraid.

Cecily mended Levi's clothes and cleaned the house for something to do and knew that Ollie was watching her as well as Levi and the stableman. And all Cecily wanted was for her old Levi, the one with the easy smile just for her, to come through the door and kiss her until she melted into his arms. A month had passed since Bernard had given Levi the photos of she and Clemmie and Levi had changed. He rarely showed her kindness, there was a constant and persistent pain in his eyes, and if she dared to speak he put his hand over her mouth, or he would walk away from her.

Cecily did what she always did in a crisis, she prayed. She had prayed when her mother was dying in childbirth. She was praying for Bernard's soul when he was threatening her. She prayed for her father as he gave all he had to keep her safe. She prayed for Clemmie and Grant and Sarah and Ollie, and now Cecily stayed on her knees praying for Levi knowing that God would answer her prayers, she just had to be patient and remember that Levi had been an answer to her prayers not long ago.

Last Sunday morning she had woken up and dressed for church, she waited on Levi to wake and then worked up the courage to ask him to take her to church. He turned his angry glare on her and said bluntly that church was no place for lying, deceiving women like her. Those words had hurt her badly, and when she had turned and seen Ollie nearby, she knew the maid had heard Levi's words to her, she felt like finding a hole in the ground and crawling into it for the rest of her life.

Every night Levi took her to bed after she cleaned the kitchen. Sometimes he would just hold her in his arms; other times he would put her in the bathtub and bathe her, some nights he would have her bathe him. Many times he would have her sit in the bed, and he would sit behind her and brush her hair the one hundred strokes before bedtime. He could be so gentle at those times, so kind; she could feel the love. Other nights he would dive into her body and take her to the heaven he promised her, he could make her wild with his mouth and with his hands, he made her beg some nights and kept it away from her only to give it to her right before she calmed down and fell asleep. One night he had taken her out onto the porch, and she sat in his lap in the rocking chair listening to the night birds and the crickets and he told her things of his childhood, of how his mother and father use to play with one another hide and seek and he and Sarah would sit and watch them find one another and then they would always tickle one another and laugh and close the door to their bedroom.

Levi would hold her at night and remind her of their childhood. Of the time her horse Dixie fell and broke its leg and how Grant took her home while Levi put the horse down. She hadn't known that she thought her father had taken care of Dixie. She listened to him tell of things she didn't know he knew about or cared about. The ragdoll she carried around with her for years that even today lay in her bed back at her father's house. How hard she cried when one of the boys at the schoolhouse cut off half her braid, and that's why he loved her hair down because he knew she loved her hair long. He really had been waiting for her to grow up, she realized. Levi had loved her forever, and she hadn't known any more than he knew she had loved him always.

Cecily sat on the parlor floor polishing the legs of the sofa and remember the night before. Levi had made love to her, and that is what he was doing to her, she knew that with certainty. He was making love to her, and she was making love right back with him. He may hate her for what he believed that she had done to him, but he loved her with his body. After he had pulled himself from her last night he had not rolled away from her as he usually did. Instead he pulled her close in his arms, and she laid her head on his chest. It had been so simple, so unexpected, yet so natural when she spoke, "I love you, Levi." He went stiff from the top of his head to the soles of his feet before he shoved her away and rolled onto his side. Cecily had remained silent afraid to speak, afraid of Levi.

"Don't you ever and I mean ever, say those words to me again, Cecily." His voice was thick and deep, and she wondered if he had been crying. Her heart fell down into the darkest, deepest corner of her stomach. "You don't love me. You thought that you loved Bernard and look how that turned out for you. Now you think you love me when all I am is your passion, Cecily. That's all you are to me as well. I wanted more from you once. Now, I'll just take your body and try and be happy with what I have. Don't give me your so-called love; I don't want it."

Cecily had reached out to touch her husband's face in the darkness and felt the tears that were there and knew, if he would only touch her face, he would feel her tears as well. Instead, Levi had slapped her hand away and rolled onto his side away from her. He had been gone from their bed this morning when she awakened.

Levi stood in the hall and stared down at Cecily polishing the legs of the sofa. Her long hair was pooled onto the floor around her, and she had unbuttoned her blouse a little way, probably in an effort to get cool and he could see the outline of her breast. She had said that she loved him last night; those words had nearly killed him. He wished that he could make her love him. Everyone believed that silly story of his father making his mother love him, but Levi knew, his mother had always loved his father; she had just not liked the fact that Ethan was a Yankee. Cecily didn't love him; he had enslaved her to him with his body and his lovemaking.

He had cried, Levi thought and hated that weakness within himself. Men didn't cry. And Cecily knew that he had cried at her words, she had touched his face last night and felt his tears. He had been furious with her. It wasn't bad enough that she had made a fool of him and humiliated him, it wasn't enough that she had shown him that he was dumber than he had ever known, Cecily had unmanned him, he was like a little boy now crying over nothing.

Cecily looked up from polishing the legs of the sofa and saw Levi as he came into the room tracking dirt all over her clean floor, she wondered if he had done that intentionally. When she looked up at his face and into his eyes, she knew, Levi had made the mess on the floor with intent. He didn't just hate her in the light of day; he despised her. She had given him her body freely and in the hopes that he would see that she loved him and still he saw her as only a liar.

"Read this to me," he demanded and shoved a sheet of paper into her face. Cecily took the paper knowing that now that Grant had gone, Levi had no one to read for him. Jamie Liston filled out the orders for the timber, but Levi didn't want Jamie to read anything of a personal nature to him. He often came to Cecily, and she would read to him what he asked.

"Dear Levi," Cecily started to read. "As you and Cecily have been married almost two months I thought that it would be all right to invite myself out for a visit. I hope you aren't too put out with me for coming so soon after your marriage, but I can't wait a moment longer. I know you've always wanted Cecily —," Levi snatched the letter from her hands. When Cecily looked up at him, she saw he was flaming red.

"Just read when they're coming," Levi said in a strained voice before handing the letter back.

Cecily scanned the letter quickly then looked back up at Levi. "Sarah and Franklin will be here the first of the week," Levi snatched the letter away from her again, and she watched as he tore it up into tiny pieces and then shoved those pieces into his pants pocket.

"Listen to me, Cecily," he said these words in a cold hard voice. "If you do or say anything to give my sister the impression that our marriage is not a love match, I'll make you sorry you ever met me, much less married me. Do you hear?"

"I won't do anything, Levi, I promise," Cecily said in a near whisper.

"I still have those photos of you," Cecily gasped at his words and shook her head. The stricken look on her face made Levi regret his words immediately. "I didn't mean that, darlin'," he said and bent down to her, she fell back away from him. "Not as a threat," he added. Her eyes were swimming in tears, and Levi hated himself. How could he let things go on this way? What the hell was he going to do about her? Fear had made him say what he had about those photos, fear that she may tell his sister that she didn't love him, that she wanted a divorce are what haunted him the most, she only married him for his money. Sarah and Cecily had grown up together; they had been best friends along with Clemmie Floyd.

Levi knew that Cecily didn't love him. He knew that he was giving her reason to hate him, but he couldn't stop himself. He could not stop this demon that had entered his soul and was wreaking havoc with his life. He should have let her go when he got those photos. He was holding her captive, and he knew that too. She had even at one time almost asked him for a divorce. Hadn't she said that she had made a mistake?

Levi reached out a hand and grabbed a hold of his wife; she had been right, he thought, she was his hell. His heart knew that he had to let her go; his body could not allow her to ever leave him. He would not be whole without her. He was only half of what he was without his Cecily. "I'm on fire for you darlin', please," he begged softly as he looked into her eyes. "Please, Cecily put out the fire."

Cecily swallowed hard. Maybe she could still make him see that she loved him, her heart cried as she let him touch her. She needed her Levi back; she could not give up on him now. "Levi, if you'll just,"

Levi pulled her into his arms and covered her mouth with his own; his tongue plunging in and out. Cecily held on to him, and he stood with her in his arms, his mouth still covering hers. He knew that she would tell him that she wanted to leave him; he could not hear her say those words to him. God help him, but he loved her with every fiber of his being. His anger had not killed his love for her; nothing she had done to him killed his love for her. "I need you, Cecily," he begged when he kicked the bedroom door closed.

Cecily held on to her husband and felt her heart bleed for his blindness to the love she had for him, a love he could not and would not accept because of her lies to him. She would love him and the only way that he would allow her too, she would love him with her body, her mouth, and her hands. And he would take her to heaven as he held her in his arms, just as he said he would.

When they lay spent on the bed together more than an hour later, Cecily looked into her husband's eyes and she knew that she had failed him and herself again. He did not see her love for him, only the pain of what she had done was etched on his face and spoke of the hell she had put him in.

"I'm sorry, Levi," Cecily spoke low, and he turned and looked at her.

Cecily was sorry; Levi thought as he jerked on his clothes and hurried from the room. Cecily was sorry that she was married to him.

"Go put your hair up, Cecily," Levi said in a hard voice as he came into the kitchen. Ollie stared at him and wondered when he was going to stop bossing and ordering Cecily around. She had known that Levi had loved Cecily for a long time, but these past weeks he had treated Cecily worse than she had ever known him to treat anyone. She had heard him, just last week, pull his torn shirt from Cecily's hand and tell his wife never to mend another of his shirts because Cecily couldn't sew well. Ollie knew Cecily sewed a fine seam; Cecily could sew better than she could. And Levi had handed his torn shirt to Ollie and told his wife to leave his things alone. He was killing Cecily by being hateful, and he didn't seem to care. First Cecily had been hurting him and now this. Ollie could not understand what was going on. She had thought that Levi and Cecily would be perfect together; these past two months had been like living in the fires of hell watching them treat one another like they were. And Levi was treating Cecily far worse than Cecily had ever treated him. Ollie knew Levi; he was a good man, he had been a good man, now he was mean.

Cecily hurried from the kitchen and Levi went to the sink and washed up. Sarah and Franklin were due to arrive anytime now. Ollie stared at Levi's back and thought of what he was doing to Cecily. He had called Cecily a bad name this morning; he told her he wouldn't take her to church anymore because she wasn't good. After he had said, the mean things and Cecily looked ready to cry Levi took her into his arms and disappeared with her into their bedroom. Ollie had stood back and watched Cecily cry in silence, she was not talking at all to anyone while Levi stormed around the house in a fit of temper and looked like he was either going bust or worse, and there was worse with Levi, The anger would fade and in its place would come a look of the worst pain anyone had suffered, as though he was dying or worse, Ollie didn't know. She had also seen another look on his face, not as often as the hurt one, but a look of fear. Something was going on with these two and Ollie felt caught in the middle. What had gone so horribly wrong that it brought the household to this? And after having worked here in this home all these years, this was a home of laughter and joy, and above all love. There was no love now, and the laughter and joy were long gone, this house was cold and empty like the two would be lovers that lived here.

"Mister Levi," she said his name and Levi turned to face Ollie. "Why are you being so mean to Miss Cecily?" Levi looked away from Ollie, but not before she saw that look of pain fill his face and eyes.

"My relationship with my wife is none of your business, Ollie," Levi said and left the kitchen. Ollie shook her head and wondered what had happened to Levi Tucker. She had known him all of his life and something terrible was wrong with him now. It was like it had been when he was in school and the other boys would call him dumb because he couldn't read. And then she knew, she had to be right, Cecily must have learned he can't read and made him feel dumb. She almost felt sorry for him, until she thought of the revenge he was having on Cecily, he was making her life very hard, and Ollie didn't like what he was doing, even if Cecily had called him dumb or made him feel dumb.

Sarah and Franklin arrived with their six-month-old son just before dark. An hour before, Cecily sat at her vanity looking at her face, everything had to be perfect tonight and in the coming days. Levi couldn't make her be quiet in front of his sister, she could say what she needed him to hear, by the time Sarah left, Levi would know she loved him, and he wouldn't make her be silent anymore.

Levi greeted his sister at the door and held it open for her family to come inside. He took his sister's husband's hand and shook it while saying to his sister, "You're looking well. Last time I saw you this one had you worn down." He took the baby Frankie from his sister's arms and tossed him in the air above his head smiling up at the baby.

"I'm feeling so much better, Levi. Where is Cecily?" his sister asked and Levi frowned. He didn't know where his wife was, all he knew was that she wasn't where she was suppose to be, and that was with him.

"Sarah," Cecily rushed to her friend, and they hugged. "It's so good to see you; I've missed you so much."

"Cecily, I always wanted you for a sister. I'm so happy. I knew someday we would be. Levi was determined to marry no one else but you." Sarah did not see her brother's face lose all color and the pain that filled his eyes, his beautiful eyes, Cecily thought as she moved to take his hand.

"He wasn't alone in what he wanted," she looked up at him and smiled before touching Frankie's cheek, the little boy was in Levi's arms chewing on his fingers and drooling on Levi's shirt. "He was all I wanted in a husband," Cecily said, looking up at her husband and she saw some of the pain in his eyes fade, and then he looked like he had when he had hit her that day, and she pulled away from him seeing his eyes were bright as well. He was so easy to read, he was angry and hurt, and she had done this to him. She remembered his easy smiles; she missed those easy smiles. She had taken those smiles away from him with her deceit.

Levi looked down at his wife. He swallowed hard and blinked twice to clear his eyes. She lied with ease, and she lied well, he never would have believed the Cecily he'd loved for so long was this way. He had seen her as sweet and innocent and loving and kind. His burning gut reminded him that she had only married him for his money and now she didn't need that money; she might leave him at any moment. He pulled his hand free of hers and looked away from her eyes.

Sarah frowned at her brother's face; she knew Levi better than anyone in the world, she thought. And her brother was not happy. He looked hurt, he looked furious, and Sarah knew that Levi, when mad, was unreasonable in his anger. She wondered what Cecily had done to her brother and hoped that it wasn't anything serious. Levi didn't forgive, and he never forgot. He could be hard that way.

No Sound The Silence Makes

She knew, her brother was the kindest, gentlest man on the earth unless he was hurt and looking at him now, she knew he was hurt. Sarah knew this marriage wasn't the one she had expected it to be.

Dinner was strained as Cecily forced herself to be happy and tried to smile at Levi and he all but ignored her. Watching him now, with his family, he was withdrawn and silent, He never smiled and she knew, what she had done to him, lying to him, allowing him to believe she married him for his money, allowing him to think she didn't love him and didn't want to be married to him, it had hurt him as much as Bernard blackmailing her. She grieved that she hadn't been honest with him, she grieved it was too late, and she wasn't making it up to him. Maybe it would take a lifetime for her to make up for what she had done. She thought of Bernard and how she could almost hate him for what he had done to her, and she wondered, did Levi hate her the same way?

She listened to Sarah talk of how close they were as children, telling her husband how they'd all been the very best of friends forever, since the cradle. And the whole time Sarah talked she looked from Levi's face to her face; Cecily knew that her sister in law was very well aware something was the matter. She also saw Franklin watching them and knew she wasn't doing a good job of convincing anyone that she and Levi were a love match.

Cecily watched Levi holding the baby on his lap and feeding Frankie mashed potatoes and mashed peas; he was enjoying his nephew. But then, Levi had always been good with babies, she knew, he was natural with all children. She saw Sarah smile at her brother holding her son and almost lost her breath with Sarah's words,

"You'll make a good father someday." Sarah turned to look at Cecily. "Soon maybe?" she smiled, and Cecily glanced quickly at Levi and saw the anger on his face, and she knew he was remembering when she had told him she didn't want a baby and she wished for the thousandth time she could go back and be honest with her husband.

Levi looked at his wife, her words weeks ago echoed in his mind, "I could never have your baby." A moan came from deep within, and he stood up handing the baby to Sarah. "I need some air; it's hot in here." He didn't see Cecily choking back tears as he reached for her hand. "You're coming with me." Cecily stood beside her husband and smiled at Sarah, or tried too.

"Don't be out long," Sarah called after them. "Once I get the baby to bed, we'll do the dishes and have a long talk, Cecily."

Levi sat down on the porch swing pulling his wife down next to him and thought of the effort that she was making to show his sister and her husband that their marriage wasn't anything other than a love match that they believed it to be. He was the one failing, Levi knew. He couldn't stop his anguish or his anger. And his fear, his fear was the worst of all. He knew that Cecily didn't love him and she didn't need his money any longer, Bernard's hold over her was gone. There was no reason for her to stay with him. She had the money in the bank he had given to her, and she could go back to her father's home, she could divorce him at any time. She hadn't wanted a baby by him because it would have tied her to him; she would never have truly gotten away from him if she had his child. He looked down at her and saw her staring up at him, he didn't know why, but he knew he had to hold her close.

Cecily felt herself getting lost in Levi's embrace, his chin resting on the top of her head, she relaxed into him and waited to see what he would do or say. She heard him take a deep breath and then another as though he were in pain. "Levi, please, can't we talk now." She felt him pull her close and wrap both arms around her before his hand came up and over her mouth.

"I can't take what you'll say," he whispered. "Let's just leave things as they are right now." He felt her head nod on his chest and breathed a sigh of relief. "You had better go clean up the kitchen," he released her and Cecily reluctantly stood. "Please, don't let Sarah,"

"Levi," Cecily put her hand over his mouth. "I promised. I won't break my word."

Sarah had cleared the table, and Franklin stood in the kitchen holding the baby when Cecily came inside, she tickled the baby and smiled up at Franklin. "He's adorable," she breathed and wondered if she might one day have Levi's baby.

"I tend to think so too," Franklin said in a teasing fashion. "He favors Levi, his eyes are going to be the same blue as Sarah's and Levi's," he held the baby so that Sarah could see into his eyes.

"Aren't they a beautiful color?" Sarah asked joining them with a dish in her hand.

"I think they're an angry color," Cecily said honestly as Levi's eyes were often angry. "Not the baby's eyes," she said with a nervous laugh.

"Just mine," Levi said as he entered the room and Cecily looked at him quickly before turning to the dirty dishes in the sink.

"I didn't mean that," she said softly.

"I'm going to put this little one down," Franklin said to Levi, and we can go out on the porch for a bit while the girls clean up. Levi said nothing to Franklin; he just turned and walked away.

Levi went around the house on the porch and stood outside the kitchen door, he had to know what his wife said to his sister, and he knew they were going to talk about him. He had put his wife in a world of silence, and now she was able to speak, he should just say what he wouldn't let her say and allow her to go home and give her a divorce.

"Cecily, tell me what's going on," Sarah demanded as Cecily washed the dishes. "And don't tell me it's nothing. I can see you and Levi both look horribly unhappy."

"I can't talk about it Sarah," Cecily said in a pathetic voice, and Levi lit a cigarette and leaned against the wall of the house listening.

She could never tell Sarah or anyone what she had done, how she had posed for photos without her clothes on for Bernard Calhoun when he was courting her and then Bernard started blackmailing her and she'd married him for his money to pay the blackmail. And now, the photos were in his possession and the plates were broken, she didn't need him any longer, and he was forcing her to stay.

"We've known one another all our lives, Cecily. You can tell me anything, and I want to help. I can see Levi looks horribly upset and you look like you're about to fly to pieces. Maybe I can help." Sarah saw Cecily shaking her head. "Well, maybe having a baby will help. Are you with child yet?"

Levi stood up straight and listened for his wife's answer and knew he had to leave her alone before it was too late, if he didn't, she may take more of him with her than just his heart when she left him. And he knew, she would leave him, they could not go on the way that they had been, they were killing one another slowly and painfully. They just were no good together. She didn't love him, and he knew that he put his hands over his face and felt like his head was killing him, it ached that bad. He had to give Cecily money, the money she had married him for and send her back to her father's house; the place was just as she had let it. He would give her money, and a divorce and this pain would have an end at last. He had no right to do what he was doing to her; he was as bad as Bernard, if not worse. He was controlling her with his desire, and he was being mean in his anger.

"I just had my cycle not too long ago," Cecily said softly. "There's no baby, Sarah." Sarah heard the gasp and the cry and then she was holding Cecily and Cecily was crying.

"Oh sweetheart, don't cry. Whatever has happened, we can fix it. You and Levi," Cecily looked up at Sarah and Sarah fell silent.

"There is no fixing this Sarah," Cecily cried, and Levi, standing out on the porch swallowed hard. "I can't fix anything, and I can't talk about it either, not now, maybe not ever. Everything between Levi and I has gone wrong."

"I'll talk to Levi," Sarah said firmly.

"No, don't do that," Cecily shook her head hard and turned back to the sink. "Please, please I beg you, don't tell Levi about my crying. He would be so ashamed of me."

"Ashamed?" Sarah frowned.

"Please, you have to promise me you won't tell Levi that I cried or that you think anything is wrong between us. We're trying to work through this, Sarah. If you tell him I've been crying – well please don't. Just let he and I work this out." Cecily had turned back to face her husband's sister, and Sarah saw the pleading in her eyes.

"I won't make any promises, Cecily. But I'll speak of this to Franklin and see if he thinks I should mind my own business or talk to my brother. But no matter what I do, you have to know I love you; I want you happy as much as I want Levi happy. I cannot believe that two people who were meant to be together like you and my brother would start off your marriage on the wrong foot." Sarah looked at the door leading to the porch; she could smell cigarette smoke and knew her brother was there listening to their every word, she wouldn't have to tell him anything that had just gone on.

"I'm not feeling very well; the dishes are done. I'll see you in the morning, Sarah." Cecily took a lantern from the stove and left the room. Sarah was standing in the near darkness staring at the door.

"I'm not leaving this room until you come in here and talk to me, Levi Tucker," Sarah said to the darkness beyond the door in a tone of voice that only a sister can use on her brother.

"Sarah, this is really between my wife and I," Levi said sternly to his little sister.

"Levi, you know how Mama and Daddy always said it helps to talk,"

"Everything has been said between Cecily and I," Levi cut his sister off. "I know you mean well, but Cecily and I aren't like Mama and Daddy were. I have to handle this in my way." He turned to leave thinking to himself, and I have to do what's best for Cecily. He had been selfish with her, he had taken from her what she hadn't wanted to give, he was forcing her to live the way he demanded, and it wasn't making her happy. It wasn't making him happy either.

Franklin Mathews handed Levi a cigarette and sat on the front porch in the dark with him, the crickets were loud, and he could hear a night bird crying out, it was peaceful here in the country, and he was glad he and Sarah had come out, but anyone could see something was going on between Levi and his wife and Franklin knew they needed to leave and let the newlyweds figure out their problem without family around.

"Cecily's a fine woman," Franklin said in way of conversation while Levi lit his cigarette.

"She's the knot in my tie," Levi said as he turned and looked out across the dark yard.

"I hope you're not upset that Sarah and I invited ourselves out here? We should have waited for you to invite us, but you know Sarah, she's always in everyone's business. A bossy little thing," he added with a smile that reached his voice.

"No, Franklin, I'm not upset. I just have a lot of stress from working too much at the mill. There have been a lot of orders to fill lately, and I'm bone weary." Levi tossed his cigarette into the yard and lit another one.

"Plus you've only been married a couple of months," Franklin added and Levi nodded his head. "It must be hard on Cecily having you work all the time."

"She wishes that I would work more," Levi said more to himself than to Franklin.

"Are you all right, Levi? Are you troubled about something? Forgive me for asking, but I know that Sarah wants you happy and if you're not, we would like to help." Franklin watched Levi's head shake from side to side.

"I'm happy," Levi said in a strained voice. He couldn't lie well; Cecily was the one that lied too well. "I think I'll go on to bed."

Franklin watched his brother in law leave the porch with a frown on his face. Levi was not a happy man; his marriage was not agreeing with him. Franklin had listened to Sarah gush over how her brother had loved Cecily for years and finally he was with her and Levi would have the fairy tale love his parents had. Franklin hoped that soon there would be truth to Sarah's words because Levi looked horribly unhappy.

Levi came into the bedroom and saw Cecily at the vanity staring at her reflection in the mirror, she looked so sad, and he had heard her crying tonight. It was him that had brought her to tears. He had to let her go; he was wrong to keep her. He closed his eyes and swayed on his feet; he couldn't let her go; he would lose her, maybe not even see her or hear from her again, or worse, see her with someone else and a baby in her arms that wasn't his baby. He lost his breath as he felt as though an invisible hand was inside his chest squeezing his heart and wouldn't let go.

"Levi," she said his name softly, and he opened his eyes to see her standing before him, she was every dream he had ever had come true.

"Look at your hair," he said in a rough voice. "Go get the brush for me and I'll fix it for you." Cecily almost smiled as she went for her brush and took it to her husband; she loved these intimate times with him even if he wouldn't let her talk.

Levi sat against the pillows of the bed and pulled Cecily against him and facing away from him, the brush gliding through her long, beautiful, soft hair. He closed his eyes and breathed in her scent; he wanted to remember this moment forever. She fit so well into him; she was meant to be here, how could he send her away? How could he let her go?

Cecily turned her face up and smiled at her husband; he was looking down into her eyes and lost his breath in the smile. He remembered when they were young, and she would smile at him, and it lit up his soul. The day down at the lake when the lake had tried to take her from him, she had smiled and played with him as they had played as children. He closed his eyes and saw her running away from him, the way she turned, and her whole face lit up in a playful smile daring him to catch her. If only they could live that way every day. If only she could love him for the man he was and not want to only be his playmate.

Cecily turned in her husband's arm, and her face was inches from his as she brushed her lips against his lips. She knew he was going to make love to her; she wanted him to make love to her, she wanted to make love to him and right everything she had done wrong by showing him she wanted him always as her husband.

"Stop Cecily," Levi said in a hoarse whisper and grabbed her shoulder pushing her gently away.

"I want to give you this," Cecily said looking him in the eyes; the anger wasn't there, only the horrible hurt.

"Not anymore, Cecily. We have to stop this. I could give you my child." Levi lowered his head, and Cecily gasped. He didn't want her to have his baby; he had before he found out about Bernard, but not now. They had been together for weeks, they had made love in so many ways, and he hadn't worried about a baby until now, now when he had held Frankie, and she knew he loved children.

"Levi, you're being dumb," the minute that she spoke these words Levi rolled her on to her back and was pressing her down hard onto the mattress causing her to fall silent. She had only meant to tell him that he was being dumb about no baby when they wanted one another so much, and this want would produce a baby eventually, but he had grabbed her not even halfway into saying what she meant to say. He really meant to keep her silent.

"Don't ever call me dumb," he hissed into her face. "I'm not dumb, do you hear me, Cecily? And the only dumb thing I ever did was marry you."

He was laying on top of her and forcing her so deep into the mattress that Cecily's back was hurting her and she was struggling to breathe with him laying on her. "I want you to leave me alone," Levi said as he moved off of her and she grabbed a long deep breath. "I want you to go to sleep. I don't want you that way anymore, not ever again." She watched him fall onto his back and put his hand over his eyes; his head was hurting worse than before; he had to get some sleep and escape this awful pain. "You will not have my child," he gasped out before he turned his back to her. "You will not have my baby," he said into the darkness after he had blown out the lantern, a night bird cried out in the distance beyond the porch door, and Cecily could hear her husband's harsh breathing. She had done this to him, she had hurt him, and nothing she could do would fix this mess she had made.

He hated her, Cecily thought as she lay lost in the darkness of the room next to her angry, hurt husband. She had taken Levi's love for her for granted and then she had killed that love. He wanted nothing from her. He had pushed her away for good and all now. Her mistake and her silence had cost her the one thing that had mattered most to her in this life, she thought. No, she knew, her mistake had cost her all that mattered to her.

Cecily had nothing. Levi would give her nothing.

Sarah lay in her husband's arms; a frown covered her pretty face. "Franklin," she spoke softly, and her husband touched her hair. "I don't think that Levi and Cecily are happy together and I thought they would be. He's been in love with her for years, and I know she's felt the same since we became young women and no longer girls."

"I know something is going on between them Sarah, but it's really not our place to butt in." He kissed the top of his wife's head, and she turned in his arms.

"Cecily said our Frankie's eyes are an angry color."

"Sarah, you know how Levi can be when he's mad. And he looks like he's mad with his wife right now. I'm sure they'll work this out in their own way and in their own time."

"I think we should leave tomorrow," Sarah said softly and snuggled closer to her husband.

"I agree, Sarah. We'll come again another time. Maybe when we've been invited." Sarah laughed while playfully slapping her husband's hand. "Don't worry about your brother, Sarah. The fact is he's loved Cecily for a long time; he'll fix what's wrong between them in the name of that love. All lovers' quarrel. Even us." Sarah heard the teasing in her husband's voice and let him kiss her.

"Franklin," she said in a serious tone when he finished his kiss. "Levi has a rotten temper when he gets mad, and he doesn't get over his anger like I do. He holds on to it like it's a living thing. Mama said her daddy was the same way. Mad and mean."

"You don't get over your anger easy either, Sarah," Franklin said with a laugh as he rolled his wife over and onto her back. "You're just like Levi that way. Mad and mean. I've just been lucky and not made you mad at me yet." He kissed his wife, and her arms went around his neck.

"I could never get mad at you," Sarah said to her husband as he reached and pulled up the hem of her nightgown. "I adore you," she moaned as Franklin touched her. Her husband knew that she spoke the truth. She loved him more now than she had the day that she married him. Every day she loved him more, Sarah thought and knew that Levi was like her when it came to loving someone as well; he gave all of his heart. All of Levi's heart had belonged to Cecily for years.

Early the next morning, Sarah and Franklin took two horses and went out for a ride leaving Cecily alone with the baby. Levi was still in the bed, and when Cecily had left the room, he was sleeping hard and fast. She was careful and dressed quietly so that she would not wake him and hurriedly left their room. Maybe if Levi got a good night's rest, he wouldn't be so angry with her. Maybe he would change his mind and touch her again.

Cecily played patty cake with Frankie and piggy toes before she rocked the little boy to sleep in the rocking chair in the parlor. The baby's small body felt so right in her arms; she wished that this was her and Levi's child, then Levi would have a part of her, a part of her that he could not turn away from or be hurt by. A part of her that he could love that would love him right back. Cecily felt the tears form in her eyes and almost let them fall. Quickly she brushed them away finding inside herself the determination to regain Levi's love and affections. She couldn't go on like this; they were tearing one another apart.

Levi had woken with the headache still hanging on. His head felt like it had been broken in two and put back together all wrong. Even his neck ached in agony. He left his bedroom and heard Cecily singing in the parlor. She had no right to be happy; he thought, not when she was the cause of all of his pain. He went to the parlor doorway and saw her sitting in the rocking chair and holding his nephew. She was smiling down at the baby and singing, and a pain filled his heart that was all consuming. She looked so perfect holding that baby; this should have been his baby, he should be able to walk into this room and share in this precious moment. He hated her when he remembered how she felt about him, how she had cost him the love he wanted to give her and have with her. He had tried to push her truth away. He had not wanted to face the truth of Cecily's feeling for him. The pain cut deep. She was killing him. And he knew, one day he would stand in church or see her in the town with a child in her arms and a husband she loved, and it wouldn't be him. He stood and watched her holding his nephew knowing she didn't want his baby, she never had. She had no right to hold a child with his blood in its veins; she had no right to anything that was his. She gave him nothing; he had already given to her too much.

"You're holding him all wrong," Levi said and went to Cecily taking the baby out of her arms. "I'm glad you won't have my child, Cecily. You would make a horrible mother. You'd probably make as bad a mother as you are wife." The look on his wife's face was enough to make him physically ill; it didn't matter that he had just gotten even with her for not wanting his child, he should not have said what he had. But it was too late now, he thought and turned and walked away from his wife. He had to send her away; he had to get her away from himself before he hated himself more than she hated him for what he was doing to her.

Ollie left the house late that morning; she could not take the sadness in Cecily's eyes any longer. And the pain that Levi was causing his wife was too terrible to stay and watch. The last weeks had been too much. First Cecily had come into the kitchen saying that she needed her husband after weeks of awful grief and then Levi comes home furious and puts Ollie from the house and the next morning Cecily's blood was on the sheets, and her face was bruised.

Ollie shook her head sadly as she remembered the hateful things that Levi had said to Cecily, and Cecily took Levi's words as though they were what she deserved. Levi's insults seemed to have no end, Ollie thought and felt like crying for Cecily. And today, she had heard what Levi had said to Cecily about the baby, the look on Cecily's face had been too awful to stay and see. And when Cecily had started to cry, Ollie had heard Cecily crying her heart out. Levi had to have some help; Cecily had to have some help. Ollie didn't want to tell Sarah, Sarah was Levi's sister, and she might not see Cecily's side. Cecily needed more help than Levi did.

Ollie knocked softly on Grant and Clemmie's front door and waited for them to answer. When Clemmie did come to the door she looked glad to see Ollie, Ollie was relieved. "Come in," Clemmie invited, and Ollie came into the house wondering what to say and what not to say. If Clemmie couldn't help Cecily, no one could. "What's wrong, Ollie?" Clemmie asked, and Ollie sat down in a chair and took the glass of tea that Clemmie gave to her. Grant came into the room, and Ollie felt hope that Cecily could be safe with these two. Grant could find out what was going on with Levi after all, Grant was Levi's best friend.

Ollie started talking, she talked fast and tried to be calm; she felt anything but calm. She did not notice the looks that Clemmie and Grant gave to her and to one another. She poured out the whole story as she knew it, everything that she had seen going on in that house up to this morning with the baby was told. The ugliness of Levi, the silence of Cecily, the pain they were giving to one another and Levi's anger, Ollie told everything she knew to tell.

"What can we do?" Clemmie moaned when Ollie finally fell quiet. "We have to get Cecily away from Levi. He's lost his mind."

"It's worse than that, Miss Clemmie," Ollie said. "He's watching her all the time, and when he's not, he has Preston down to the stables come up and watch her. He's holding her prisoner in that house. He won't take her to church neither; he won't even let her talk, not one word," she told what she'd already told wanting them to understand the situation.

"We have to get her out of that house," Clemmie said again and started pacing around the room.

"Getting her out of there isn't the only problem," Grant said. "Where would she go? She's Levi's wife. He has a right to force her back home. And we don't even know if Cecily wants out of that house."

"I think that she would go if she could," Ollie spoke. "She can't stay there; she's dying; Mister Levi is killing her with his words."

"We have to hide her," Clemmie said and paced faster. "We have to get her out of there, and we have to hide her from Levi." Cecily had saved her, Cecily had given her a safe place to stay, Cecily would have done anything for her and Clemmie knew that.

"I came here because I knew Miss Cecily needed help. I can't do nothing. Please, help her." Ollie looked Grant in the eye, here sat a man and men saved women, that was the law of nature.

"I've tried to see Levi several times these past weeks; he pulled a gun on me the last time I went to the sawmill and told me if I came back he would shoot me. He's really not in his right mind." Grant didn't add that Levi had told him to go home to his whore wife. "I wonder what has happened to him. He loved Cecily so much; he was always a happy man with a good heart."

"I know what happened," Clemmie said softly. "He's blaming Cecily for what Bernard did to her. He doesn't believe what really happened."

"He's mean," Ollie said in a firm voice. "And he's hurting Miss Cecily."

"Has he hurt her physically?" Grant brought Ollie's eyes back to his own with this question. He kept remembering Cecily's lip and the blood and was more certain now than before that Levi had hit Cecily.

"I don't know," Ollie said and shook her head. "He hasn't hit her while I've been around. But I think he might have hit her."

"Aunt Louise," Clemmie said and looked at Grant. "My mother's friend from over in Thomasville, Louise Crandle. We could send Cecily to her. Cecily's met Aunt Louise before, and they got on famously. I know Aunt Louise would take her and keep her safe."

"How can you be sure Clemmie?" Grant asked with a frown hoping that this would be the solution, Thomasville wasn't too far away but far enough for Cecily to be safe from Levi.

"I know Aunt Louise would take her in, she lives alone and never married, and she has tons of money. She has been after someone to come and keep her company for a while now, she asked mama for my little sister Jean, but mama said no. And besides, Aunt Louise would do anything for me."

"But how do we get Miss Cecily away from Mister Levi?" Ollie almost cried out, they were so close to helping Cecily and yet so far.

"Grant will think of some way to get her out, Ollie," Clemmie said and looked at her husband. "I know you won't let us down," she said to her husband.

"If you say so Clemmie," Grant tried to smile, he didn't feel like smiling. They were talking about taking a wife from her husband; they were talking about taking his best friend's wife away and hiding her, he didn't like this idea at all, he couldn't. Someone might get hurt. And then he thought of Cecily who was already getting hurt.

"And when Mister Levi comes to his senses we'll tell him where to find Miss Cecily, and she can come home and be happy like they should be already," Ollie said with a smile, glad now that she had come here.

"I doubt that Levi will have any sense when he finds out what we've done to him," Grant said. "And we still don't know if Cecily wants to leave him."

"I'll sneak over there later today and talk with Cecily myself," Clemmie said. "If she wants to leave Levi, we'll get her out of there somehow, someway."

Ollie didn't go home as she had planned when she left Clemmie and Grant's place. Instead, she went back to Levi's house, back to Cecily. She had to be there to help find a way to sneak Clemmie in when the young woman came later this afternoon. She prayed that all went well and that Mister Levi turned back into himself soon.

Franklin and Sarah left in the early afternoon, Levi was glad they were gone, he needed time alone, he needed time to think. He looked back at the house as he walked down the road and saw Cecily standing at the parlor door watching him, he thought that she hated him now, he had given her all the reason in the world to hate him these past weeks. He could not take the sadness in her eyes any longer, sadness that he had put in her eyes. He could not take what he was doing to her any longer, this had to end, and he had to end it.

He should have let her talk to him, Levi thought. He should have let her tell him that she wanted a divorce, and then he should have let her go. He should have never have kept her after he got those photos of her. He had been wrong. He had not wanted to live without her; his brain screamed in reminder of why he had kept her. He wanted her to love him as he loved her; he thought that he could make her love him. She was his Cecily. She had never been his Cecily. If only he could go back, if only he hadn't forced her to silence, if only he hadn't forced her to stay with him when she had wanted to leave.

Levi stopped under a tree and lit a cigarette. He would go home, he would talk to Cecily, without anger and he would tell her the truth, that he loved her still, that he wanted her as his wife without anger and pain and lies, then he would listen to her. He would let her tell him what she wanted, how she felt. He would plead for a second chance. He would tell her that there would be no more wrongs between them. He could accept what little she may feel for him. He would try and trust her again. He loved her enough to take her any way that she came to him. And he would be good and kind to her again. He wanted to be good and kind to Cecily.

Levi closed his eyes and took a deep breath knowing that by facing her, by allowing her to talk, this could go another way. She could leave him today, go back to her father's, and demand never to see him again. He deserved that after the way he had treated her.

All he could do now was be open and honest with her and beg her to forgive him as he should have forgiven her.

Cecily stood at the parlor door and watched Levi walk away. His words this morning about the baby had been so hurtful that she had felt like her heart had been broken. He was trying to destroy her as she had destroyed him. He could not be mad forever, she thought. At some point, forgiveness had to take place. She thought again that she wanted her Levi back, and she closed her eyes now and saw his smile, the sparkle in his eyes right before he kissed her. She had to find her old Levi; she needed him.

"Cecily," she heard her name whispered from behind, and she turned to find Clemmie standing in the shadows of the parlor. "I had to come," Clemmie said as she rushed to Cecily and they hugged.

"Clemmie, oh Clemmie, I'm so glad you come," Cecily hugged her friend quick. "You can't stay though if Levi were to find you here, I don't know what he would do. He's not like he use to be Clemmie; he's changed." She stopped speaking and turned to look back out the door, the yard was empty.

"I want to help you, Cecily," Clemmie said and pulled Cecily to the sofa. "Please, let me help you."

"I'm all right, honest I am. Levi is just mad about the photos and Bernard," her voice broke, and she almost started to cry.

"Ollie says that he's been hurting you," Clemmie looked sharply at Cecily's face.

Levi entered the house through his bedroom door and went to find his wife. He couldn't wait; he had to tell her now how he felt about her, he had to know if she would stay with him or if she would leave him. He would beg for a second chance, and he would give her a second chance. He would go down on his knees and beg her to stay if he had too.

"I don't think I even like Levi any longer," Cecily said to Clemmie. She was glad that at last, she was free to talk with someone. "He's been awful, Clemmie, nothing like he use to be," she added softly.

Levi stopped in the hall and heard his wife talking, her words cut him like a knife, and he knew they were true. He felt like she had punched him in the gut; he knew she didn't want to be here, he knew now that he had lost her. All this time he had kept her silent because he knew her words would kill him; her words always hurt him. The silence had been better.

"I'm free of Bernard, but now I'm being tortured by Levi. He won't let me speak; he's holding me, prisoner, here. And Clemmie, it's like Levi has no brains at all. He can't see what's right in front of him, staring him in the face. I've tried so hard, but he's just being so dumb –." Cecily broke off speaking when she saw her husband take two steps into the parlor; the look on his face made her swallow whatever words she meant to say.

"Get out," Levi said in a low firm voice to Clemmie. Cecily didn't move, she had never seen him this angry, not even when he knew of Bernard's photos of her. "Out!" he screamed and grabbed Clemmie by the arm pulling her from the sofa where she sat beside his wife to the front door.

"What are you doing, Levi?" Clemmie cried as he shoved her hard and she fell onto her knees on the porch floor.

"You gave yourself to Bernard just like she did," Levi said in the worst voice Cecily had ever heard him use. "Grant wants you still near him; I do not want you near me or my wife." He slammed the door in Clemmie's face as she realized, he doesn't know the truth, he doesn't know that she nor Cecily willingly allowed Bernard to take the photos. Why hadn't Cecily told him what happened to them? Clemmie knew she couldn't think of Levi right now; she had to tell Grant that Cecily was in danger, they had to find a way fast to get Cecily out of this house. Clemmie ran down the road afraid for her friend, her mind on finding Grant as soon as she could.

Cecily stood in the parlor doorway; her eyes were huge with disbelief. Levi had just thrown Clemmie out of their home and away from her. She shook her head as he came toward her and she fell back a step into the parlor. She squeezed her eyes shut certain that he was going to hit her again.

"I was going to trust you again!" Levi screamed at her and Cecily opened her eyes and shook all over. "I wanted to trust you, and you won't let me. Why do you continue to betray me? Why?"

"Levi," she said his name, but that was all that he let her say.

"Shut up!" he yelled and grabbed a hold of her arm. "I heard you, I heard you tell Clemmie that you didn't like me, you never liked me. You never gave me a chance. And all I ever wanted was you. All I ever wanted was to love you." He pulled her close to him and looked down into her crystal clear blue eyes. "You slept with Bernard, and I said that it didn't matter, I wasn't going to let it matter. You posed for those photos and every time I look at them I feel sick inside because I know you don't want to pose like that for me, your husband. You don't want me, you never did. You shut me out and turned me away, and I hurt you," Cecily saw him hang his head and tears slid down his nose. "And God help me, I've said things to you these past weeks that I never dreamed of saying to anyone, hurtful things, mean things. You make me hate myself as much as you hate me. And all along you think I'm dumb for loving you. All this time you've been laughing at me and hating me and all I wanted was to love you."

Cecily was sobbing along with her husband; he was tortured by the lies Bernard had told him, by the lies she had told him and what she hadn't told him. She felt like doing what Clemmie had done, better that than have left this wake of destruction upon her husband. He only knew what he knew; she should have shouted on the night that he took her virginity that he was the only man she'd laid with and there was the evidence. Instead she allowed him to believe it was her time of the month. He had loved her; he still loved her. All she had given to her Levi was hurt.

"Oh, Levi," Cecily said brokenly, her eyes staring up into her husband's eyes.

"You hate even the color of my eyes," he cried and hung his head; his hot tears fell onto her. "And you are right; I am dumb, I've always been dumb."

"I didn't mean that," Cecily said softly and touched his face; he jerked away from her hand.

"You unman me, Cecily. You may not love me," he said looking back into her eyes. "You may not want to be my wife, but your body wants mine." Levi pushed her to the floor, and Cecily cried out as he fell on top of her. "You gave to Bernard; you loved Bernard, you married me to save yourself from the humiliation of Bernard and what he had on you. I know you don't want me, but by God, you want this."

Cecily pushed on her husband as he pulled up the hem of her skirt and tore her underclothes. His tears were falling onto her face as he shoved himself inside of her and she screamed. Levi heard her scream and knew she had not been ready for him, he was hurting her, and he knew he should not be taking her this way, not in anger, but he couldn't stop himself. He had to put the fire that she made burn within him out before he let her go. And he had to let her go. He would never let her go; he thought as he fell on top of her, his cheek against her cheek where their tears met, where their pain became one.

Cecily heard her husband crying, his face was buried in her neck, and his tears were hot on her chest. She kept her eyes closed as he rolled off of her and then she rolled onto her side, still hearing him sob. She hadn't wanted him when he shoved himself into her, she hadn't been ready, and she ached in the worst way a woman could ever ache. He heard her words to Clemmie; she had said he was dumb, that was all he would ever hear, he was deaf to what her heart had been showing him for weeks. He would never hear her heart with all this anger inside of him; he was full of anger at her. And he had a right to his anger; she had shut him out, she had pushed him away. She knew as she lay here on the floor hurting that she had hurt him as badly as he had just hurt her. But why, why did he have to do this to her? This was unbearable.

Levi stood and stumbled before he fell against the knotty pine wall. He turned his face against the paneling. "God help me," he cried and couldn't look at what he had done to his wife. "Oh, God, please help me," he spoke as if in prayer. He had raped her; he had raped Cecily when all he had ever wanted to do was love her. He had just dishonored her and himself. He wasn't fit to love her, not now, not after what he had just done to her, not after the weeks he'd been mean to her

Cecily stayed still and listened to Levi cry, her own tears fell and washed her face. She had loved him for almost all of her life, she had wanted only him and because she had never told him how she felt she had brought them to this. She should have told him that she loved him. She should have looked into those dark blue eyes long ago and told him that she could never hate him as he had said she did, and she should have trusted him, not only with her heart but with the truth. She should have forced him to listen to her when she told him the truth. She should have screamed the truth in his face after he found those photos and then she should have pulled him into her bed and never let him out until he was certain of her love for him.

Levi leaned against the wall for a long time; he couldn't think anymore; all he could do was feel the heartache that had been tearing him apart for weeks now. The heartache was unbearable. His anger had hidden his hurt; his hurt was worse than any anger he had ever felt for Cecily. He looked down at her small on the floor where he had violated her, and the guilt of what he'd done to her almost took him to his knees. She cried softly, not hard as he was, she should have been the one crying hard; she was the one that had been hurt physically. And then he knew, his pain was as physical as hers. He had been trying to live with a broken heart for weeks now.

"Cecily," he finally bent toward her and said her name; she got on her hands and knees and tried to crawl away from him. Levi went after her and caught her around the waist. She kicked at him and shoved him, but Levi held on to her tight allowing her to hit him. "Don't hurt me again, Levi," she cried with each shove and push and kick she gave. "Don't hurt me again, Levi." When her fist was shoved into his left eye, and the pain was blinding, he still held on to her, she still hit him and kicked at him bruising him as he knew he had bruised her.

"I won't hurt you again," Levi cried as he finally got a firm hold on his wife and pulled her into his arms. "I won't hurt you anymore, Cecily. I swear," he pleaded with her to believe him.

Cecily fell against her husband and cried; she couldn't believe that she was hugging him tight. She should tell him everything right now, the time was right. "I made a mistake, Levi," Cecily sobbed, and Levi pulled her into his arms as he stood with her cradled against him.

"I know you did darlin'," he said as he carried her into their bedroom.

"No," Cecily whimpered. "Don't hurt me again, Levi," she cried, and Levi stood her on her feet realizing that she believed he meant to take her to bed.

"I won't," Levi said tenderly. "You need a bath. The water will help ease what I did to you."

Cecily stood still by the tub and watched Levi turn on the water. "I never thought of Bernard when I was with you. I never thought of Bernard when I was with you," her voice broke, and Levi turned her around.

"It doesn't matter right now, Cecily. Hush." He undid the buttons of her dress; glad that now she was not fighting him.

"I was wrong, Levi. I was so wrong," Cecily cried as Levi lifted her up and placed her gently into the tub full of warm water. "It was always you; it was always you."

"Be quiet, darlin'; everything will be all right." He said softly as he lathered up the washcloth with the soap and gently washed her body, a body he had just abused.

"I never meant to hurt you, Levi," she said when his eyes met hers.

"I know. It doesn't matter right now darlin', just be quiet and rest." Cecily closed her mouth and fought not to cry. They would talk later. Levi wasn't mad at her right now. He was being tender; he was being kind.

Levi reached down and carefully took her into his arms, heedless of the fact that he was getting soaking wet. He dried her off with a towel before he helped her into her nightgown. He noticed she was quiet now; he had broken her, he should have never have broken her. No matter what she had done to him, she did not deserve what he had just done to her on the parlor floor; no woman deserved to be raped.

Cecily stood still in the middle of the room and watched Levi as he changed his pants and threw his wet shirt onto the floor. He came back to her when he was dry and picked her and carried her to their bed. She watched him go and pick up her hairbrush and climb onto the bed behind her pulling her up and back against him he started to brush her hair. "I won't hurt you again, I swear," he said softly as he brushed her hair five hundred strokes. She was still and quiet against him, and he put his mouth on her ear as he use to do and felt her turn her head for more. Even after what he had done to her, he knew he could still seduce her. "I'm sorry Cecily, I'm so sorry," he said against her ear, the brush held in his hand and on her stomach.

"I have to tell you, Levi. I should have told you long ago."

"Hush, darlin', hush," Levi interrupted her. He knew that she wanted to tell him that she didn't love him, that she wanted to be free of him. He was going to set her free.

"I have to talk to you," Cecily said in a pleading voice.

"Never," Levi said and held her closer. He would keep her tonight, he would hold her in his arms all night, and then he would do what he should have done weeks ago. He was going to give her a divorce and let her be free.

Levi wouldn't listen to her, Cecily thought. He would never listen to her. They would have no marriage; they would have no life together unless he heard the truth and the only way that he would hear the truth was if she forced it onto him.

"Can't you believe anything I might say to you?" Cecily asked. "Can't you hear my heart?"

"You lied to me, Cecily. You hurt me, and I hurt you worse. You never trusted me; you never will trust me now, not after what I did today. And I don't blame you. I can't take your words, Cecily. I can't take your words. Let's go to sleep now." He buried his face in her hair; she was leaning against him as he was leaning against the pillows. He wished that she could see that she didn't have to ask him for a divorce; he was going to let her have one, he was going to set her free. She didn't have to tell him that she hated him; he knew that she hated him; he hated himself more. And her mistake, he could not hear that her mistake was in marrying him, he knew already.

Levi closed his eyes when he heard her even breathing and tried to go to sleep himself. He lay there holding his beautiful wife, wracked with pain and sorry for the injury that he had done to her today. He never should have raped her. Everything he had done since finding those photos had been wrong.

She was running, her hair was down the way Levi liked it, and she was running. She looked back over her shoulder and saw him running after her, he was almost to her when she stopped and laughed, and he caught her and laughed with her. He was the old Levi, looking down at her with that easy smile of his and then his head bent, and he covered her mouth with his. The kiss was heaven, and she moaned deep and long before he let her go. She laughed again and turned to run, he tried to catch her, but she ran free with him laughing behind her. She was safe and home in his arms as he caught her again. "I love you, Levi," she said in her dream and heard him say, "I love you, Cecily." She didn't wake up from the dream for a long time.

Levi was up with the dawn, he had slept, but not much. Cecily lay still on the bed; she had not moved throughout the night. Levi went to the strong arm box and opened it with the key he had hidden in his drawer. Inside were the photos of Cecily that Bernard had taken and his mother's rings. He had found the rings in the box that Bernard had thrown at him that day that he had lost all of his dreams. He knew that Cecily would never wear those rings again. Not now, not after what he had done to her yesterday. He had lost any hope of his dreams, Levi thought, and yesterday he saw that those dreams died a sure and certain death and could never be reborn. He reached down into the box and picked up one of the photo postcards of his wife without her clothes on and put it into his wallet. He turned back and looked at Cecily, small on the bed. He hoped that when she woke she would not hurt from what he had done to her. He didn't know how he was going to live with himself. Yesterday he had been a monster to his small wife that hadn't deserved that.

"You'll be a good man, just like your father," Levi heard his mother's words from long ago when he had been a boy. Lilly Tucker would be ashamed of her son if she knew what he had done to his wife. He was ashamed of himself, and his shame was deep.

Levi stood over Cecily and thought about how much he loved her, enough to have put aside the fact that she had been intimate with Bernard before she had even accepted his proposal of marriage, he loved her enough to forgive her anything. And then he realized that he had forgiven her nothing. He remembered her terrified look yesterday, the fear in her eyes now made him sick as he stood and remembered that fear and knew he had put it in those crystal clear eyes. He was not a good man; he did not deserve Cecily or her love if she had given it to him. She had said that she was his hell, only because he had made her his hell. He could have stood beside her when he found those photos. He had the choice to forgive her and try to make their marriage good despite whatever reason she may have had for marrying him. He could have tried to help her learn to love him.

Levi looked away from his wife on the bed, his eyes staring out into the distance by seeing nothing. He had committed an unforgivable, unpardonable act yesterday against Cecily. What he had done had been a sin and a crime against her and himself. And why had he done that to her? He asked himself in anguish. He had cried for what he had done to her; he had begged God to help him. God would not help him for having hurt Cecily. God would no more forgive him for what he had done to his wife then he would ever forgive himself. And now, today he knew, he would have to live out the rest of his life living with what he'd done. He would hate himself for all time, even in eternity; he would never forgive himself for what he had done to his Cecily. No, she wasn't his, she never had been. She had been meant to be his heaven; instead, he had taken her to hell.

"Ollie," Levi said his maid's name as he entered the kitchen. "I have to go to Madison for the day." He didn't have to go anywhere; he wanted to go, he wanted to put money in Cecily's bank account, enough money for her to live free of him on when she chose to leave him, be it today or the next day or whenever she felt up to going away from him. She would never want for anything; he would see to that. He would make up to her in any way that he could for the hurt that he had caused her. His money would be a start.

Levi saw Ollie's head nod, but she said nothing to him. "Take care of Cecily for me," he said before going out the door. Ollie said nothing to him, only stared at his black eye and wondered if Cecily had given it to him.

Levi left his home, taking his guilt and shame and the horror of what he had done with him. He had too much guilt to carry and enough shame for ten men. His regret was endless.

Cecily woke from her dream calling out for Levi; he wasn't in the room. Levi had put her to bed before dark last night, and she'd slept for more than fifteen hours, but she still didn't feel rested. Her eyes were swollen, and when she looked in the mirror, she found them red and puffy. She dressed slowly and left the room going to the kitchen and hoping that Levi had gone to his sawmill, she didn't think she could face him right now. The kitchen was empty; Ollie wasn't here. After walking through the whole house, stopping at the parlor and staring at the floor for a long few minutes, she knew that she was alone in the house.

A knock sounded at the front door, and Cecily went and opened the portal to the outside world. What she saw beyond that door made her fall back into the house and gasped out loud.

"Hello, Cecily," Bernard Calhoun smiled at her and Cecily covered her heart with her hand, thinking that she could not deal with this, not after what Levi had put her through yesterday. "I heard Levi tell the Reverend Bidwell that he was on his way to Madison for the day, so I knew you would be alone."

"What do you want?" Cecily asked and took a deep breath while standing firm. Bernard could not hurt her anymore. Levi had seen to that. Levi had saved her from Bernard. Levi, she thought of her husband and felt like crying.

"I just came by to ask you how your marriage was," Bernard smiled even more, and Cecily narrowed her eyes while she stood still and looked at him.

"My marriage and my life is no concern of yours. Go away," Because of this man her life was a shambles. She hated Bernard; she would always hate Bernard for what he had caused Levi to believe of her.

"I wanted to tell you what I told Levi," Bernard took a step toward her, but Cecily did not move. She refused to be afraid of him anymore. She had been ruled by her fear for too long; she would never let fear control her like it had, not ever again.

"I don't care what you told anyone, Bernard. I want you to leave, I want you to leave me alone forever, and Levi too." Cecily stood up straight and stared Bernard in the eyes. When he made no move to leave her, Cecily tried to close the door in his face. Bernard held the door open, and her strength did not match him, she could not close the door.

"Did you know that Levi can't stand to be told he's dumb?" Bernard asked, and Cecily looked at the floor remembering Levi's reaction when she had used that word in reference to him, but not in the way he had taken her use of that word. She wasn't about to tell Bernard what she knew or didn't know. "I told Levi you said that living with him was like living with a big dumb ox." Bernard laughed when Cecily gasped. "That got to him. You should have seen his face when I told him that you couldn't stand his touch."

"Why?" Cecily whispered, and Bernard laughed.

"You always thought you were too good for me. And Levi, just because he has money and his daddy was a damn Yankee, he thinks he's somebody special. He isn't anything. He can't even learn to read." Bernard gave Cecily one of his cruel smiles; it was an even uglier smile with his nose ruined like it was. "I also told your husband that you could teach him a few things in bed, does he know yet that I lied to him about that too?" At Cecily's stricken face

Bernard gave a shout of laughter. "He really is a big dumb ox. He thinks that you posed willingly for those photos; that you were in love with me. Poor bastard believed everything I said to him."

One moment Cecily was standing in the hall staring in total horror at Bernard, then the next moment she was screaming her head off and running at Bernard, he wasn't laughing at her when she flew into him. Cecily hit Bernard; she kicked him, she caught him so unaware that she had the advantage over him. And when her knee hit his most sensitive spot, he fell to the floor of the porch and screamed in agony. She was glad he was in agony.

"I hate you!" Cecily screamed as she kicked Bernard in the stomach. "You should have killed me and been done with me. I should have killed you." She fell down to her knees and bit him so hard on the arm that his blood was on her mouth when she got back up and kicked him again. "I should have killed you! I wish that I had killed you!" Her small foot flew into Bernard's face, and blood squirted from his nose. "I hate you!" she screamed again.

"Mrs. Tucker," Preston, the young stable man that Levi had watching Cecily ran up onto the porch and grabbed her from behind by the arms, but that didn't stop her from trying to kick Bernard again.

"You filthy scum," Cecily screamed at Bernard as he tried to stand.

Bernard looked at Cecily as he covered his face and felt blood on his hand. Cecily was red in the face with her anger and hatred of him. He had never seen Cecily look so strong before. But she couldn't do anything more to him; a young man held her tight from behind. "I think I won our game, Cecily. I taught you for looking down on me. Good luck in your marriage." Bernard turned with his blood covered face and hand and left the porch.

Cecily pulled free of Preston, tears bright in her eyes; the tears did not fall. "Levi! Levi!! Levi, I need you!" she screamed her husband's name over and over, but he did not come to her.

"Mrs. Tucker," Preston touched her arm, but she shoved him away before running into the house and slamming the door.

Cecily leaned against the door and let her tears fall. Bernard had explained Levi's anger to Cecily. She had refused her husband's right to their marriage bed, she had turned him away, and Bernard had told him that she couldn't stand his touch. If she had been in Levi's place, she would have thought the worst of her as he did. She had denied her husband everything. She had shut him out of her life, just as he had said yesterday. Levi had given her everything, she had given him nothing in return but her silence, and he kept her silent. She pushed him away; she had even told him she didn't want his child. She had driven Levi to hurt her; she had driven him to hate her and now himself. She came into this marriage with silence, with secrets and caused her innocent, loving, handsome husband pain and now it was too late to make anything right. Levi had used his body as a weapon against her body and in anger. He had invaded her with pain, a pain that she still felt. And he had said that he would never let her talk. He would go on believing Bernard's words and never hear the truth from her. Bernard's lies had wrecked her marriage. Because of Bernard, she and Levi were doomed, they had been from the start.

"Miss Cecily," Ollie appeared out of nowhere and grabbed her hand pulling her into the kitchen pantry and closing the door.

Ollie, what are you doing?" Cecily asked the maid within the darkness of the pantry. For a long few moments, Ollie held tight to her hand, and they stood in the stillness.

"I've been to see Miss Clemmie and Mister Grant. They think they can get you out of her and someplace safe. Do you want to leave, Miss Cecily?" Cecily gasped and covered her mouth with her hand.

"Leave Levi?" she asked in disbelief. "I have nowhere to go, Ollie." Levi would never let her go, she thought. He had to punish her for what he believed she had done to him; he had to hurt her for Bernard's lies of her.

"If you had a safe place to go where Mister Levi can't find you, would you leave here then?" Ollie all but begged to know of Cecily.

Cecily stood silent for a long time, lost in her thoughts. She could not make Levi see that she loved him. He could not feel the truth within her. And he would not let her tell him the truth. They were hurting one another; they had been for a long time. The hurt had to end; she couldn't take this life she was living anymore. Lies and half told truths kept a wall built solid around both she and Levi, neither of them could reach the other. And yesterday. She closed her eyes tight in the darkness as she remembered what Levi had done to her yesterday. She may have driven him to hate her, she may have driven him to anger, but he had no right to do what he had done to her yesterday.

Cecily didn't want to leave her husband in spite of everything that had happened between them. She wanted to stay and make everything right. But in her heart, she knew that Levi would never let her make anything that she had done wrong to him right. Not now. He hated her; he hated himself. She wanted her old Levi back, she wanted his love and his concern, but the old Levi was gone. Thanks to Bernard Calhoun and that man's lies, she had lost her good and tender husband. She would never have her Levi back, and she knew that their marriage had to come to an end. She could end their marriage right now. Levi's pain would be over the moment she left him, and he would smile again, he would be all right again like he was before he married her.

"Do you want to go?" Ollie asked more u urgently, and Cecily opened her eyes..

"Yes," she said more firmly than she had thought she could. "Yes, Ollie, I want to go. I have too. But how? The stableman watches my every move. "

"Don't worry about that; it's all planned. Just be ready to run when I say run."

"But what about Levi?" Cecily asked with her heart pounding in her ears. She loved Levi; she didn't want to leave him. If she left, she might never see him again. He would be lost to her forever. She caught her breath and a sob.

"He's gone to Madison," Ollie said, and Cecily remembered Bernard having said something about that to her earlier.

"How much time do I have left?" she asked with her voice filled with both fear and shock that she was prepared to run away from Levi. He had been the only man that she had ever wanted. She was leaving him so she couldn't hurt him anymore. She had hurt him far too much, as much as he hurt her. She didn't want her Levi to hurt anymore.

"About one hour," Ollie answered and opened the pantry door.

"I better go pack some things," Cecily said and started to hurry from the kitchen. Ollie grabbed her hand.

"No, don't." Ollie held Cecily's eyes with her own. Ollie could see that Cecily didn't really want to go. Ollie could see that Cecily loved Levi in those clear eyes. The love that they had wasn't a good love; they had done nothing but hurt one another. Cecily had to leave. Levi would realize that he had lost her, he would change, and Ollie would tell him where to find Cecily, and they could make things right and find happiness. "You'll get new things where you're going, Miss Cecily. Just be prepared to run when I saw.

Cecily nodded her head. She did not ask Ollie where she was going. She didn't care. All she could feel was the pain around her heart that she was leaving Levi and probably for the rest of her life. Once she was gone, he would not take her back, even if she chose to come back to him. This was the end of her marriage to Levi, she had killed his love for her and lost him; she had nothing left. There was nothing left for her to do but run away from him and not look back.

Cecily left the kitchen and went to her bedroom. She had less than an hour left; she thought as she tore everything out of Levi's drawers and threw his things onto the floor. Her hands shook in her search, but she knew that the key was here, the key had to be here. The strong arm box was on the dresser before her, locked up tight, if she had too, she would take the box with her when she ran. She could not leave it for Levi; he may use what was in that box to hurt her. He had hurt her enough, what was in that box had destroyed all her happiness, had put her father in the grave, she wouldn't leave it behind.

The key was sent by God as a sign that she was doing the right thing, Cecily thought as the key fell out of a handkerchief and right into the palm of her hand. She let out the deep breath that she had been holding and hurriedly opened the box. All the photos of her were there; she knew that the plates had been destroyed; Levi had broken them in front of her. She lit a match and put that match to the pictures in the empty fireplace and watched as her shame went up the chimney in red flying flames. That was over; she thought as she stood before the dying fire. She was finally safe from both Bernard and from Levi. Those photos would haunt her no more.

Cecily went back to the strong arm box to lock it up again and saw her rings. All of this time Levi had had her rings, and he had not given them back to her. Because he did not want her as his wife, she thought and hung her head in sorrow of what they had lost. In the next instant, Cecily snatched up the rings and put them on her finger; they were hers, Levi had given them to her. She knew that Levi would be furious with her for taking them, but she didn't care. Levi would be mad at her whether she took these rings or not. Her heart jumped in her chest as she thought that maybe Levi would see that she really did want to be his wife by her having taken the rings. Maybe he would see that she did not want to be his wife in fury and pain, but his wife in love and truth. He would search for her, and when he found her, she prayed that he would no longer be mad and would listen to her words and to her heart.

"Fire!" someone cried out from the yard, and Ollie rushed into the room where Cecily stood.

"Time to go, Miss Cecily," Ollie said and grabbed her hand pulling her into the kitchen and out onto the porch. "Run to your pa's old house and be quick. Mister Grant and Miss Clemmie are there waiting for you with a horse." Cecily turned and hugged Ollie quick.

"Thank you for everything that you've done for me, Ollie. And take care of Levi for me, please. Take care of Levi for me." Ollie pushed her away.

"Run child. I don't know how much time we have." Cecily turned and ran for the woods that led to her father's house. Ollie's heart was pounding the word, *go go go* as Cecily disappeared into the trees.

Cecily mounted the horse that Grant held ready for her and kicked hard. She didn't know where she was going or what her future may hold, but she knew that she was safe from the past. "I burned the photos," she said to Grant and Clemmie. "They're all gone. Levi can't hurt me anymore."

Grant swore low and furious. He would kill Levi when he saw him; Levi had been using those photos against Cecily just as Bernard had used them.

"I won't hurt Levi anymore either," Cecily said, and Grant looked at her face. She was pale, tears covered her cheeks, and she stared straight ahead. "I'm leaving my heart with Levi," she grieved. "I hurt him so badly. I'm so sorry I hurt him." Neither Grant nor Clemmie said anything to her; they didn't know what to say. They both believed it was Levi hurting Cecily.

Chapter Eight

"Mr. Tucker," Preston called out Levi's name, and Levi stopped in the yard to see what the stableman wanted of him. "We had a brush fire down at the sawmill today, sir. It wasn't much, and we put it out pretty quick. There was no damage to the mill."

"That's good, Preston," Levi said and started to move toward the house. He had thought all the way to Madison and back about what he was going to do about Cecily. The first thing he was going to do was go to her and beg her to forgive him for what he had done to her, for all that he had done to her. And then he was going to tell her that he did not want to live without her and that he would spend the rest of his life making up to her for all the hurt that he had caused her. He felt sick that he had raped her, that he had violated her body with his own. Of everything that he had done to her these past weeks, that had been the worst. He had a lot to atone for.

"There is a problem, sir," Preston said from beside him, and Levi stopped walking and took a deep breath prepared to give Preston his full attention for the moment. "While we were fighting the fire, your wife ran away." Levi's mouth fell open from shock of Preston's words.

"She's gone," Ollie said from the porch, and both Preston and Levi turned toward her.

"We were only gone for a few moments, Mr. Tucker," Preston continued while Levi stared at Ollie.

"Where is she?" Levi demanded to know, Ollie only shook her head at him.

"She's safe," Ollie said with her head held high.

"That's not all sir," Preston said, and Levi wondered what more could have gone wrong with the day while he was gone. "There was a man here earlier today, a man with a crooked smashed nose."

"Bernard Calhoun," Levi said and went pale. Cecily couldn't have run off with Bernard; the man had blackmailed her for two years. Surely she wouldn't leave him for Bernard, he reasoned and then knew, Bernard hadn't raped her on the parlor floor.

"I don't know who the man was," Preston continued. "But your wife attacked him, sir. She kicked him in a place where no man would want to be kicked." Preston blushed and looked away from Levi for a full second. "Well, once the man was down, Mrs. Tucker beat him up, she was wild. I had to pull her off of him."

"Why did you pull her off of him?" Levi asked in amazement that his tiny wife would hit anyone, but then he remembered her hitting him yesterday and he had the black eye to prove it.

"She was hurting him, sir," Preston answered simply.

"I wish she had killed him," Levi said to Preston, then turned back to Ollie. "Where is she Ollie?" he asked in a calm tone.

"You ain't gonna find her, Mister Levi. Not until-."

"You're fired, Ollie," Levi interrupted his maid. "Get off my place now." Ollie looked shocked for a few seconds, then she pulled herself together and nodded her head.

"Fine by me," she said and turned to go down the porch steps at the back of the house. She had lived here all her life, she was getting old now, but she had no regret for what she had done. She had done the right good thing. And there were plenty of people that wanted her; she was the best cook in the state. She would find another job.

Levi hadn't meant for Ollie to take his words seriously. He had thought for sure that she would tell him where to find Cecily before she ever left him. She had been with his mother all her life; she had helped raise him; he loved Ollie. Levi stood in total shock as he watched Ollie leave him. She would be back, he thought. And she would tell him where Cecily was. Ollie could never leave him for good.

"Where have you looked for my wife?" Levi asked, turning back to Preston. He knew that Cecily couldn't have gone far; she had nowhere to go but back to her father's house.

"I went to her father's place sir; there's no one there. I left Jacob at the house to keep an eye out in case she showed up.

"Have you been to Grant's house?" That was where Cecily was; he felt certain.

"Mrs. Whittaker offered me a glass of tea while I searched the whole place. She even took me up into the attic. Mrs. Tucker wasn't there either. I looked everywhere after that. The Reverend Bidwell hasn't seen her; no one in town has seen her. She just disappeared.

"Well, keep looking," Levi said and went into the house. Cecily would be back, she wouldn't leave Cherry Lake forever, this was her home, and everyone she knew was here. He went into their bedroom and found the mess on the floor, clothes were thrown everywhere, and the strong arm box sat on the dresser, the key was on top of it. Levi went to the box and opened it up; the photos were gone. He reached into his back pocket and pulled out his wallet; he still had the one photo of his lying wife.

"You deceived me, Cecily," he whispered. "You never meant to give me any kind of a chance." He sat down on the edge of the bed and put his face into his hands. Once he had been full of dreams and hopes and happiness for his future. Cecily had taken all of that and more away from him, and now she was gone and he didn't know where she was. She was gone and with a ten thousand dollar set of wedding rings and his damned heart.

Cecily sat on the train headed west and looked out the window at the world going by. She was going away, away from Levi, far away from Cherry Lake and home. She would probably never go back to see Levi again. Levi. She saw her husband's face as he looked down at her hand touching his in the churchyard all those weeks ago, the day that she had fallen in his lap. How happy he had been, and she brought him down when she married him. She closed her eyes tight and saw him kissing her, remembered his touch and how gentle he had been with her until yesterday. She saw him hitting Bernard and breaking Bernard's nose in defense of her. She saw him at the graveyard with her, concern on his face, concern for her, how loving and gentle he had been with her, and she was betraying him and his love.

She remembered their childhood, Levi almost a man, her not quite a woman, he was chasing her down the road, she was looking back at him, her hair loose and flying behind her and around her face. She saw him throwing the garden snake he was chasing after with on the ground, the look in his eyes as he came up to her, the way he looked at her was like it was the first time he had ever seen her. He pushed her long hair away from her face and said in his calm, cool way, "Hey you." She had loved him then in her girlhood with a crush, and she never stopped loving him as a man. Even now, going away from him forever, she loved him. He had held her face within his hands with tenderness and care. He had loved her. She had betrayed him.

Cherry Lake faded fast in the distance, she had left him, Cecily knew, left and no going back, this he would never forgive her for. She touched her chest and knew her heart was not making this journey with her; her heart was at home, would always be at home, with Levi. She felt like Levi really had owned her body and her soul. She could almost feel his arms around her, strong and protective and loving.

Cecily bowed her head and saw in her mind's eye Levi's face filled with anger, anger at her as he had shattered those plates at her feet. She remembered the look of raw pain in his eyes when she had said yes, that she had only married him for his money. She had trampled all over his heart, and he hated her. Now he would always hate her.

"Are you all right?" a young man across from Cecily asked her. She looked up at the man and tried to nod her head. She couldn't. Her eyes were filled with the image of Levi's tear-covered face as it had been yesterday when he had believed that she didn't like him when he heard her tell Clemmie that she didn't like him. And Bernard's lies to him had seemed all too real because Cecily had kept him away before he found those pictures. "Here, take this," the young man across from her held out a handkerchief, Cecily only stared at the handkerchief, he forced it into her hands.

She had not realized that she was crying until the tears fell onto the handkerchief that she now held in her lap. Cecily covered her face and sobbed, the linen square she pressed to her face was soaked in tears. God had dropped her into the lap of the answer to her prayers, a savior; if only she had done everything differently, she could have spent a lifetime with Levi. But it was too late now. She was going away from her husband forever. There was a forever, after all, Cecily thought. Forever was having to live without Levi. Forever was leaving Levi.

"Still water runs deep, that's what I say," Jamie Liston said to Grant. "And Levi has always been still water."

"Laid back and easy going, is what I thought," John Hyde added. "So he fired you, Jamie?"

"He put everyone off the place. Even Ollie," Jamie said. "I've know Levi my whole life, and I've never seen him like he was today. Ya'll know how quiet he's always been, and always smiling, and nothing was a big deal. Well, he wasn't quiet today, and everything was a problem. He was tearing the sawmill down and screaming at everybody to get out. He had some of the men afraid of him. And I always thought that he was overly sensitive and tender heart, he wasn't today. Ya'll remember that baby bird we found that time and Levi took it home and tried to save it. He cried when the bird died for hours."

"My God, Jamie," Grant said. "We were all of maybe six years old then. What are you fellows drinking?"

"Some of my daddy's corn liquor," John Hyde said and held up a jug for Grant to see.

Grant had been passing by the lake when he had seen Jamie and Jon sitting under an old oak tree that they had all climbed in when they were boys. Jamie had called for Grant to stop and visit and he had, he never imagined they were both drunk, it was the middle of the day.

"I heard that Ollie took a job with the Prichard's this morning and left for Jacksonville. Levi went and asked her to come back to him, she told him the only way that she would ever come back to him was if Cecily came home," Jon said before taking a sip from his jug.

"You know, everybody always said that Levi was too good, a giving, caring compassionate man." Jamie took the jug from Jon while he spoke. "Lord, if ya'll had seen Levi today, ya'll wouldn't be saying those things about him. He called me stupid and I ain't the one that can't read. He also said that I was lazy because I needed half the county to put out a little brush fire. I burned my hand putting that fire out." Jamie took another sip from the jug. "And the word is that Cecily left Levi because he beat her."

"You two had better stop drinking," Grant advised as he stood to leave.

"I think Levi was drunk today," Jamie said and passed the jug back to Jon. "I ain't never seen Levi drunk, he's seen me drunk, but I ain't never seen him drunk. Nicest fellow you ever wanted to meet or know, but something happened to him, and he got mad." Jamie leaned against the tree.

"And they say that he beat poor Cecily," Jon said shaking his head.

"Levi didn't beat Cecily," Grant said and hoped that his words were true, but he couldn't be sure. "You two shouldn't be drinking like this. Folks will stop talking about Levi and start talking about ya'll."

"People ain't gonna quit talking about Levi no time soon," Jamie said and gave a loud burp. "He's a scandal now that Cecily has left him."

Grant turned and mounted his horse. "Still water runs deep," he heard Jamie say again as he started for home.

"Tell me where she is Clemmie," Levi stood on Clemmie's porch, she stood still in the doorway and wondered if Levi would hurt her if she didn't tell him what he wanted to know. He looked furious, and he looked drunk. She wished that Grant were home, for the first time she was afraid of Levi. "Go away, Levi," Clemmie said, and he shook his head. "She's safe and where you won't find her." Clemmie looked into Levi's eyes, eyes that she had looked into all her life, he had been one of her dearest friends, there had always been laughter and happiness for anyone to easily see. She could remember when she and Cecily were sixteen he and Grant would run after them, and she could see how Cecily smiled and hear her laughter, Cecily had been in love with Levi even back then, and he would catch Cecily and turn her around in his arms, his laughter was one with Cecily's. They had all been so close, more than friends, more than family. And now that was all gone, and the look in Levi's eyes was one she never dreamed she would see. His eyes were not kind today; they were red and swollen and too bright from drinking. "You can't hurt Cecily anymore, Levi. Just go home. She's not here, I swear."

"I just did to her what she did to me," Levi said in a choked voice.

"Cecily was never mean to you," Clemmie stepped forward and put her finger in his face. "You insulted her, you tore her down, you took her away from her friends, you held her prisoner in your home, and only you and she know what else you did to her. And why? Because of Bernard?"

"Don't say that man's name to me," Levi grabbed Clemmie's finger and she pulled it from his tight grasp. "And Cecily did do me wrong."

"Because she married you for security?" Clemmie nearly shouted this question at him. "That's what we women have to do, Levi. It's what your own mother did. Cecily was in trouble, she needed help, I knew that, and I think you knew that too. Remember how it was just a few years ago, us always together, Cecily laughing and us running around the lake and down these roads, how we use to horseback ride and race, and you always let Cecily win. Then she stopped playing with us; she stopped leaving home? Don't you remember? I think we all saw the fear, but we put it off as grief when her father died. If we had only known what was happening to her, we could have helped her."

"You don't know what she did to me, Clemmie. She never gave me a chance."

"No, Levi, I'm sure she didn't. She was too afraid. I never would have dreamed that she would have to be afraid of you too." Clemmie's voice was filled with disappointment. "When she left you, she told Grant and me that she had destroyed those horrible photos and you couldn't hurt her now." She saw Levi turn pale and fall back on the step. The look on his face made her grab a hold of him. "Are you all right, Levi?" she saw his head nod.

"I never would have used those photos to hurt Cecily." The way he said these words made Clemmie believe him.

"Well, you gave Cecily reason to believe that you would," Grant spoke from the yard behind Levi and Levi turned around. Grant had never seen Levi look as haggard as he did now.

"I was mad, Grant. How would you feel if you married Clemmie thinking that she loved you and then found out that she didn't love you."

"I wouldn't have locked her inside my home and have treated her bad as you did our Cecily," Grant answered. "Ollie told us some of what you said to Cecily."

He had just wanted to get even with her for having lied to him, Levi thought and then knew, it was because she believed him to be a big dumb ox. He did feel bad for the things he had said, he regretted them as soon as they were out of his mouth and he wished now he could take every word back. "She's my wife, Grant. I want to know where she is, please."

"Why? So you can tear her apart one piece at a time? You've done enough to that poor girl; you won't do one thing more, not while we have her safe from you." Grant stepped closer to Levi. "I've known you all my life, Levi. I thought I was your best friend. I never, not once ever have seen you hurt anyone or anything with the intentions to do so unless it was in the schoolyard and some kid was picking on you about being dumb because of your issue with reading." Grant saw Levi's eyes look up and into his, the pained look in his eyes caused Grant for a moment, think that Cecily had told Levi he was dumb because he couldn't read. "Levi," he said his friend's name and Levi hung his head. Dear God, Grant thought, Cecily was so loving and gentle and kind, he couldn't imagine her being that cruel and never to Levi, Cecily had always loved Levi best of everyone in their little group. "No matter what she did to you Levi, you've been wrong and done wrong by her. She's better off without you, and you're better off without her. You won't find out where she is by coming here. I want you to leave and not come back.

"She didn't want me," Levi said in a broken voice. "I married her, I loved her, I trusted her, and she didn't want me." He stepped up to Grant. "I know I've done her wrong, I know that I hurt her," he thought of the last day with her and flinched both inwardly and outwardly. "But I never lied to her, and that's all she ever did to me. Right from the start."

"Then you should be glad to be rid of her," Grant faced Levi. "I'm sorry that you're hurt, Levi. I know you've always wanted Cecily and maybe if she hadn't been scared out of her mind, she would have made you a good wife. But she left you, and it's over. It's over Levi."

"What do I do?" Levi asked, his eyes red from more than the liquor he had drank. "Wait for her to divorce me?" He didn't let Grant answer his question, he turned and threw a bank book at Clemmie, "See Cecily gets that, she'll never want for anything all her life," he said before he got onto his horse, kicked the animal hard and tore off of Grant's land at breakneck speed.

"Good Lord," Grant said when Clemmie came to stand in the yard beside him, and they watched Levi disappear in the distance. "I think Cecily told Levi he was dumb."

"No, that's not the problem, Grant. He's mad as fire because Cecily married him for his money. She had to pay Bernard, and she had no money to do that with. Her father had paid everything they had to Bernard before he died." She looked up at her husband as he put his arm around her.

"So that's why he was so mad. Poor Levi. I thought it might have been something else," Grant took a deep breath glad that Cecily hadn't called Levi dumb.

"Poor Levi?" Clemmie asked in amazement. "Have you forgotten that he tortured Cecily?"

"No," Grant said, and he pulled his wife close. "I know Levi; he's always felt dumb because he can't read. And all Cecily wanted from him was his money, she made him feel like he was dumb for loving her."

"The only thing Levi Tucker was dumb about was hurting Cecily," Clemmie said and shook her head, feeling sorry for Cecily and for Levi before she opened the bank book, gasped and fell against Grant. "Oh heavens," she breathed looking at the bank account Levi had opened for Cecily in Madison.

"One hundred thousand dollars," Grant almost whistled. "If Cecily married him for his money, she just got it."

"Why would he do this?" Clemmie asked.

"I don't know. But it's really sad the two of them ended this way," Grant said to his wife. "It started out as money, and it ended as money. A crying shame."

Levi rode home to his empty and lonely house. He knew that he had been out for revenge; that's what he did to Cecily; he got his revenge on her for having hurt him. He should have let her go right from the start; he had no right to keep her knowing that she didn't want to be his wife, that she had only wanted his money to hide what she had allowed Bernard to do with a camera to her. He saw her face before him when he closed his eyes, those large crystal clear blue eyes of hers, filled with fear and tears and yesterday he had added pain. He had forced her to stay with him when he knew in his heart that he should have let her go. If only he could go back and do everything again. He would have let her go.

No, he had to be honest with himself; he would never have let Cecily go. He had wanted her too badly. He remembered the day at the lake when the weeds got tangled around her legs and they were pulling her under, She had been on the verge of drowning and he'd swam out fast and grabbed her, it had been in a battle with those weeds, a battle he meant to win and he had pulled her to shore with the roots of those weeds wrapped around her leg. They had not won, the lake had not taken her from him, he wanted nothing to take her away from him.

He thought of Bernard. How could Cecily have ever loved that man? He was rotten to the core, and in the end, he showed how evil he was by taking photos of Cecily that she had posed for with love in her heart for Bernard and used them against her. Before Bernard had come into her life, Cecily had appeared to be sweet on Levi; he remembered all the boxed lunches of hers that he bought at the church social and how she had eaten with him and laughed, and they were happy together. Bernard had changed Cecily, he had broken her heart by leaving her and moving to Madison, and she never looked at Levi the way she had looked at him before.

She was a part of his very soul. He had wanted her, and he had kept her knowing full well that he had no right to her. Levi went inside the house thinking this and fell back onto his bed, staring at the ceiling. He would not look for her anymore. She was safe from him now. His only regret was that she would never care for him, that she had not loved him or trusted him or given him a chance to make her happy. But then he knew, he had done nothing to even try and make her happy, he had been too hell-bent on getting revenge for the wrong she had done him. He was dumb, he knew now without doubt. He had been dumb all his life; he couldn't even learn to read.

The house was filled with silence. He had sent Ollie away, and she wouldn't come back to him. He had closed down the sawmill; he didn't need it, he could earn plenty of money from his horses. He knew that he could live a lifetime on the interest he had earned on the money he had in the bank. There was no one to provide for; there would never be anyone to provide for now. He was alone, and he would stay alone forever. He would have no wife; there would be no children, this house would not know laughter again in his lifetime, he had no future. There was nothing left of him that made life worth living, nothing but his money. Money had been what had brought him to this sorry state. He didn't need more money.

Levi felt like he didn't know himself anymore because of Cecily. He would have given her everything; he would have laid the world at her feet had she loved him. But she hadn't loved him, and she hadn't wanted his world. He had forced her into his bed; he moaned out loud and fought not to cry over what he had done to her. He had done everything that he knew to do to make her body want him. But that wasn't love; desire wasn't love.

Dear God, he had shamed her, and in doing so, he had shamed himself far more. He had dishonored himself by keeping her; he had shown her neither love nor honor by forcing her to stay with him, a prisoner in his home. And then he had raped her, taken her body against her will, forced himself on her in the cruelest act known to mankind. It would take him ten lifetimes to forgive himself for that. No, he thought, he would never forgive himself for raping Cecily. Not ever.

Levi had been living in a fool's world. He knew the truth now. Cecily hated him, she did not want to be his wife, and she never had wanted to be his wife. And he hated himself and her for making him turn on her with his anger. She was gone now, and that was for the best. He had been killing her slowly, and she had been killing him too. He had to find some way to live with himself. He had to.

All Levi wanted right now and forevermore was to be alone. He had cost himself the only thing in the world that had ever mattered to him. He was alone.

Chapter Nine

January 1898
Thomasville, Georgia

Cecily walked slowly up the stairs of Louise Crandle's home; she felt tired and wished that Louise was not forcing her to take a walk outside even if it was a beautiful winter day. But she knew, she needed to be out, the fresh air did both her and Louise good, and she was starting to feel strong again. The moment she had arrived here months ago, Cecily had felt awful, her heart had broken, she had thought she would never smile or know joy again, and frankly, she didn't know joy yet, and she was still struggling to smile. Every day she thought of him, she thought of Levi, her husband.

  Cecily entered Louise's bedroom and looked for the older woman's shawl, she had her own shawl downstairs already, but Louise had forgotten to bring one down earlier. Her eyes searched the room, and she smiled when she found what she sought on the floor near the vanity. Cecily reached down and picked up the shawl, then turned to leave the room, but not before her eyes fell onto the envelope with the familiar bold handwriting that was on the vanity. Clemmie, she thought as she turned back to the letter. She almost felt like she might cry, she had written Clemmie months ago and told her best friend not to write her anymore for a while. She needed time to adjust to her new life and hearing from Clemmie had only made Cecily think of Levi. Cecily thought of Levi every single day anyway.

When she first arrived at Louise Crandle's home, she had been a wreck. She missed her home, her friends and most of all she missed and mourned the loss of Levi. She had wished that she could write him a letter and explain everything in great detail like Clemmie had done with Grant before her dear friend had sliced her wrist open. But Levi couldn't read her words any more than he would allow her to have spoken them. Anything that Cecily might have put to paper would mean nothing to her husband, and she could not stand the thought of Jamie Liston reading her private words to Levi or anyone else for that matter. Only Levi could ever hear what her words were to him; her words were from her heart and were locked up inside of her with no way to be released.

Clemmie had written her a letter months ago after she left and told her that Levi wasn't even looking for her, he was probably glad she was gone, Cecily grieved. After all the pain she had caused him he was probably happy to have seen the last of her. She closed her eyes and saw his face in her mind before she had hurt him before she had married him. He was so handsome with his deep eyes and his easy smile, he had always been so gentle and kind and good until she had destroyed him.

Cecily reached for the letter on the vanity knowing that she should not touch it much less read Louise's mail from Clemmie. Her hands shook for even thinking of doing so, but she wanted to hear the news of home, she wanted to read if Clemmie had written anything of her husband. She needed to read this letter; she had to know if there was any word of Levi and she was growing more desperate to open it by the second, and she finally did, pulling out several pages.

"Dear Aunt Louise," Cecily read aloud as if that would make it alright for her to be reading someone else's mail. "I take pen in hand to thank you for letting me know that Cecily is well and adjusting to her new life. I hope your next letter tells me that she's happy at long last, it would be good to know she is no longer sad over what took place between her and Levi.

"Speaking of Levi, I know you inquired about him and whether he might have started searching for Cecily or if he had petitioned the courts for a divorce," Cecily closed her eyes and gasped, she never dreamed she would be a divorced woman, would Levi do that to her? She forced her eyes open and continued reading the mail that was not meant for her. "Levi is not looking for Cecily, nor has he filed a divorce petition. The Reverend Bidwell, our local pastor, went out to visit with Levi shortly after Cecily left and Levi told the Reverend that there was no place in his life now for Cecily, that he was alone and he wanted to be alone. Other than the one time that he came to see Grant and me and asked where Cecily was, he has not been back, and that was months ago.

"Aunt Louise, if only you had known Levi before he married Cecily, he was a good and kind man, he was caring of all of us around him. He was like my big brother, and I knew he would watch out for me, my parents knew he would as well. And it's so odd; everyone was very well aware that Levi loved Cecily, since they were young it's been obvious. I've wondered just what went wrong and I can't figure it out. But it was a catastrophic event that hurt them both.

"I can hardly write this as I still can't believe what I was told by Jamie and until Grant went over and saw Levi for himself, I wouldn't have believed it, but Grant came home and told me that what Jamie said was true. And it's so sad."

"Levi is dying," Cecily stopped reading and dropped the letter as she sat down hard on the vanity stool holding on to the vanity and breathing hard and fast, tears welling up in her crystal eyes. She forced herself to pick up the letter and wiped her eyes so she could see. "Last week Levi's sister, Sarah came out to see her brother and went back to Madison for the new doctor there that is supposed to be the very best. The doctor told Sarah that if Levi didn't start to eat something and taking care of himself, he had only a few short months to live. Jamie said that Levi looked at the doctor and said that if he were any kind of a man, he would have taken a gun months ago and blown his head off." Cecily gasped and closed her eyes. How could this have happened? Why would Levi say such an awful thing? Would she be responsible for his death? Was he killing himself because she had hurt him so badly? Cecily prayed that that was not so. She went back to the letter,

"I asked the doctor myself, Aunt Louise, when I went to Madison and he told me that Levi is wasting away. He said it happens sometimes when people are broken emotionally; they lose the will to live and give up. He said he had never seen this in someone so young before. As I wrote earlier, Grant went to see Levi, my husband, and Levi use to be best friends, they grew up together, and the news of Levi's health upset Grant so greatly. Levi met Grant at the door, and Grant said he didn't even recognize him, a man he's known all of his life Aunt Louise. His eyes are red-rimmed and bloodshot, his cheeks are predominate in his face, and he's lost so much weight that he is only half the man that he was just a few short months ago. Grant said that he looked like he was dying. And when Grant asked what he could do to help him, Levi said that he just wanted to be left alone. He said he wanted to die in peace. Grant tried to tell Levi to eat, Levi said for Grant to eat at his funeral. He said that he would set Cecily free to his own way and no one would be sorry that he was gone. Grant said he broke down and cried that Grant and I were right, he had been hurting Cecily, he told Grant that here on earth was hell because of what he'd done to his Cecily and he wanted to die. He said he couldn't wait to die. Then he told Grant not to come back and locked the door behind Grant.

"Grant went straight down to Madison to see Sarah. Levi's sister cried and said that Levi had put her off the place and told her not to come back until he was dead and he would see that that was soon. She said that she asked him to let her find Cecily and he told her that if he ever saw Cecily again, he would blow his brains out right in front of his wife and set her free.

"Jamie Liston went over to see him yesterday as Levi's cattle is wondering all over Jamie's land and Jamie thought Levi might hire him to round the cattle up for him. Levi told Jamie to keep the cattle. He said that dead men have no use for owning anything. Of course, Jamie has the biggest mouth around these parts and told everyone what Levi said. I don't know what happened to him, Aunt Louise, honestly Grant and I have no idea. He was the nicest person I ever knew. He smiled all the time and;"

"No good ever came from reading other people's mail," Louise interrupted Cecily's reading aloud about her husband.

"I've killed him," Cecily whispered in horror.

"No," Louise said while walking into her bedroom. "You should have taken a frying pan to his hard head when you had the chance; then you could have taken credit for having killed him." Louise tried to lighten the mood, Cecily looked far too serious and hurt, Cecily's health couldn't handle this, she shouldn't have seen or read that letter.

"Levi's too tall, I'd never have been able to hit him on the head," Cecily said before she covered her face with her hands and fought not to burst into tears.

"Well dear girl, you should have attacked when he was sitting down," Louise went to Cecily and put her arm around the younger woman's shoulders. "Don't cry; there isn't one thing you can do for him right now. You have to take care of yourself, so you can be strong and well." Louise reached for Cecily's hand and took the letter from Clemmie, she didn't know how far Cecily had read, but no good would come from reading the whole letter.

"If you want to talk or if you need me, just call out." Louise watched Cecily leave her bedroom, then she went to the fireplace and threw the letter in watching it burn, she should have done that after she finished reading it. Cecily had been working hard to make a new life for herself here with Louise, reading that letter wasn't a good thing to have done; it brought back the past and the pain. Cecily had been in too much pain.

Cecily lay down on her bed and turned onto her side. Levi didn't want her in his life. Levi hated her. Levi was killing himself to set her free. She didn't want to be free. She wanted to go home; she wanted to go back to her old Levi, the one that adored her and that she loved. She closed her eyes and knew that she had killed her old Levi months ago. Why would he want to die? She asked herself and stared at the window across her room. Because he had no one, she thought. She had left him and come to Louise Crandle. Louise had helped her find a new life. She had friends, a place to call home; she was almost happy, but not really happy at all. She had a reason to go on; she had all the reason in the world to live.

Levi had stayed in Cherry Lake; he was probably known as the man that's wife had left him, he was probably ashamed. Shame was a hard thing to live with; she knew that all too well, she had lived in shame for more than two years in her life. And now she was safe and had a life. Levi wasn't safe; he had no life.

Cecily wished that she had given her husband something. He had given her his love, freely and gladly. She had taken his money, his concern, his tender care, and his mother's wedding rings. She had given him nothing but this desire to die. There was no way for her to go back to him; he didn't want her. There was no way for her to change what she had done to him. She closed her eyes and saw his tormented face and felt sick inside. If only Levi could have forgiven her, but that was something that he would not give to her.

And she had left him to live with her lies and her humiliation for having left him.

She didn't want Levi dead, Cecily thought. No matter what had come to pass between them, Cecily didn't want her husband to die. She loved Levi; she had always loved Levi; she would only love him until the day she died. It didn't matter what had happened those two months of their marriage. She remembered and knew the Levi she had known all her life, the one that had shared a picnic lunch with her and tapped her on the nose calling her a silly little girl, the one that had kissed her in the field at her father's house, the one that had pulled her down onto his lap. She loved him, he hadn't raped her, he just hadn't prepared her for him, he hadn't made love with her, it had been rough, and he had cried, he had been so sorry, she knew that then, she knew it more so now. She didn't want him to die; she had married him, she had deceived him, his death was really on her.

Cecily sat up in bed quickly, and her heart was beating fast. She could save her Levi; she had a way to make him live. If anything were to happen to her, if she were to die, she held within her body Levi's salvation. She didn't want to die, but she knew she wasn't well, she knew she was having a very difficult time and she was even aware enough to know that she was afraid that what had happened to her mother would happen to her as well. Louise knew she was fighting for her life; the doctor had told her and Cecily had overheard. If she should lose her life, she would be sure to give Levi a life. She could and would give her Levi something to live for after all. She just hoped it wasn't too late for him or her.

"The pain is so bad, Louise," Cecily complained from the bed and grasped Louise's hand in a death grip. "I don't want to die like my mother did," she cried pathetically.

"You are not going to die, dear," Louise said in a firm voice before she looked at the doctor's worried face. "Just hang on,

Cecily. Hang on to me and try to bear up under this pain for a little longer." Louise's voice was soft now, and she watched Cecily draw blood as her small white teeth sank into a pale lower lip.

"She's bleeding far too much," the doctor said to Louise in a low voice as Cecily fought another terrible pain and cried out.

Cecily knew that she was dying. For the past two days, she had been swollen, her skin was too pale and too dry. And she had been so physically ill; she had even vomited blood this morning. The doctor's concerned face and Louise's terrified look only added to Cecily's belief that she was dying. Cecily wasn't afraid to die, but she didn't want her baby to die. She closed her eyes and remembered her baby brother, her mother.

"Louise," she said when she could speak past the pain. "I need for you to make me a promise." Louise reached for a cloth and wiped Cecily's face.

"Not now, dearest. Rest when you can now, we'll talk after the baby comes."

"Louise, I probably won't be here after my baby comes," she said this looking at the doctor and knew soon she would be with her parents and brother.

"Hush dear, hush," Louise said in a tear-filled voice.

"I need you to promise," Cecily cried harder, her tears rolling into her ears. "Please, promise me."

"I'll do anything that you want me to do dear, anything in the world. You have my vow." Louise was worried half to death and felt she was too old to deal with this. Cecily was dying in front of her eyes, and she could do nothing about it, and the doctor didn't even know what to do. Cecily needed a miracle.

"My baby," Cecily cried out in an awful pain, and the doctor told her to push hard and push now.

"Your baby will be fine. I'll take care of it for you." Cecily shook her head while pushing.

"No," she cried out as she fell back onto the bed. "Levi, I want you to take my baby to Levi." She was breathing hard and fast, the doctor ordered her to push again, and she did. "I owe him," Cecily said when she could speak again. "I owe him this."

"You owe that man nothing, Cecily," Louise looked back at the doctor, his hands were soaked in blood, and he ordered Cecily to push harder this time. "You aren't going to die. Do you hear me? You are going to live and raise this baby yourself and grow to be a little old lady like me with Grandchildren filling your lap. You're not going to die, Cecily." Louise looked down at Cecily's white lips and pale skin as she pushed with what little strength she had left, trying her best to get this baby out of her body, a baby she intended to give to her husband.

"Levi," Cecily said her husband's name. "Louise, he gave me everything." She looked into Louise's eyes. "I gave him nothing but a handful of hurt and lies. I want him to have his child. He needs his child. Please, Louise. I love him. And he'll love his baby; I know he will. He'll live Louise; I want one of us to live," she whimpered. The doctor demanded that she push again. Louise saw all the blood and knew this wasn't good. "Please," she screamed as she arched herself into a push.

"All right, Cecily. I promise to take your baby to Levi Tucker," Louise said, and Cecily continued to push. Louise saw how deathly white she was and knew, Levi would raise this child alone, his wife was going to die today.

"Levi!" Cecily screamed with the last ounce of her strength. The screams of the baby filled the room while Cecily fell back on the bed and was too still. The doctor saw Cecily fall back onto the bed and shoved the baby into Louise's arms and then pushed Louise out of his way as he leaned down and put his ear to Cecily's chest. Louise started to cry with the newborn baby and walk the floor begging God for Cecily's life and knowing that one life had come into the world and another had left. Cecily should have lived to love her baby and grow old. And Cecily, begging her to see that this child was given to a man that Louise could never like, to give this sweet, beautiful baby to Levi Tucker. Louise closed her eyes and realized that Cecily had cried out for her husband with her last breath. Levi Tucker needed to be brought to his knees for what he had done to this sweet innocent darling girl that had been his wife. This baby's screams could bring anyone to their knees, Louise thought and cried all the more.

February 1898
Cherry Lake, Florida

Levi Tucker fed his horses and chickens and milked the one cow that he had kept in his barn. Those were his only chores these days. The sawmill was still closed down and had been for a long time, ever since Cecily had left him. His steer roamed free; the calves were free of his mark as he didn't care to take the time to mark them. He didn't care about anything, least of all himself. He had nothing; he was nothing. The only thing that he had ever wanted in this world was gone, and he would never get her back.

Levi waited for Cecily to divorce him. She had been gone for months; he wondered how she was living. He didn't want to think about her, and he tried to push her from his mind, but he couldn't. She was haunting him. And everywhere that he went he saw her, everything that he did brought her to mind. He could not escape her. He could not put her from his life.

His sister Sarah had come out with a doctor not long ago; the doctor had said that he was dying. He wanted to die. Living with what he had done was too hard. The words that he had said to Cecily came back to him even in his sleep, and he would be plunged into endless guilt for those words for weeks at a time. They would burn his gut as he knew that they had hurt Cecily when he had said them. What he had done to her in his parlor faced him every time that he tried to enter that room of his house. Her ghost walked the floors of that room and tormented him; it was a ghost of the living, the worst kind of ghost. Everything that he did reminded him of the hell that he had put Cecily through, he hated himself. He wanted to die, and he welcomed his coming death.

Levi's hair was long, down on his shoulders, he had grown a beard that he never trimmed, he had lost so much weight that he couldn't keep his pants on without suspenders, permanent dark circles were under his eyes, deep and purple in color. He looked worse than walking death, and he knew that too, but he didn't care. The only person that he had ever wanted to care about him was gone, and she hated him as she should. Cecily was never coming back, he knew that, and yet he sought her out in every room, praying she would forgive him, praying she would one day come back. He loved her.

Grant and Clemmie had refused to tell him where Cecily had gone; they were right not to tell him. He had no right to even beg them to know after what had happened in their parlor. Wherever she was, Levi knew she was safe, safe from him as she should be. He would see that she stayed safe if and when she came home because he would be dead. He wanted her to return to her home in Cherry Lake.

Levi went into the bathroom and looked at himself in the mirror above the sink. If Cecily were to see him now, she would not even know him. She would probably run from him in fear. He looked like the monster she knew him to be. He leaned his head against the mirror and remembered raping her, her words to him after he finished with her, "It was always you, Levi. It was always you." He wondered constantly what she had meant by those words. He should have let her talk to him. He shouldn't have made her be quiet. No, he thought, he couldn't take her words. Her words had broken him; her words were cruel; he couldn't live with the words that Cecily said to him. "I could never have your child," she'd said, and he lost his breath at that memory. And when he asked if she had married him for his money, one answer, one single word for an answer and it tore him apart — "yes." He grabbed a deep breath and felt his hands shaking again; his hands always shook these days. He was weak all over; he was glad to be weak; he didn't deserve to be strong. Cecily's words made him weak.

He had never understood his wife. He only knew that her words had broken his heart. His heart was now and had been bleeding to death; he wasn't wasting away as the doctor had said. Cecily's words were killing him. He might not want to die like he did, not if Preston, his stableman hadn't come to him a few days after Cecily left and told him that Cecily had been screaming for him after her attack on Bernard Calhoun. He had told Levi that she screamed his name over and over again and was crying in the worst way. And then she had run away from him. Why had Cecily been screaming for him? She hated him.

"I never thought of Bernard when I was with you," he heard Cecily's sorrow-filled voice in his mind and squeezed his eyes closed. "Can't you hear my heart?" she had asked him in her soft way. He knew her heart, he knew there was no place for him in her heart, and he had kept her, he had forced her to take him. That first night that he had entered her body, she had not wanted him, he had taken her anyway. He remembered her scream when he shoved into her on the parlor floor and went to his knees now on the bathroom floor, shaking his head and trying to push the memories of what he had done away.

Grant had been right; he had been tearing her apart a piece at the time. She had said that he was dumb; she was right; he had no brain when he was with her. He knew he had controlled her, he had tried to possess her soul, he had tried to own her, and he shouldn't have done any of those things. She had wanted nothing to do with him; he was nothing to her. Even in the field at her father's house, the kiss in the field had meant everything to him; to her, she had said she wouldn't marry him.

Someone was knocking constantly on his front door interrupting his thoughts and memories, but Levi stayed in the bathroom on the floor on his knees, his head in his hands while he rocked slowly back and forth and remembered Cecily. Cecily wasn't his hell; he had made his own hell by having to have her when she didn't want him to have her. He had to find a way to escape his memories. He had to find a way out of this hell on earth. He didn't want to live this way; he would live this way as long as he filled his lungs with air.

The knocking became more insistent, and Levi pulled himself up while holding on to the bathroom sink. Whoever was at his door wasn't going away. Someone really meant to see him. For a gut-twisting moment he thought that it might be Cecily and he nearly went back down onto his knees.

Cecily wasn't at his door; Levi saw when he answered it a few seconds later. There was an elderly woman in her fifties standing on his porch, and she looked put out, her lips were pinched together like she had just finished eating sour grapes. He wished that she would go away and leave him alone. He didn't know her; he didn't want to know her.

"Well young man, it certainly took you long enough to answer your door," the woman gave him a look like his school teacher used to when he got in a fight over a child calling him dummy. "Are you Levi Tucker?" she asked, and Levi could only nod his head slowly, she spoke to him like he was a boy in trouble. "I would say it is a pleasure to meet you, but as I know that it is not, I won't waste my breath." Levi gave a sharp laugh. "You certainly aren't pretty like Cecily told me you were," the woman said, and the laugh Levi had given became caught in his throat and chest. "Cecily lived with me for a time; she told me that her father's house here was empty. I would like to rent that house from you."

"What?" Levi's mind had gone blank after the woman had said his wife's name. What had she asked him? He tried to clear his head and think.

"Are you deaf? I said I want to rent Cecily's father's house from you. If you would remove all that hair," she waved her hand at his head, and Levi stepped back from her, "from covering your ears you could hear me," the woman said sternly, and Levi raised his eyebrows at her.

"Who the hell are you?" Levi asked as he regained his senses.

"My name is Louise Crandle, and I was a friend to your wife. I made her certain promises, Mr. Tucker and I intend to keep them; I will not fail her. Are we clear on that?"

"I'm – um – sure that you won't fail her, Mrs. Crandle," Levi frowned feeling confused and weak.

"It's Miss Crandle," she corrected him his mistake and frowned back at him. "Do I or don't I get the house, Mr. Tucker."

"I don't give a damn about that house," Levi said harshly. "Take it."

"Thank you," Louise said in her dry, harsh voice. "You are too kind, I'm sure." She turned and went down the porch steps. Levi thought that she was leaving and grabbed a deep breath. This woman could not leave; he had to know where Cecily was.

"Wait," he called out and followed her trying to catch his breath; he was too weak. "Do you know where my wife is now?" Louise turned from her buggy, a small bundle in her arms. She handed that small bundle to Levi, and he took it, not knowing what else to do other than to look at Miss Louise Crandle and hope she would tell him Cecily was here with her. "Please, ma'am, do you know where my wife is?"

"Yes, Mr. Tucker, I do know where Cecily is," Levi stood holding his baby and looking at Louise Crandle. He's so anxious to know where his wife is, that he doesn't even realize that there is a baby in his arms, Louise thought and stared hard at Levi. "Cecily is in the graveyard. She died giving birth to your son." She saw Levi fall back at her words and nearly drop the baby. Louise saw the shock her words had caused him and reached quickly to take the baby away from him before some harm fell upon the infant.

Levi turned away from Louise after she had taken the baby from his arms. He was going to be sick, his stomach lifted up into his throat and then fell down fast to his feet, and he bent forward, his arms wrapped around his sunken belly and he fought for several breaths. Cecily had her monthly cycle, and he hadn't touched her afterward because he didn't want her to become with child. He didn't want her to take more with her when she left him than his heart. And then, he had raped her on the parlor floor, and she had taken his child with her when she fled that day from his home. He had forced his child onto her and then she died having his child. She hadn't wanted his child.

"I killed her," Levi said in a voice that was sheer agony.

Louise heard his words and remembered Cecily saying the same thing not long ago of him. They were star crossed lovers; their relationship was doomed to fail right from the start. It was a shame, Cecily deserved better than this, and Levi Tucker didn't look a bad sort of person at all. All that was left of any love the two might have was this little baby, and that was sad.

"Mr. Tucker," Louise Crandle's voice interrupted his thoughts, and he turned around to face her. "Cecily made me promise to bring this baby to you, and I have done as she asked. But now I must have a promise from you." Levi could only stare at Louise; he could not have spoken even if he had wanted to; he was too busy fighting down the nausea that burned hot in his throat. "I want to see this baby every single day for at least three hours. You will bring him to me from nine in the morning until at least noon time. I must insist on seeing this baby every single day until he's at least six months old. I won't just abandon Cecily's baby to a man like you without first being assured you are worthy of the child."

"I was not worthy of his mother," Levi stated while looking down at his baby held in Louise's arm. She saw him looking and handed the baby to him. "I'll bring him to you every day as you ask."

"Good, then I'll go move into the house now," Louise looked as Levi gently held his son.

"Did Cecily," his voice cracked and broke when his wife's name was said, and he took a deep breath before he continued. "Did my wife give him a name?"

"She did," Louise looked straight into Levi's eyes, she had been determined not to like him, and she found herself being drawn to him. "Ethan Daniel Tucker."

Levi squeezed his eyes shut tight. Cecily had named their son after their fathers, he would have wanted that, and he was glad she had as well.

She was dead, Levi thought over and over again. He could never correct all the wrongs that he had done to her now if he might ever have been able to correct them. He had treated her too badly. He had forced her to run away from him and hide. He had forced her to die having his child. He had killed her. When he opened his eyes Louise Crandle stood with a severe look on her face; he wondered if she were wanting to read his mind, to know his thoughts? She looked like she did, but said nothing and he was glad of her silence.

Louise had been prepared to hate Levi Tucker; she had hated him for hurting Cecily. But the look of pure torment on his face right now was as bad as the look on Cecily's face in those last few seconds before Ethan had been born. Levi Tucker was a man full of pain, he looked haunted, and Louise thought that she almost felt sorry for him.

"Cecily told me that you struggled with reading, so listen closely to me young man." Levi gave Louise a nod as his eyes left the baby and settled on her. No wonder everything went wrong between Cecily and Levi, Louise thought further to herself as she looked at the horribly thin pale man before her. He was as quiet as Cecily had been, a man of few words. The two young people probably never sat down and had a heart to heart talk, she knew for certain that Cecily had secrets from Levi, secrets are not a good thing to have and an even worse thing to have in a marriage. Well, Louise thought, there were two things for certain. First Cecily and Levi may not have talked but they were together as evidence was this baby, and the second thing is that Ethan Daniel Tucker was not quite like his parents and Levi would find that out soon enough. "This baby is not yet two weeks old, he eats every two hours, do not forget to feed this baby," she said in her stern voice that was making Levi feel like a schoolboy. "In his bag are bottles to feed him from, one is prepared, look at it closely so you'll know how to fix the next one that he needs. There are also diapers and clothes in his bag. He must be changed often, his diaper, not his clothes, or he'll get a rash on his bottom, and we don't want a rash on his bottom. He eats no food," Louise Crandle emphasized the word food and gave Levi a look that matched the Reverend Bidwell's in sternness. I'll let you know when he's ready for food. You're to do as I say, Mr. Tucker. Cecily loved this baby before he was born, she had a horrible time giving birth," Louise felt quiet and swallowed looking away from Levi. "It was a nightmare for her really." She looked back up into his eyes and saw the stricken look on his face; she hadn't expected him to have taken Cecily's death like this, he looked crushed, to say the least. "I'm available to you night and day, young man. Night and day," she shook her finger in his face. "That's why I want Cecily's old home, it's nearby, and you can come for me when you need me. From the looks of you, you'll be needing help." Levi blushed; he knew he looked haggard at best.

"You're welcome to stay here, Miss Crandle," Levi surprised himself by his offer.

"Thank you, but no thank you. I've had my own place for too long, and I like my privacy. Remember what I tell you, anytime that you cannot care for this baby; you're to bring him to me. I love this little man and will take him home with me to live forever. So don't feel yourself saddled, I can take him now if you don't want him."

"I want him," Levi said quickly and held the baby closer. "He's my son. And Cecily's." He looked down at the baby trying to see if he favored his wife, he just saw a beautiful baby. "I'm sure that I can take care of him. What I don't know; he can teach me." Levi looked back down at the sleeping baby in his arms and knew, here was a part of Cecily that he hadn't hurt, a part of Cecily that would accept his love, a part of Cecily that would love him.

"You will allow nothing to happen to him," Louise ordered, her finger back wagging in his face. "I gave Cecily my word that I would keep this baby safe. I also promised to bring him to you, and I have. You will help me keep my word to Cecily and keep this baby safe, or you'll answer to me. And I can assure you, young man; you do not want to answer to me."

"I'll guard him with my life," Levi said softly and earnestly while touching the baby's soft pink cheek and saying his name.

"That you had guarded Cecily with your life," Louise said, and Levi's eyes collide with hers, and then he glanced quickly away knowing she was right in what she said. "Cecily told me when she first learned that she was with child that you wanted a child of your own. As she lay dying, she said that she owed you." Louise stared intently at Levi's face watching for his reaction to her words.

"Did she say why she owed me?" Levi asked and looked back at Louise.

"I don't remember her exact words, Mr. Tucker. It was a terrible time as you can well imagine. Cecily was in horrible pain; she was bleeding to death in my arms." Louise saw Levi's face turn white and reached for the baby afraid that he might drop Ethan.

"No, I'm fine," she heard Levi say in a strained voice and pulled her hands back down by her side.

"Cecily had spoken of you often before she died," Louise continued speaking and watching Levi's face. "She said that you were good to her when she needed goodness in her life. I know most of your story, Mr. Tucker. Cecily had nothing but regret for what she did to you." Louise saw Levi close his eyes and wondered what he was thinking.

Levi held his son closer and wished that Cecily had never had anything to regret; he knew that he hated the regret that filled him. He had more to regret than his Cecily ever did. And he was going to have to live with his regret for the rest of his life, Cecily was at peace. As she could not forgive him for what he did to her, Levi would never know peace.

Cecily said that you loved her," Louise words made Levi focus his eyes back on her face. "I don't understand; if you loved her why did you hurt her as you did."

"I'm dumb, Miss Crandle," Levi said looking down at his feet with the most awful look on his face that Louise had ever seen. "That is all the excuse that I have, and as it is no excuse at all, I guess I'll pay for what I did to Cecily in hell."

"It looks to me like you've been there," Louise said, and Levi frowned at her. "Hell, young man. Look in the mirror sometimes, hell looks like you do right now." She heard Levi give another sharp laugh and smiled for the first time with him. "I think at the end of her life, Cecily wasn't afraid of you anymore. I think had she lived she would have come back to you if she would have thought that you would take her back." Louise saw the look on Levi's face change again to intense sorrow; he looked to be in physical agony. Would he have taken Cecily back with love? Or would he have taken her back with anger and pain and too much silence? These questions were all too late now, Louise thought, and that was the real horror of this. The decisions had been made. Cecily had given her baby to her husband, and Levi had lost his Cecily forever. The baby also lost his mother to his birth. Louise felt sad for them all, but most of her sadness was for Cecily. Cecily had lost the most.

"I want to thank you for everything that you've done, for Cecily and Ethan," Levi finally spoke as he and Louise stood in his front yard staring at one another. And thank you for bringing my son to me. You may have the house for as long as you want to stay."

"And the rent? I would like to settle that with you right now," she said in her stern voice but found herself softening toward this man. He wasn't even aware tears were falling down his face; his grief was obvious.

"The last thing I need is more money, Miss Crandle," Levi said with a strained laugh that sounded more like a cry. "Take the house, and you're welcome to it. It was Cecily's home, never mine."

"Then I'll see you in the morning," Louise said before she turned to leave Levi Tucker holding his baby son in his front yard.

"Miss Crandle," he called as she started to pull away. "Did she suffer having him?" Louise saw Levi close his eyes and bow his head, "she suffered at my hands," he sobbed, and Louise reached out to touch his shoulders.

"She was in agony with the birth, and I don't know if she suffered him or you. What I do know is the last word she said was your name. She was calling for you, I think she wanted you there at the last, and in a way, maybe you were." Louise turned away from the grief-stricken face of Levi Tucker and started down the road she had been told would lead to Cecily's old home calling out as she left him, "nine in the morning, Mr. Tucker."

Levi watched Miss Crandle drive down the road to Daniel Walker's farmhouse. A few long moments passed before he looked down at the baby within his arms, his son was fast asleep. He turned and went inside his house with Ethan's bag held in his fist under the baby's back. He placed the bag on a chair in his bedroom before he sat down on the edge of the bed; he was feeling like he had just run a race and won. He was trembling and out of breath and lightheaded, and he had to get a fire going, this room was cold, he thought.

"Hello, Ethan," Levi said to his sleeping son as he gave the baby a good look. Right now Ethan didn't look like anyone he knew, except for the small dimple in his chin, like Levi's own dimple. He felt he could see no resemblance to either himself or Cecily. Ethan was too tiny, smaller than Levi could ever have dreamed his baby would be. He closed his eyes tight and looked to be in prayer as he thought that Ethan was his now, Ethan was his to take care of for a lifetime.

"I could never have your baby," Cecily had said to him months ago. Levi gave a cry and laid the baby down in the middle of the bed and then laid down himself staring up at the ceiling. Cecily was gone, he grieved. He shook his head at his thoughts. Cecily was more than gone; she was dead. She would not have died having his baby if Levi hadn't raped her on the parlor floor that awful day. She had taken his heart to heaven, she had died from his sin against her, and she had left him this most precious of gifts, his son. He had driven his wife to her death and his wife, the woman that he had hurt worse than anyone had ever been hurt, gave him his son to raise. Levi knew he didn't deserve this gift Cecily had bestowed upon him. He should have been the one to die. He had wanted and even tried to die.

He had to start a fire; the baby would get cold. Levi moved from the bed and put a fire in its place before going to look at his little son who was now on the bed fussing. Levi reached for the baby and turned him on his back, intent on changing Ethan's diaper. It wasn't an easy job, the baby was screaming bloody murder, and he was muddy. Levi wondered how often this would happen and hoped it was always when the stern looking Miss Crandle had the baby. Ethan continued to fuss while Levi went to the bag and pulled out the prepared bottle and with Ethan in his arms, he went into the kitchen where he sat down in the rocking chair near the stove and fed his son.

Ethan opened his eyes and looked up into the eyes of his father; Levi sucked in his breath and gasped loudly as he stared down into Cecily's crystal clear blue eyes. His heart ached as he saw the complete trust that was in Ethan's eyes as he looked up at him. Levi knew that Cecily had never looked at him with trusting eyes.

Levi held his son and tried to breathe slow and even; he needed to find some strength, he had so little strength. He saw Cecily, his Cecily's face as a little girl offering him a cookie, those crystal eyes of hers looking up into his own with laughter and kindness. He saw her, his Cecily running up to him to show him a fish that she had caught down at the lake, she was only seven or eight years old, even at that tender age she had been beautiful and one of his best friends. He saw her down at the lake running from him as he chased her with the green snake, the way she looked back at him and smiled, her hair loose from the ribbon that held it back from her face and flowing down to her hips. He had fallen in love with her that day, she was fourteen, and he was nineteen, and he knew he'd wait for her to grow up; she was the only woman he ever wanted to marry. She had lived so close to him, all her life only a short walk away from him. He had waited for her and hoped she would see his love, but she only wanted to be his friend. He should have left her alone, he never had any right to her, and she had died having his baby, she hadn't wanted his baby.

The baby was sleeping in his Levi's arms, and he stood slowly and carefully not to awaken the little fellow before taking the baby back to his bedroom. He felt weak and was trembling. He hadn't eaten right in a long time; he could not even remember his last good meal. He had to do better, Levi thought as he put the baby on his bed and went back to the kitchen to have the same dinner that Ethan had. A large glass of milk.

Levi washed his glass and saw how Ethan's bottle was put together; then he washed the bottle before going back to his room. He looked at Ethan tiny on his bed. Cecily had given him his son; he nearly went down on his knees with the full realization hitting him like a fist in the gut. Cecily had trusted him in the end. She had known that she was dying and instead of giving Ethan to Louise Crandle or her friend Clemmie or anyone else, Cecily had sent Ethan home to him. She couldn't have hated him too much, not in the end. She must have felt something for him, something other than hate. He wished that she had known that he was no longer angry with her. He wished that she could have known that he had forgiven her and needed for her to forgive him. She could never forgive him now.

Levi forced his eyes away from the baby and went to unpack the bag. The baby had a lot of things, Levi thought as he filled all the drawers on one side of the dresser. For someone so small, Ethan needed a lot. Levi almost began to worry that he might not be able to take care of his son; he was sick; he had been sick for a long time. He decided then and there to get well, for Ethan and for himself.

The rings! Levi nearly fell down when he pulled the wedding rings out of the bottom of the bag. Cecily hadn't sold them as he had thought she should or would have. He held the rings in the palm of his hand and remembered the day that he had slid them in the name of love and honor onto his wife's finger. He had loved Cecily that day; he loved her still. He would always love her. He went to the strong arm box and put the rings inside, no longer feeling that they were cursed, they had been a token of his love for her, of his father's love for his mother. One day he would give these rings to his son. He hoped that Ethan did better in marriage than he had done in his own. He prayed that Ethan did not have his temper.

Levi woke to the most panic causing noise he had ever known in his whole life. It was pitch dark both inside and outside, and his son was awake and screaming as though the world were coming to an end. Levi stood and lit a lamp before going to pick up the baby. The baby was soaking wet, so was the bed. Ethan continued to scream as Levi slowly changed the diaper, then took Ethan to the kitchen where he fixed one of the bottles with only one hand. Ethan became quiet the second that Levi put the bottle into the baby's mouth. "Dear Lord," Levi said in a startled voice as the baby was drenched in milk, so was Levi's shirt. He took the bottle away from Ethan, glad to see that he hadn't drowned his son with the milk and Ethan began to scream again. This baby could scream, Levi thought. The bottle wasn't as easy to put together as Levi had thought. A few moments later, Levi had the bottle back in Ethan's mouth, and his shirt was laying across the kitchen table. He sat down again in the rocking chair and looked down at the baby sucking on the bottle for dear life.

"This isn't going to be easy; is it?" Levi asked his new son. "I know I'm going to make a lot of mistakes like this one, but I swear, this time I won't mess up with a life. I'll love you, Ethan, always. No matter what. And I'll be good to you. I'll always be good to you." The baby blinked up at him, and Levi felt tears burn bright in his eyes. He should have never messed up with Cecily. He swore before God and man that he would not hurt Ethan like he had hurt Cecily. The job of raising Ethan was going to be long and hard, but he would not fail. Levi would never fail someone that he loved again.

The father kissed his tiny son's head and prayed that in heaven the mother had forgiven him, the father. That she knew of his deep and endless regret and guilt and constant shame for all that he had put her through in their marriage. He prayed that now she knew that he had really loved her, it hadn't been a good love; he knew that in his heart. If he had loved her good, she would never have died having his son. She would be alive now and happy with the man that she would have chosen for herself. A man that was intelligent enough to always forgive those he loved.

Levi felt a tear fall onto his face and did not feel like he was any less of a man for that tear. He needed to cry; the tears might cleanse his soul enough for him to be worthy of Ethan and this gift Cecily had given to him as she lay dying. Levi cried so hard that his sobs shook his little son in his arms.

"I'm sorry, Cecily," he cried out loud and rocked in the chair. "I'm so sorry, Cecily." He wished that she was here; he wished that she could see his sorrow. Levi was full of sorrow; he had been for a long time; his sorrow had been killing him.

Someone was trying to beat his front door down, Levi thought as he sat up in the middle of the wet bed. Ethan had to have a bed of his own as soon as possible, or Levi wasn't going to smell so good in the mornings, he decided. How could one tiny baby make a bed so wet? He wondered as he stood up beside the bed, intent on going to the door and sending whoever was there away. Company was the last thing that he needed right now. He saw Ethan's eyes were open before he turned to go answer the door and Ethan let out the loudest noise he had ever heard. This baby of his could wet the whole bed and make enough noise to wake the dead and Levi didn't think Ethan weighed ten pounds even in a wet diaper. The baby was all fluid and lungs. Levi smiled as he bent and picked up his son.

"What a noise," Grant said as he looked from Levi to the baby. Levi stood in the doorway with a shocked look on his face. "Are you going to invite me in this time or slam the door in my face?" Levi didn't answer Grant's question, he stepped back and out of the way, and Grant entered his home. "So, how is it going?"

"Fine," Levi said as Grant followed him into his bedroom.

"Where did you learn to do that?" Grant asked as Levi changed Ethan's soaking wet diaper.

"He taught me," Levi said as he added the wet diaper to a pile growing on the floor. "Can you get the fire going and make a pot of coffee for me while I feed him?" Levi asked as he went to the kitchen and saw Grant go to the stove out of the corner of his eye. "How did you know I had a baby?"

Grant turned and looked at Levi. "Clemmie's Aunt Louise told us she had brought him to you." Grant looked away from Levi and went to fill the coffee pot up with water.

"Louise Crandle is Clemmie's aunt," Levi said more to himself than to Grant. "That explains how she knew Cecily. Did Miss Crandle send you over to check on us?"

"Louise was a little concerned," Grant confessed.

Levi only nodded his head and fell silent for a long while, the baby in his arms sucking noisily on the bottle. Thanks to Grant and Clemmie, Cecily had found a safe place to live away from him, he thought as he looked down at his son. Ethan's eyes were closed, and he wondered if the baby was going back to sleep. He thought that he remembered his sister slept all the time as a baby. A smile touched his face. Sarah hadn't been a baby in nearly twenty years, he was only five years older than she was. Sarah, the same age as Cecily would be or would have been if she were alive, which she wasn't, he had killed her.

"Have you had breakfast yet?" Levi finally looked back up at Grant and found Grant staring hard at his face.

"Yes, at about six this morning. It's after seven now; I think that I could use a snack. You look like you need some food too Levi." Levi smiled at Grant's words. When they were growing up, they use to raid the kitchen all the time. Ollie would chase them out with a broom at least ten times a day. Ollie, he thought and took a deep breath, his unforgiving ways, his temper, had cost him more than just Cecily.

"I can't remember the last time I ate breakfast," Levi said in a low voice, and Grant believed his words. "Want to go hunt us some eggs while I put Ethan back to bed?" Levi saw Grant smile and knew that he would have breakfast soon. "While you're out there hunting eggs for our breakfast, would you mind feeding my horses and milking my cow. I think I'm going to have to find some help around the place. I need Ollie."

Grant left the house and Levi went and put Ethan on a small dry spot of the bed. He put on a clean shirt which was too big for him, all of his clothes were too big, he grabbed the suspenders to keep his pants up. He had a son to raise; he couldn't go on like he had been, Levi had to eat again. He would have to live. He almost felt afraid to live; he didn't want to hurt anyone else in this life as he had hurt Cecily. He wished that she was here and that he could correct all the mistakes that he had made with her.

Levi went back into the kitchen and sliced some smoked ham that was hanging in the pantry. Grant came back inside with a pail full of milk and eggs, and Levi thanked him while Grant poured them each a cup of coffee.

"Do you know of any woman that would come out here and work for me?" Levi asked as he started to fry up the ham and eggs.

"Mrs. Liston is looking for work now that her husband is dead. But she'll only come in the day, what are you going to do in the night if you have a problem with the baby?" Grant sat two plates on the table while he talked to Levi.

"I'm not looking for someone to take care of Ethan; I'll do that. But I do need someone to help with the laundry and to do the cooking and cleaning. When you leave here could you stop by and ask Mrs. Liston to come see me, the sooner, the better. And ask Jamie to come over too. I'll need help with my animals; I think I'm going to be too busy with Ethan to do much else." Levi sat the eggs and ham on the table between him and Grant and suddenly remembered the times he sent Cecily here to eat, and he ate alone in the dining room.

"What's wrong Levi?" Grant asked seeing how pale Levi suddenly became.

"I'm going to be sick," Levi sat down and put his face in his hands.

"You need to eat Levi," Grant ordered him, and Levi took a fork full of eggs. "You need to get your strength back; you look awful."

Levi couldn't forget what he had done and said to Cecily; he ate trying to not think, trying to just eat and get strong to take care of Cecily's son, a son she gave to him. "I feel pretty bad," Levi said. "And if I eat another bite, I really will be sick. I haven't eaten this much since before Cecily left me." Grant knew that Levi was speaking the truth. "Besides, I have work to do." He stood up and went to the dirty pile of diapers; he put them in a huge pot on the stove to boil while Grant washed the dishes. "I need to go up into the attic for the baby cradle; can you listen out for Ethan?"

"Listen out for Ethan?" Grant shook his head while he said this. "I'll go up to the attic; you listen out for the baby. I wouldn't know what to do if it started crying or something." Levi almost laughed at Grant as he watched his best friend climb the attic steps. He was glad that Grant had left him, he was feeling weak and dizzy and sick, and his hands shook so bad that he held on to the edge of the table to make them stop.

When Grant came back down with the cradle and a small feather tick mattress, Levi found sheets in the hall closet to fit the baby bed and put Ethan down on the bed with several blankets under him and over him. "If he wets the bed now, I want the bed to stay dry," Levi explained to Grant as he pulled the sheets from his own bed. "Can you help me get this mattress outside? It needs to dry." Grant took the mattress out without Levi's help. Levi had to sit down and let his head stop spinning. "I haven't done this much work in months," he said when Grant came back into the house.

"It shows," Grant said as Levi stood on unsteady feet and went back to the kitchen.

"I hope that Mrs. Liston can come to work right away, I have laundry," Levi spoke as he removed the diapers from the pot and put them in cold water in the sink. "Do you think I should bring the cradle in here? My bedroom is cold."

"Hell Levi, I wouldn't know what you ought to do. I know you put enough blankets on the kid to cook him. You better find someone to take care of that baby."

"I take care of Ethan. Cecily gave him to me." Levi rung out the diapers and put them in a basket to take outside.

"Cecily didn't know you are sick, Levi," Grant said when he followed Levi into the yard to the clothesline and watched his friend struggle to hang the diapers out to dry. Levi was so weak he was wearing himself out just bending and reaching to hang the diapers, Grant thought.

"I'm not sick," Levi said and hung onto the clothesline to steady himself before he started the walk back to the house which wasn't that far away but seemed like a million miles away to Levi in his weak state. "What time is it?" he asked Grant when they finally reached the back door.

"Almost nine," Grant said putting his watch back in his pocket.

"I have to get Ethan to Miss Crandle," Levi said and went to fix a couple of bottles to take with him for the baby. "Will you stay for a while, I need your help?" Grant nodded his head as Levi went to get the baby. "I need to borrow your horse," Grant followed Levi out into the yard and watched Levi stand still looking at his horse.

"What's the matter?" Grant asked, and Levi turned to face him

"You're going to have to hold the baby while I mount up," Levi said and held Ethan out to Grant. "You aren't afraid of the baby, are you Grant?" Levi asked as Grant stood and started at Ethan in his arms.

"Give me the kid," Grant said and took Ethan. "And no, Levi, I'm not afraid of the baby, I just haven't been around them much before. Don't let those bottles leak in my saddle bag." Levi laughed at Grant and Grant liked the sound of Levi's laughter. It had been a really long time since his friend had laughed.

Levi rode slowly to Daniel Walker's house; this was the first time out other than to feed up his animals in months. He realized the weather was mild for winter and nice, it was almost like spring out here, and he wondered if it would be an early summer. He stopped his horse in the yard and looked at the house; it was still the same as when he had seen it last. He wished that Cecily was inside waiting for him. He could almost see her at the door waving to him and calling his name; she was young again and full of laughter and happy to see him. He would miss her forever.

"Miss Crandle!" Levi yelled out again, and Ethan jumped in his arms and started to scream. "Miss Crandle," he yelled louder and knew that the woman would hear Ethan if she didn't hear him and would come soon.

"What are you doing, Mr. Tucker? Yelling your head off and making that baby cry," Louise asked as she came out of the house and onto the porch. The look on her face reminded Levi again of the stern and serious Reverend Bidwell. He didn't think Miss Crandle liked him and he didn't blame her, she certainly had reason to not like him, he didn't like himself much.

"I need you to come and take the baby. I can't get down off this horse with him in my arms." Louise hurried to him, and he gave her Ethan. "I brought a couple of bottles, the milk is fresh," Levi said while he got down off of Grant's horse and fell against the animal.

"Mr. Tucker," Louise said his name in grave concern. "Are you all right?" Levi tried to stand up straight and hated his weakness.

"Just a little tired. I'll be fine." He reached into the bag on the back of the horse and took out the bottles.

Louise saw Levi's nearly white face and shaking hands as he got back up onto the horse. "Are you sure that you can take care of this baby, Mr. Tucker?" Levi looked at her and nodded his head.

"Despite having a lot of laundry this morning, we're doing fine so far. I just need to eat more. I'm a little weak is all."

"Wait just a moment," Louise said, and Levi watched her hurry into the house. When she came back she didn't have his son in her arms; she held out a paper-wrapped package for him to take. "These are freshly made this morning. The sugar will give you energy. And remember, I'm here should you need me," Louise's voice was gentle; her face had a softer look. "I know that you've been ill, if you need rest and want me to keep the baby longer than three hours a day until you're strong again, don't worry and come back when you can." This man won't live out the month, Louise thought as she looked up at Levi Tucker. He had starved himself near to death and all because of the love of a woman he couldn't forgive.

"I'll be back by noon,' Levi said firmly. "I want to care for my son; I'll be fine." He kicked the horse and Louise watched him race down the road.

Levi looked in the mirror above the bathroom sink and touched his clean-shaven face. He was clean completely now as he had taken a bath. He felt a little stronger as well, but not much. He left the bathroom and found a mirror and the scissors and a comb. "I need you to cut my hair," he said to Grant as he stepped out onto the porch.

"I've never cut hair in my life, Levi," Grant said as Levi forced him to take the scissors.

"Just cut my hair, Grant. This mess has got to go." He ran his hand through his long hair. "Do you want to get a bowl like our Mamas use to do and put it around my head to cut?" He laughed at the look Grant gave him. "Just cut it and be done with it, if you mess up, it'll grow back. I don't have anyone I need to be pretty for."

"All right Levi, but don't complain to me when I completely ruin your good looks," Grant said and cut a piece of long hair that fell over Levi's forehead.

"I've already ruined my good looks,' Levi gave a soft laugh. He was so thin he didn't look like himself anymore.

"How do you feel now about Cecily?" Grant asked while he cut more hair.

"Cecily's dead," Levi said in a hoarse voice. "I can't change anything now, so there is no use in talking about her."

"I'm sorry that I didn't tell you where she was before it was too late," Grant trimmed the sides around Levi's ears. "We didn't know, Clemmie and me, that Cecily was in the family way. If we had known, I'd have told you where she was. I should have told you anyway Levi. Instead I let you starve near to death. I'm sorry."

"It's too late now. All of this is on me, Grant. I made this happen. Cecily didn't want my child, she told me so. I should have let her alone."

"What happened to you, Levi?"

"You know how I always got picked on for being dumb when we were in school?" Levi looked up at Grant.

"You fought anyone that called you dummy if I remember right. After a few fights, no one picked on you because you couldn't learn to read. You may not have been able to read Levi, but you sure could fight."

"Cecily made me feel dumb, and I got mad. She lied to me, and the whole time that she was lying to me I was feeling sorry for her and loving her. I thought that she was grieving over her father. I think now that I might have known all along that she was keeping something from me. I never dreamed it was that she had only married me for my money. I was so sure that she loved me like I loved her." Levi looked away from Grant and Grant went back to his hair.

"You aren't dumb, Levi. You never were, you just couldn't learn to read. You are good with that kid. I wouldn't know what to do with a kid, but you're so natural." Grant handed him the mirror; it was Cecily's mirror, Levi thought as he took it and looked at his reflection. "So, what do you think?"

"I think you should open up your own barbershop," Levi said as he stood and brushed the loose hair from his clothes. "I'll be sure to always come to you when I need a trim. Thanks, Grant."

"Does this mean that you're my friend again?" Grant followed Levi into the house and accepted a cup of coffee Levi poured for him.

"I never stopped being your friend, Grant. I just lost my mind, I guess. The day I drove Cecily from me I knew that I had to come to my senses if I ever meant to get her back." He closed his eyes and saw his wife as she had been that day on the parlor floor. "And I knew too that I would probably never get her back. You were right that day when you said that I was tearing her apart."

"I wish now that I had been wrong," Grant said and looked at Levi from over the rim of the coffee mug that he held to his lips.

"What's done is done. I can only feel terrible guilt and shame for what I did, I always will, and talking won't help. It's over." Levi stood and went to the sink. "I am glad that you got Cecily away from me, Grant," he said softly without looking at Grant. "I wish you'd gotten her a few days sooner," Grant said nothing more and Levi was glad for the silence.

Late that afternoon, Mrs. Liston and Jamie came to see Levi. He hired Mrs. Liston to take care of his house and Jamie to take care of the animals. He also told Jamie to get Jon Hyde to work rounding up all of his cattle. Levi knew, he now had someone to provide for; he had Ethan and a future again. He owed Cecily; he could never repay his debt to her. His wife had given him a reason to live when she had died.

Levi put Ethan into the cradle and went out onto the porch to smoke a cigarette. The stars twinkled bright in the night sky, the moon was full and bright and hung low. The outside world seemed huge, Levi felt alone, even with Ethan. He wondered if he would ever get over Cecily, would he ever stop thinking about her all the time. He knew that he wouldn't, not even if he lived to be one hundred years old. He had known her all his life; she was more than a lover; she had been a playmate and friend and the girl that lived down the road. No, he would never get over her, ever.

He went back inside the house and into the kitchen. He took one of the rocking chairs by the stove and brought it into his bedroom. He filled the oil lamp and put matches by the lamp. He would be ready when Ethan woke for his next feeding; Levi thought as he filled a bottle with milk and placed it on the dresser.

After he had done all that he could think to do before going to bed, Levi lay down and closed his eyes. He was worn out. He hadn't done so much in one day as he had this day in almost a year. And he had eaten three good meals today as well. He rolled over onto his side and took hold of Cecily's pillow and hugged that pillow tight trying to fight off his unmanly tears. He had cried that day that he had hurt her, he remembered. He had cried for what he knew was lost to him, for something that he had never had. He cried now; he still wanted Cecily to love him. Cecily was dead and would never love him now.

Chapter Ten

Levi found that a routine worked best with Ethan. Every morning he was up by six and had the baby changed and fed. He had learned to pat the baby's back after every feeding to avoid gas. Gas was a God awful thing for a baby to have, he had found that out the second night that Ethan was with him and neither of them got even a moment of sleep due to Ethan's constant crying from an ill stomach. After he had Ethan settled every morning he would eat breakfast, at first he had only been able to eat a very little bit, but slowly over time, he was able to eat more. By the time that he finished washing his morning dishes, Mrs. Liston would be there, and Ethan would need changing again. He would then take Ethan to Miss Crandle's house by nine and in the first six weeks that he had Ethan, he would go back home and back to bed. He didn't know how he had survived those first six weeks. He had been dizzy and weak so much of the time that he worried he would not be able to wake up in the night and take care of his son, he was that tired. But as time passed, he got better, and now after he would drop Ethan off with Miss Crandle, he would join Jamie and Jon in gathering up his herd and marking all the calves that had been born in the past year. Grant would often come and help with the herd in the morning, and it was good to be around his old friend who knew him so well and had forgiven him.

By noon every day, Levi would return to Miss Crandle's and get Ethan and take the baby home for a change and a nap. At first, Levi had had to force himself to eat a decent lunch, Miss Liston was a good cook, and she urged him to eat well, and he did as she said, he wanted to be strong again, for his son.

His sister Sarah had come out for the day and held his son while he held little Frankie, she cried over the loss of her friend and the mother of this sweet little baby that she thought favored his mama. "She died, and when she did, she saved my brother," Sarah said. "So much like our Cecily." Levi looked at his sister; she was right. Cecily had always been unselfish and good, everything he wasn't, she was caring, had empathy and compassion and was sweet. "We were blessed to have had her in our lives, she was always family," Sarah continued. "We have to honor her Levi; we have to raise this little boy to know he had a mama that adored him. She loved him so much that she saved his daddy's life. She loved you that much Levi. Promise you'll tell him how wonderful his mama was every single day forever."

Sarah held the baby tight and heard her brother gasping; she looked over and saw he was crying. "Don't cry Levi; I didn't mean to make you cry.

"I don't want this little boy of mine to be anything like me, Sarah. I hurt her; I was mean to her. I got mad." Sarah left her chair on the porch and put her hand over his mouth.

"Listen to me, Levi. Think about what I'm saying to you. You lived with Cecily; you loved her. She tried to make everyone around her happy; I know she did. She gave you this baby to make you happy. You can't go back and fix what you did; it's in the past. All you can do is move forward. I know Cecily; she forgave you before she died. I know she did because you have this darling baby in your life."

Levi looked up at his little sister. "She couldn't forgive me; you don't know what I did to her."

"I don't need to know; I know Cecily. She was the most loving, forgiving soul I ever knew. Let go of what you did to her Levi; she would want you too. And the proof of my words is in my arms."

"Thank you, Sarah," he said taking her hand.

"I wish I were the mother you are," Sarah laughed. "You're so organized, and everything around her runs so smooth." Levi laughed; he liked being a mother. Sarah liked the sound of his laughter. Cecily had given her not just a nephew, but her brother back.

Life was going on, Levi was alive and living his life again, a life that Cecily had given to him. He spent his afternoons with the baby; he enjoyed his time with Ethan. He would put the baby on a blanket on the floor and watch Ethan. At first all Ethan did was sleep and eat and need his diaper change, but as the days came and went Ethan started noticing his world. The baby found his own hand was an amazing thing to look at, and Levi would sit and watch his son for hours and never be sorry that he was tied to the house by his darling baby boy.

By the middle of April, Levi was healthy again. He had gained back all the weight that he had lost and was able to do anything that he wanted to do without shaking all over in weakness. Ethan was big enough for him to take out for a walk, Ethan loved to be outside, and Levi liked having his son with him. Together they were exploring the world and Levi was seeing the world for the first time through his son's eyes. He still felt sick when he thought of Cecily, he still grieved and hated himself for what he had done to her, but he was thankful she had given him his child, and he knew his sister was right, Cecily would have forgiven him, that was just who she was.

"Woolgathering," Miss Crandle said as she came up onto the porch and saw Levi sitting on the swing with Ethan in his arms. She would walk over every Sunday morning and go to church with Levi and Ethan; then she would take the baby home with her for the afternoon. The reason she came over to Levi's house was because Ethan was a wiggler and Levi could not hold the baby and drive the buggy too.

"I guess I was," Levi said and handed her the baby. "I was thinking about how the past three months have gone by so fast." He smiled at Louise and saw her eyes grow wide. "Did I say something wrong?" he asked her and she shook her head.

"No, not at all. I was just surprised. When I first met you, I couldn't believe that you were the man that Cecily described to me. She said that you were very handsome, almost beautiful and she said that you had an easy smile that you gave often. She said that she loved your smile. And just now, when you smiled at me, I realized that you really are a handsome man." Levi felt himself blush at Louise's words.

"I had better get the buggy," Levi said softly and hurried past Louise after he gave her Ethan to hold. She watched him until he disappeared inside the barn, a frown on her face.

Levi hitched up the buggy with clumsy hands; Louise's words of Cecily had upset him. Cecily had told Louise that he was a handsome man. She had told Louise that she had loved his smile. Cecily should have told Louise that he was a monster and that the very thought of him made her sick. And then Levi paused in what he was doing and caught his breath. Cecily had loved his smile. Cecily had loved something about him when she should have had nothing but hate for him. And he kept remembering that she had given him Ethan. Cecily must have felt something more for him than he had ever known. She had loved his smile after all that he had put her through. He wished that she were alive; he wished that he could have another chance. Cecily had loved his smile.

Levi brought the buggy into the yard and helped Louise in while he held Ethan in one arm; the baby was awake and making baby noises. "I hope he's quiet in church today," Louise said after Levi got into the buggy and started down the road. "What I said earlier," her words brought Levi's eyes to hers. "I didn't mean that you aren't a handsome man when you don't smile." Levi started to laugh, and she stopped speaking.

"Thank you, Miss Crandle," he said when his laughter died down

"Don't you think it's time you started calling me Louise?"

"Only if you call me Levi," he offered.

"Cecily missed you very much," Louise said and waited to see his reaction to her words. She had been here for three months, and she had visited with Levi often, she had shown him how to burp the baby, and she had made sure he had clothes for Ethan as the baby was growing fast, she had even fed Levi in the beginning in an effort to help him regain his lost strength. And they had never, in all their time together, just sat and talked of Cecily. The time had come, she needed to know how he felt about his wife, and by the look on his face, he felt terrible.

"She shouldn't have," Levi said in a near whisper.

"If you had it to do all over again, would you do things differently?" Louise watched the tortured look cover Levi Tucker's face.

"Cecily's dead," he said in a whisper. "I killed her." Louise sat in silence by his side, when she thought to say something to him of Cecily; the church had come into sight.

Levi sat in the church with Ethan leaning back against his chest and facing the Reverend Bidwell. He did not look forward to the ride home with Louise; he didn't want to talk about Cecily. Everything that Louise had said had hurt him in some way. Cecily was dead, and he couldn't change what he had done in their marriage, talking about her missing him and loving his smile when it was too late for him to change what he had done to her only made him feel worse than he had before. He wanted to forget Cecily, forgetting his wife was the only way that he could live without hating himself every second of every single day for the rest of his life.

Levi looked down at the top of Ethan's head and saw his wife's hair, that soft brown hair that he ached to touch as he had ached to touch Cecily for years while he had waited for her to grow up and become his. He thought of the times that he had held her on the bed and brushed her four hundred strokes rather than one hundred before bed. He loved her hair loose and flowing and long, around her body when he made love to her. He looked down at his baby and saw crystal clear blue eyes looking up at him; Cecily would haunt him every time he looked into his son's eyes.

The Reverend Bidwell finally finished his sermon, and as Levi sat in the front of the church now, it took him a long while to get outside. Several people stopped and talked to him and Louise in the long line headed for the door, and he tried to smile and put Cecily from his thoughts.

"He's a natural mother," Mrs. Liston said to a group of women outside in the churchyard. "I've never seen a father as devoted to his child as Levi is."

"He certainly looks better than he did a few months ago," Althea, the Reverend Bidwell's sister said to Mrs. Liston. "You're feeding him well."

"He eats everything I cook and then some," Mrs. Liston said with pride. "I can't understand why Cecily left him; he's such a fine young gentleman."

"She had the baby brought to him after she died," Mrs. Albertson the pianist for the church said.

Levi came out of the church and once down the steps and in the churchyard, he lifted Ethan above his head and laughed up at his son while the baby smiled down into his eyes. "He won't stay single for long," one young woman in the group said, and every one of the women turned and stared at Levi Tucker.

"My nephew, Preston worked for Levi, and he told me that the day Cecily left Levi, that horrible Bernard Calhoun came out to their place. Preston said that Cecily went crazy, kicking Bernard and hitting him. Preston had to pull her off of Bernard; she was trying to kill him. I think that nasty Bernard had something to do with her leaving here," the Reverend Bidwell's sister Althea said.

"I don't know," Mrs. Albertson said. "If you'll remember after Levi and Cecily married we didn't see much of them. They only came to church a couple of times. And Cecily was always in church; she liked to sit up front."

"I still think that Bernard was the problem, Althea Bidwell said and her twin sister Eva agreed. The ladies smiled as Levi and Louise passed by walking toward their buggy. None of the women noticed how pale Lydia Masterson had become at the mention of Bernard Calhoun, or how closely she looked at Levi when he went by them.

Levi helped Louise into the buggy praying that she would say nothing more about Cecily while he handed her Ethan. Louise saw Levi's face and decided to keep quiet on the ride home. She needed to talk to him about Cecily, but she didn't want to hurt him, and she could see the hurt on his face when she talked of his dead wife.

Levi took Louise home and watched her take his son into her house; it would be a long lonely Sunday afternoon. He went home, and after having put up the horse and buggy, he went inside and fixed himself some lunch. After he had eaten, he went out onto the porch and smoked a cigarette. Levi was relaxed and thinking of how he planned to reopen the sawmill this coming week. Grant, Jamie, and Jon were all coming back to work for him, and he had five orders to fill already. They would be busy for at least the next two weeks. He had six acres of pine trees ready to cut, and three men hired to cut the trees starting tomorrow. His thoughts were interrupted when a buggy pulled up into his front yard.

Lydia Masterson saw Levi sitting on his porch and left her buggy to go up the steps. "May I speak with you, Mr. Tucker?" she asked, and Levi stood. He wondered what she could want with him; he hardly knew her.

"May I offer you a seat?" he asked hoping and praying she would refuse. He didn't want her here; she wasn't Cecily and Cecily was the only woman he wanted to be near. Cecily was dead; he reminded himself.

"I need to ask you a question," Lydia said, and Levi waited for a long moment while she stared up at him. "Did Bernard Calhoun hurt your wife?" Levi's eyes grew wide, and he took a deep breath, he had not expected this question. "I need to know, Mr. Tucker." Lydia's voice was filled with pleading, and Levi frowned.

"Why?" He did not want to talk about Bernard, and what Bernard had done to Cecily, he tried never to even think about Bernard being with Cecily.

"Because I heard some people talking today and they said that your wife left here because of Bernard. I have to know if he might have hurt her. He wants to court me, and I've heard a rumor he hurt Mrs. Whittaker as well."

Levi tried to think if Bernard had actually hurt Cecily, he had courted her, he had taken photos of her that she allowed him to take without her clothes on, Clemmie too for that matter. The only way that Bernard had hurt Cecily was to blackmail her, and that had hurt her and Levi.

"Stay away from Bernard Calhoun," Levi said firmly.

"That's what Mrs. Whittaker told me to do, she wouldn't tell me why," Lydia said.

"Listen to me," Levi said in a voice almost as stern as the Reverend Bidwell's. "Stay away from Bernard; you're too nice a young woman to get mixed up with that kind of man.

"Are you saying that Bernard hurt your wife, Mr. Tucker?" she pressed Levi for a firm answer, and he nodded his head.

"That's just what I'm saying," he confirmed.

"Thank you, Mr. Tucker," Lydia said and turned away from him. Levi watched her go and hoped that she would stay away from Bernard Calhoun.

Levi rushed to his horse after having told Grant he would see him tomorrow and started for Louise's house. He was going to be late as it was already noon. He decided to take a short cut through the woods and turned his horse off the road. The sawmill was up and working all the time now, and Levi had to hire two more men so that they could get all the orders filled on time. And still, they were behind schedule. He had even been taking Ethan out to the sawmill in the afternoon and watching the work he missed doing himself, but he didn't want to give up his time with his son.

One moment Levi was on his horse and the next he was staring up through the trees at the blue sky above. He had been so lost in his thoughts that he hadn't even seen the tree branch that felled him. He turned his head and saw his horse eating the green grass between the trees and wondered how long he had been unconscious. He grabbed his head when he tried to sit up, and the whole world went mad around him, both twisting and turning. He let go of his head as it hurt to touch and saw blood on his hands. He felt a knot starting to form and knew he had hurt himself. He felt like a fool; he hadn't fallen off a horse since he had been a small boy.

After a long while of sitting still, Levi stood up and fought the dizzy pain in his head as he went to his horse and awkwardly mounted. He had to ride slow so that he would not jar what was left of his brain and continuously had to wipe the blood that flowed into his right eye away with his handkerchief.

"What happened to you?" Louise cried while pulling him into the house.

I fell off my horse," he said, and Louise forced him to sit down in a chair at the kitchen table. "That hurts," he complained as she pressed a cool cloth to his forehead.

"I'm sure that it does," Louise continued to wipe the blood from his face and forehead. "This needs stitches Levi," she said as she touched the growing knot on his forehead and saw him flinch.

"I'll be fine," Levi said and took the cloth from Louise. "I've been hurt worse than this. I can't believe that I rode right into a tree branch. I was in a hurry to get here because it's near Ethan's lunchtime. Where is he?"

"I fed him and put him down for a nap. I thought that you might have gotten busy at your sawmill and would be later than usual." Louise offered him a cup of coffee.

"No, thank you," Levi said of the coffee and stood. "I think I'll just take Ethan and go on home."

"You need to go into town and let the doctor see to your head, Levi." Louise wiped more blood away that ran down his face. "I'll keep Ethan for you."

"It's nothing," Levi said firmly, and Louise rolled her eyes.

"All right, when you have a horrible scar on your forehead in a few weeks, just remember that I tried to prevent it by begging you to go and get stitches."

"I'll remember," Levi tried to smile but couldn't, his head hurt too bad. He felt like he had run head-on into something. He had a tree branch.

Levi went home and put Ethan down for a nap. He looked at the bump on his forehead before he went and explained to Mrs. Liston what had happened. She bandaged it for him after telling he needed to go let the doctor set in a few stitches. Levi assured her that he was fine.

He spent the afternoon sitting on the porch swing with Ethan lying on a blanket at his feet. His head hurt so much that after Mrs. Liston left for the day, he fed Ethan and went to bed. This was the first time he had missed a meal in almost four months, but he couldn't eat, he felt sick.

The baby was screaming, the screams heartbreaking. The full moon shone into the bedroom and made it almost as bright as day inside, and she could see, no one was going to the baby. The double doors that led onto the porch were open wide and worried about the endless cries of the baby, she slipped inside the room and picked the baby up out of his bed, unbuttoned her blouse and put the baby to her aching full breast to quiet him, something she did almost every single night.

Levi heard his son crying and fought to open his eyes. His whole face hurt and he couldn't get his eyes to do like he wanted them to do and open. He had to get to Ethan, he knew that, and he forced himself to sit up. Ethan had stopped crying by the time he had his eyes open, and he looked toward the cradle and blinked hard. "Cecily," he said his wife's name softly before he passed out and fell back onto the bed.

She slipped into the darkest shadows of the room; she knew where they were as she came every night to feed her son. She stood now staring at the figure of her husband on the bed. Something was wrong, and she didn't know what to do. She did know that she had to deal with the baby first. Ethan knew that she was real and not a ghost, the man on the bed thought that she was dead.

After she had the baby back in the cradle and asleep, she walked softly to the bed and looked down at her husband, a man that was better off without her. A man that had once loved her and then hated her more than he had ever loved her. She had nearly killed him, and then she had saved him by dying to everyone that mattered in the world except for her child and Louise Crandle.

Cecily reached out a hand and smoothed the hair away from Levi's face. He had changed a lot since she had given Ethan to him. He was strong now; he was well again. Then she saw the bandage on his forehead and remembered having him tell Louise that he had fallen from his horse from where she had been hiding in the back of the house. Levi was in trouble; he needed help.

Levi opened his eyes and saw Cecily standing by the bed, he felt her hand touching his face, or he thought that he felt her hand touching his face. She was real; he wasn't being haunted. She was here with him. He had to tell her; he had to tell her he was sorry before she disappeared into heaven again and away from him forever. "I never should have raped you. I'll burn in hell for that," Levi said softly and felt his mouth was too dry if he could only get a drink of water he could say all that he needed to say to her before she left him. "Forgive me that day," he whispered and felt her hand leave his face.

"I forgive you, Levi," Cecily said softly and backed away from him with wide eyes.

Levi groaned as his wife moved from the side of the bed and he tried to sit up, he rolled over to the edge of the bed where he vomited. Cecily knew that he needed help and turned and ran out of the house. Levi saw his wife running away from him and reached out his hand to her calling her name in a broken and weak voice, and he knew that the night had taken her from him, he had lost her again. He had lost her for the rest of his life.

"Cecily," he said her name in a choked voice and looked out into the darkness. "Come back to me, Cecily. I need you." The darkness remained empty.

"Louise!" Cecily called out as she busted up into Louise Crandle's bedroom in the wee hours of the morning. "Louise, wake up," Cecily cried out while she lit a lamp. Startled awake by Cecily calling out her name Louise sat up on her bed and rubbed her eyes. "You have to go to the doctor right away," Cecily said as she hurried to the bed. "Levi is sick, very sick."

"What are you going on about?" Louise asked and stared at Cecily's worried face.

"I heard Ethan crying, I went into the house, and Levi was ill in the bed. Very ill. I think it's his head from where he fell off his horse today. He should have gone to the doctor like you advised but he didn't, and you have to go get help for him. You have to get up now."

"I cannot go and get the doctor, Cecily. Sit down and get a hold of yourself and think this thing through," Louise ordered

Cecily. "Making these nightly visits there to feed that baby from your breast has just been taking a risk. Maybe you want the man to know you're alive, I don't know what's going on in your pretty little head, but sometimes you make me think you have fluff for brains."

"Do stop talking about my brain and get dressed, you have to go for the doctor. Levi needs help; he could be dying."

"And just how in the world am I going to explain to the doctor that I knew at two in the morning Levi Tucker needed help and when I'm at home, in my own bed, asleep?" Louise looked at Cecily and shook her head.

"You can say that you went for a walk because you couldn't sleep," Cecily offered helpfully.

"Little old ladies do not go for walks in the middle of the night, Cecily. And I have paper curlers in my hair; I wouldn't be caught dead out in public with paper curlers in my hair." Louise said firmly. "And besides," she raised her eyebrows and stared hard at Cecily, "Only the dead walk in the night," Cecily stared in confusion at Louise and shook her head hard.

"But you have to go," Cecily begged. "He can't take care of Ethan." Louise left the bed reaching for her clothes.

"Why didn't you tell me that to begin with? That foolish man," Louise said as she was pulling on her clothes. "I told him to go to the doctor, and he wouldn't listen to me, and now he's put our little Ethan in danger because he can't take care of him."

"Oh, please," Cecily begged. "Don't talk, just hurry. Levi might be dying."

"And you would know about dying," Louise said as she started removing her paper curlers.

"Don't do that, there isn't time," Cecily said to Louise and reached for her hat. "Here, put this on, it'll cover the curlers."

"I will not leave this house with curlers in my hair, Cecily," Louise said, and Cecily stood still holding her hat. "This is going to be embarrassing enough to explain without looking like a total fool with curlers in my hair. Go back over to Levi's and hide in your dark corner and care for the baby. When you hear knocking on the door, run into the dark as you do every night, I'll hurry with the doctor as fast as I can." Cecily kissed her cheek before she ran out of the house.

Louise left her house walking fast with her lantern in the dark thinking that the doctor was never going to believe for one second that she, a little old lady, had been out taking a walk at this ungodly hour and just happened to stop by Levi Tucker's home and found him ill in his bed. The Doctor was going to think she was a crank. This was worse than embarrassing. If it weren't for Ethan, Louise knew she would not have made one move from her bed until morning, and Levi Tucker could just wait for help to come.

Cecily snuck back into Levi's house by the kitchen door and then softly slipped into his room reaching into the cradle for her baby. Every night she had been doing this to relieve her aching breasts and had never feared she would get caught, Levi slept hard she knew. She went to the bed and checked on Levi, he was still breathing, and she breathed a sigh of relief before turning her attention back to Ethan.

Even in the dark Cecily could see his light colored eyes so, like her own staring up at her. She had nearly died giving him birth, he was worth it she smiled, he was so beautiful. The past few days she was seeing Levi in her son, the dimple in the center of his chin, the slant to his eyes, he was going to be as beautiful as Levi one day. And she wouldn't be here to see him grow up. She had given this baby to her husband, and she was going to have to one day too soon walk away from them both. Cecily had no delusions that she could stay here; she was dead and in her death, Levi lived. Levi was growing strong and healthy and happy with their son; she had no regret in what she had chosen to do.

Cecily saw her husband sit up on the bed and moved with Ethan into the darkest corner of her old bedroom to where the vanity stool. Ethan started to coo, and she quickly put the baby to her breast holding her breath. Levi stood on shaky legs and walked to the bathroom, Cecily heard him vomit again and then silence.

Louise and the doctor knocked several times on Levi's front door when after a few moments there was no answer; Louise took hold of the knob and with a quick turn entered the house. They found Levi on the bathroom floor, and Louise realized that Cecily had been right, Levi was very sick.

"Levi," the doctor called out his name and Levi halfway opened his eyes only to close them tight as Louise's lantern was blinding him after having sat in the dark. "Let me help you back to your bed."

"Can't," Levi moaned. "I'm sick."

"I need to look at your head," the doctor said in an easy manner, and Levi turned his face where the doctor could see what the tree limb had done to him. "It's a good thing you came for me Miss Crandle; he has a concussion. Levi, you need to be in your bed," the doctor said these last words to Levi and all but forced him to stand.

Louise stood outside the bathroom and gasped when Cecily touched her shoulder and handed her the baby, she saw Cecily disappear out the door into the darkness and Louise put a hand over her heart, these nightly visits to Levi's home to feed her baby were more than risky, she could have easily been caught by the doctor. But looking down at the baby, Louise's heart swelled with the love his mother had for him, to not just take chances of getting caught, but to have given this beautiful baby to a husband that didn't want her in his life any longer.

"A head wound is nothing to ignore," the doctor was saying to Levi as he helped him into bed.

"Louise," Levi said her name, and she hurried to him. "I can't take care of the baby. He was crying earlier, but Cecily got him to stop." The doctor gave Louise a wide-eyed look.

"I thought Levi's wife was dead," the doctor said, and Louise nodded her head. "Head wounds sometimes do this kind of thing; I had a patient with a head wound once that couldn't remember his own name for days on end, then one day was back to himself as though nothing had happened to him.

"I'll take care of Ethan," Louise spoke to Levi when the doctor turned and started cleaning the wound on his forehead. "You just rest Levi."

"It was a very good thing that you woke worried about him, Miss Crandle and came over here," he needs someone to be with him at all times for the next twenty-four hours." Louise could say nothing; the doctor had accepted her ridiculous story; she didn't want to say anything now that would cause him to disbelieve her.

"Is he all right?" Cecily worriedly asked Louise as the elderly woman came in the front door of Daniel Walker's house just before dawn with Ethan in her arms. Ethan was screaming his little head off, and she handed him to Cecily who quickly undid her nightgown and put her baby to her breast.

"Ethan is fine now; he was just upset because his night's sleep was disturbed, as was mine." Louise had a put outlook on her face and kept shaking her head.

"I know Ethan is fine," Cecily said as she followed Louise into the kitchen. "Is Levi going to be all right?"

"He has a head injury, Cecily. He should have done what I told him to do yesterday and gone to the blasted doctor in the daylight hours. Instead his stubborn nature has caused all of this uproar." Louise went to the stove to put the coffee on but stopped when she saw the look on Cecily's face from the corner of her eye. The younger woman was terrified for her husband. A man that she had died for. "Do calm down dear, the doctor has stayed with him, and

I'm sure in a day or two he'll be fine. And we get to have this little man all to ourselves while his daddy gets well." Louise smoothed down Ethan's hair while smiling at the baby; she had grown very fond of him.

"I was afraid, Louise. I don't want anything to happen to Levi," Louise turned back to the coffee.

"You think I don't know that? You've given the man your baby, and I'm still not certain he deserved to have that little one, certainly not more than you. But anyway, the doctor is with him and Ethan is safe with us. There is something you should know; Levi told the doctor and myself tonight that you were there taking care of Ethan. So he did see you, but the doctor seems to think it was normal for Levi to have seen his dead wife and brushed it off. I know the truth, as do you. We can only hope Levi will accept the doctor's attitude." Louise put two cups of coffee on the table, and Cecily sat down holding her son up to be burped. "How long do you think you can go on this way?"

"Forever," Cecily said while patting Ethan's back.

"You should never have given that baby away, and I was a fool to go along with this crazy plan," Louise stated, everything about this situation was wrong, and from what she had seen and heard, everything had been wrong between Cecily and Levi for a long time. She loved Cecily like she was her own child and she adored little Ethan and being honest with herself, she knew she truly liked Levi Tucker, he wasn't what she had expected, and he adored his son and was a wonderful, devoted father. Why hadn't he been a devoted husband to Cecily? She looked again at Ethan; the baby was innocent of the way his parents were behaving.

"I did what I had to do, Louise. Levi was dying because of me. I left here because I was hurting him. I gave him Ethan because my lies were killing him. And you can see the change in him. Levi is alive. He's strong and happy, and Ethan is well cared for and loved."

"And what about you, Cecily? We can't stay here forever, and you know that. One day Ethan is going to call out for his mother if we stay here much longer. He's almost five months old. You made it where you are going to lose Ethan forever. He'll never know his own mother." Cecily squeezed her eyes shut tight at Louise's words. She knew the truth; she knew that she had given her baby away and was going to lose him very soon.

"I saved Levi's life," she said when she opened her eyes and looked back at Louise, her heartache plain to see on her beautiful face.

"And at what cost?" Louise demanded slapping her hand on the table and causing Ethan to cry for a few moments. "You've destroyed your own life," Louise softened her voice

"I did what I did in the name of love, Louise." Cecily swallowed to keep from crying. "I did an unselfish act of kindness for the only man I've ever loved my whole life."

"Oh for God sake, Cecily. And what about that little man?" Louise pointed to Ethan. "Listen to me; it's not too late to fix this. Go to that man, tell him that you want to be his wife and work things out, you love the fool, and I think he loves you too. And there in your arms is the tie that binds you both one to the other. Do not leave this baby behind. Do not give up this little boy." Louise was pleading in her firmest voice. She knew that this young mother needed her child; she needed the father as well.

"You think that I don't want to go to Levi?" Cecily nearly cried out. "He doesn't want me, you saw Clemmie's letter, he said he'd shoot himself if he ever saw me again. I'm what was killing him. He hates me, Louise and he has reason."

"You will lose your son!" Louise raised her voice in desperation.

"Not right now I won't. We still have a little time left here."

"And when the time comes to leave what are you going to do? Take Ethan and run away?" Louise put her face in her hands for a moment and thought. "go to him, Cecily. Go to Levi and end this foolish game that you are playing with him and his affections for this child. One of you are going to lose a son if you don't."

"Louise, I made my choice to lose Ethan months ago. I knew what I was going when I did it. I love Levi; I want him happy and healthy and safe. And I want him to have a part of me. He wanted me to give him a child, and I told him I wouldn't. Well, now I have. I finally gave something to Levi, something that he can see and feel and hold in his arms and love, love Louise without fear of betrayal and deceit. Don't you understand? All I gave to Levi were lies, and half told truths. I can't go to him now, he hates me, and he has that right. I've brought him so much pain. I can't take Ethan from him now; he loves Ethan."

"You are seriously going to give up your child," Louise said in a harsh voice. "And Levi Tucker thinks he killed you. Did you know that? I've seen that man's face, Cecily. When I spoke of you, he was tormented with grief and pain. I think in my heart he would take you back and be glad in the taking."

"He's too poisoned by the things Bernard led him to believe of me to ever hear any truth I might tell him. He might take me back in the anger and hurt of before; I don't know if I can go back to that. I've watched him from the trees and seen he's like he use to be," Cecily fell silent seeing Levi's smile in her mind. "My old Levi is back."

"Good, he's back," Louise said in a disgusted voice as she took the baby from Cecily. "So when the time comes, you and I will take Ethan and run. And if or when your Levi follows us, I'll hire the best lawyers in the State of Georgia to fight him for this little one." Louise kissed Ethan's cheek.

"No Judge would give Ethan to me," Cecily said as she looked down at her son. "I abandoned my husband, my home and now my child. Please, let's not talk of this anymore. It's over. Ethan belongs to Levi, and when we leave, I won't even be a memory to my baby."

Ethan stayed with Louise and Cecily for two days before Levi came for the baby. He had six stitches in his forehead and a long bruise down the side of his face, but he felt much better than he had the last time he had seen Louise. He sat at her kitchen table with Ethan playing on the floor in the sunshine that came through the back door of Daniel Walker's old home, Louise placed a cup of coffee in front of him and sat down facing him across the table.

"I want to thank you for coming to check on me that night, Louise. I was so sick I couldn't take care of Ethan. When I saw you in the darkness pick Ethan up out of the cradle, I thought you were Cecily come back to me in whatever way the afterlife allows us and was taking care of our baby for me." Louise felt her face turn red; she should tell this young man right now that his wife was flesh and blood and in the next room listening to his every word and loving him and she was just being idiotic and so was he.

"I'm just glad you're better," Louise said to fill the silence and trying to find some way to get these two back together again.

"Louise," he said her name softly, and she looked up at him feeling sorry for him and for Cecily. "That night, when I thought you were Cecily, did I say anything to you?"

"You only asked that I take care of Ethan for you. Why?"

"I was just so certain I saw Cecily," he almost whispered. "She was touching my face; it felt so real. If I said anything to you, I'd like you to tell me now, please." He needed to know if any part of that night had been real, if he had asked Louise thinking she was Cecily, to forgive him.

"I don't know what you think you think you might have said to me, Levi, but I can assure you, all you did say was for me to take care of Ethan for you."

"I must have been dreaming," Levi said more to himself than to Louise. He wished it hadn't been a dream; he wished it had been real. Cecily had forgiven him.

"I'm certain you were, Levi," Louise took a sip of her coffee staring over the rim of the cup at Levi. He hadn't been dreaming, Cecily had been there that night with him, and she wondered, what had he said to his wife? She wasn't about to ask him in order to find out the answer to her question. And Cecily had not said one word about her nightly visit other than that she had gone into the room to feed Ethan and found Levi ill. Whatever Levi thought he had said to Cecily it couldn't have been of importance as neither were telling her what might have been said.

"I guess I should be going," Levi said and stood up before going to Ethan and picking his baby son up off of the blanket on the floor. "I'll see you in the morning, Louise. Thanks again for watching over him for me, I'd have been lost and him too without you."

The second Sunday in June was hot and beautiful. Bees filled the air with their buzzing, birds called out from the trees, and a gentle breeze blew off the lake giving some relief to the heat of early summer. Levi had gone to church with Louise and Ethan that morning, and now he had the afternoon alone and to himself while his son visited with Louise at her house. He sat in a rocking chair on the front porch and smoked a cigarette thinking that he hadn't been haunted by Cecily since that night that she had come into his room and touched his face. Maybe she really had forgiven him, and he was going to know peace in this life after all.

The doctor had removed the stitches from his forehead and other than a slight discoloration and a small scar above his brows, anyone looking at him would never have known that a few weeks ago he had ridden his horse into a low lying tree branch.

The weather must have been agreeable to the Reverend Bidwell also, Levi thought. This morning's sermon had not been filled with hell and damnation, and they had all been released from church a full quarter of an hour before noon. The Reverend almost never let his congregation go early.

Levi was thinking his life was now almost happy when he saw Grant and Clemmie pull up in his yard and leave their buggy. He stood up as they came onto the porch and offered them both a smile. He hadn't said much to Clemmie since the day he had come to her house demanding to know where Cecily was the day after he had thrown Clemmie out of his house and then raped his wife. Clemmie smiled at Levi, and he was glad, there might be some hope that their relationship was going to get better, he had always cared for Clemmie and what she had done with Bernard was none of his business, that was between Grant and his wife.

"Hello," Levi said with an easy smile. "Come inside and have a glass of tea.

"We can't," Grant said and looked from Clemmie to Levi. "We need you to come with us."

"I can't go anywhere, I have to go and get Ethan from Louise in about half an hour," Levi said and noticed for the first time that Clemmie looked concerned. "What's going on?"

"Lydia Masterson's has killed Bernard Calhoun," Grant said as he put a protective arm around his wife's shoulders.

"Bernard needed killing," Levi said softly.

"You don't understand, Levi," Clemmie spoke in a strained voice. "Lydia was being blackmailed just like Cecily, and I were."

"Then she had a good reason for killing Bernard." Levi's eyes were as cold and hard as his voice. He didn't want to stand here and talk about Bernard and Cecily; he tried never to think of Bernard and his wife together. He didn't like the way he felt inside of himself when he remembered that Cecily only married him for the money she needed to pay Bernard. Cecily had once loved Bernard.

"They will put poor Lydia in jail forever. She could die in jail." Clemmie looked into Levi's eyes, and her eyes pleaded with him for help. "If we go and tell the sheriff what Bernard was doing to Cecily and me, poor Lydia could get out of jail and go home where she belongs."

"And you want me to go and tell the sheriff about Cecily and Bernard's relationship?" Levi shook his head. "No, you two go. I want no part of this."

"How can you say that, Levi? You know what Bernard did to poor Cecily and for two long years." Clemmie pulled free of Grant's arm and stepped closer to Levi.

"He didn't do anything to her that she didn't allow him to do. You either for that matter." Clemmie slapped his face so hard that Levi's head turned to the side. Grant took a step closer to them, and Levi thought that Grant meant to hit him as well.

Clemmie stepped back away from Levi and stared into his angry eyes that also held too much hurt. "Oh," she breathed. "Oh, dear God in heaven," she looked at her husband who was looking at her; she knew he came to the same realization that she had just come too. She looked back at Levi's pain filled eyes. "You don't know." Grant shook his head hard in disbelief looking from his wife to Levi.

"He can't not know," Grant spoke only to his wife.

"No," Clemmie never took her eyes off of Levi. "He doesn't know; he really doesn't know."

"But Cecily had to have told him," Grant was standing closer to his wife also staring at Levi.

"She didn't, Grant. He doesn't know," Clemmie asserted.

"What the hell don't I know?" Levi demanded and heard Clemmie take a deep breath, Grant as well.

"Bernard, when he took our photos, mine for Grant and Cecily's for her father, he offered us a glass of tea, it had a bitter taste. Cecily and I we both just put it off as Bernard couldn't make tea." Clemmie stopped her explanation and looked at her husband, Grant came behind her and put his arms around his wife knowing that this was not an easy thing for her to remember, much less tell.

"He drugged them, Levi," Grant picked up the telling of this for his wife. "After they were unconscious, Bernard undressed them and took their photos. Didn't you see, in all the photos they appeared to be sleeping? They were sleeping. God knows how many other women Bernard did that too before Lydia finally killed him. She was protecting herself, something Cecily could only do by marrying you for your money, and my Clemmie almost lost everything, I almost lost her because of that dirty no good snake. And poor Daniel Walker, he lost everything, including his life to protect his child from Bernard. You would do no less for Ethan, Levi and you know it. We have to go to the sheriff, and we have to tell what Bernard did to Clemmie and Cecily. It's our duty."

Levi couldn't move or speak for a few long moments as he stood and thought of what Grant was telling him. If Cecily had been drugged as Grant said, then why hadn't she told him? Because he wouldn't let her, he had forced her into silence with his rules. He had been out of his mind over her reason for having married him, and he never let her explain anything to him. He remembered all the times that she had asked him to let her explain and he wouldn't. But then, it may have been different with Cecily; she had courted Bernard, she had been in love with Bernard.

"I don't know if Cecily was drugged or not," Levi finally said. Clemmie gave him a murderous look.

"She was Levi. She went to Bernard to have her photo made for her father, and he did to her the same thing to her that he did to me. No, he did more. Cecily wrote to me from Aunt Louise's months ago and told me everything. Bernard wanted to better himself, he had Cecily's father's money, and he thought that people would respect him if he were courting a decent woman, so he forced Cecily to court him. And she was so afraid of him exposing those horrible photos of her that she did everything he told her to do. She hated him, Levi and she was scared to death of him every minute of every day for two years. Cecily had more reason to hate and fear Bernard than I ever had. I still have her letter if you want to see what she wrote to me."

Levi stood and stared at Clemmie. He couldn't believe what he was hearing. And to see Cecily's letter, that was a laugh; he couldn't know one word written on the paper.

"Bernard came to me with those photos of Clemmie and tried to make me believe that Clemmie had been intimate with him," Grant said and saw Clemmie turn a fiery red before she hid her face against her husband's shirt. "Well, anyway, I found out on the night that we married that Bernard was a liar." Clemmie moaned, and Grant hugged her closer.

Levi's eyes grew wide as he stared at his friend, then he took three steps back and away from Grant. He put a shaking hand over his face as he remembered the bloodstains that had been on the sheets the morning after he had forced Cecily to take him as her husband. "God forgive me," he whispered to himself and his Lord and even Cecily. She had come to him pure. Cecily had come to him pure and he, Levi stopped thinking and shook his head hard fighting to breathe.

"Levi. What's wrong?" Grant asked and reached out a hand to steady his friend. Levi was swaying on his feet as he broke free of Grant's supporting hand and leaned against the house still fighting to breathe.

He had not let her talk; he had thrown every one of Bernard's lies to him about Cecily into her innocent face. He had been rough and quick in the taking of her untouched body. He had been far worse to Cecily than he had known. He really would spend eternity and beyond in hell for what he had done to his wife. And he had been so stupid to believe everything Bernard had told him. And he knew what Bernard really was; he had known what Bernard was since they were children.

"I have to go," Levi said and tried to stand upright.

"What about the sheriff?" Grant asked as Levi was leaving the porch.

No Sound The Silence Makes

"I'll go with you tomorrow. I'll ask Louise to keep Ethan for the day." Levi hurried down the road not looking back at the concern and confusion on Grant and Clemmie's faces.

Cecily had only known his body! He had been the only man to ever touch her! And his words to her, they had abused her as much as his body had! He was a monster! Levi thought. He had no right to Ethan. And Cecily, she had given him Ethan and then died. She hadn't wanted his child! His heart cried, and he thought that organ was going to burst inside of his chest for the crimes he had committed against his innocent wife. She had told Louise that she loved his smile; he had wiped any smile that she had ever meant to give him from her face. No wonder she had told Clemmie that day in the parlor that he was dumb. She had known he was dumb.

Levi started to run; he tried to escape the awful things that he knew he had done to his wife. He tried to run from the words he had used to hurt her, from the horror that he had made of her life. Cecily had never been his hell. He had been her hell from the moment that he learned of those photos and took Bernard's lies for truth.

Levi stopped running and leaned against a tree. Cecily had married him because she was afraid of Bernard. He had seen her fear that day in the church. He had seen her fear when Bernard came near her at her home; it was why he had followed Bernard into the yard and beaten him up. Cecily had never loved Bernard Calhoun. "Why?" Levi asked himself why he had never given his wife a chance to explain.

He had seen her ghost that night in his room when he had been too sick to care for Ethan. He had begged her ghost to forgive him for raping her. He should have begged her for more forgiveness. He hadn't known. He hadn't known because he wouldn't let her tell him. And he had hit her for a crime that she had not committed. He had punched her in the face.

Levi let go of the tree and started running down the red clay road again. Louise opened the door to his knock, and Levi ignored her concerned face as he reached down and grabbed up his son from the blanket on the floor. He buried his face in his son's soft brown hair, hair the color of Cecily's.

"Levi, whatever is the matter?" Louise asked him in concern as she followed him out of the house.

"I have to go to Madison tomorrow for the day," his voice was hoarse from having run the mile from his house to here. "Can you keep Ethan for me?"

"You know that I will," she said and touched his arm. "Is there something more that I can do for you, Levi?"

"Pray for my soul," the seriousness of his voice made Louise take a firm hold of his arm.

"What has happened, Levi. What's happened that has you upset like this?" He shook his head and gave a bitter, harsh laugh; Louise didn't like the sound of his laugh.

"All my life I tried to be good. There goes Levi Tucker; he's such a good man, I wanted people to say of me. Dumb, but good." He gave another bitter laugh. "I'm not a good man, Louise. I get mad and stay mad forever. That doesn't make me good. And I got mad over a pack of lies." He fell silent, and Louise watched as he hugged Ethan close.

"Does this have something to do with Cecily?" Levi looked at Louise with that tortured look on his face that she had seen before.

"Cecily," he almost cried his wife's name and looked at the floor.

"Do you hate her that much, Levi?" Louise asked while studying his tortured face.

"I know in heaven, she has to be hating me," Levi said and looked up at Louise with bright blue eyes. "And I'm the one that hated her," he whispered and turned away from Louise Crandle to take his son home. A son he knew he didn't deserve.

Louise stood in her doorway watching Levi Tucker walk down the road. He was taking Cecily's baby from her, and she was letting him. And now he's saying that he hated Cecily. He had no right to that baby while hating its mother; Louise wished that they had never come here.

"Cecily, pack your things, we're leaving here tomorrow. We're taking Ethan, and we're going to go home."

"No," Cecily said in a calm voice as she watched her husband walking away from her with their son in his arms.

"Levi is giving me Ethan for the whole day tomorrow while he goes to Madison. We'll have time to get out of here. We can go to my niece in Texas for a few years; you can stay in Texas, you have that money he gave to you in the bank, you've not touched it. We can hide from Levi forever if we have too." Cecily was shaking her head from side to side, and Louise sat down hard on the chair knowing that she wouldn't change the younger woman's mind. "He hates you," Louise stated as she stared at Cecily's back.

"But he loves Ethan. And Louise, I love him. I'll always love him."

Chapter Eleven

"How do I know for sure that Bernard Calhoun did to you what he did to Lydia Masterson?" The sheriff asked Clemmie as she stood nervous and frightened before him. She didn't want anyone to know what Bernard had done to her, but telling the sheriff was the right thing to do.

"Because she said he did," Grant stepped closer to his wife and the sheriff.

"The Judge won't take just her word, Grant, even if I do believe her. Where are the photos?"

"Cecily burned them," Clemmie answered the sheriff's question softly as he looked at Levi standing alone by the door.

"Without the photos, you won't be much help for Miss Masterson. Her story is the same as yours Miss Whittaker, but all I have is a dead man's photos of a young woman that aren't fit to make public and I won't. And her word and your word that the photos were done without consent."

"Here," Levi stepped forward and removed Cecily's photo from his wallet. "You show that to anyone other than the judge and yourself sheriff, and I'll kill you." He handed the photo to the sheriff while Clemmie stared up at him. All of this time he had been carrying Cecily's photo around with him and Cecily had thought she had burned them all the day that she left him.

"Now I have proof of your story, Mrs. Whittaker," He took the photo of Cecily and turned it upside down on his desk. "And you say that your wife and her father paid Bernard blackmail for two years, Mr. Tucker?"

"Bernard took almost everything Daniel Walker had and drove the man to an early grave," Levi said. And he had forced Cecily out of mourning clothes when she had all the reason in the world to mourn her father. Daniel had been trying to save his daughter. Daniel had loved Cecily and done the only thing that he could have done to keep her safe.

"Can Lydia get out of jail?" Clemmie asked the sheriff while still looking at Levi.

"If it's a matter of self-defense," Levi said softly, "I can tell you now that Bernard threatened Cecily physically," he remembered the day he had seen Bernard touching his wife, he had thought she wanted that touch. The look she gave him in the graveyard that day, Cecily was afraid, she was afraid of Bernard. Her trembling beside him while they ate together that evening in her father's house. So many times he had known she was afraid of Bernard, she had even tried to step into the grave when they went to lower her father, she had felt that unsafe.

"The Judge will have to hear the case, and an inquest will be held," the sheriff said to Levi. "I'm going to let Miss Masterson go now, Miss Whittaker, she'll be home with her family by dinner." The sheriff looked back at Levi. "You'll have to tell the judge of the physical harm you saw Bernard Calhoun do to your wife, Mr. Tucker. You can tell behind closed doors in the judge's chambers; no one else needs to know, sir. And I'm sorry that happened to your wife, what a nightmare she lived through. You were both very brave to come forward like this if it had been my wife; I'm not sure I could or would have let her tell what happened to her."

"Cecily would have wanted us too," Clemmie said. "She was sick when she found out that Bernard had done to me what he had been doing to her. She kept telling Grant over and over again that she should have told."

"And I told her that I wasn't her God, I wouldn't sit in judgment of her," Grant said while watching Levi's face. "She's dead now, and I know God didn't sit in judgment of her for this. She never did anything wrong. She was scared. She needed help. She was Bernard's victim daily for years. I wish she had told us so that we might have all helped her. Her Daddy would be here now if she had." Clemmie saw the pain that covered Levi's face at her husband's words and knew he had hurt Cecily; she didn't like that he had, but she forgave him because that's what Cecily would have done.

"I'm your hell," Levi heard Cecily say those words to him loud and clear inside of his head. She had thought that she was going to ruin him as she had ruined her father. Those first weeks of their marriage she had never been laughing at him for being dumb, she had been dying inside because she was afraid she would have to give all of his money to Bernard in order to be safe. She hadn't just married him for his money; she had married him so that his money could keep her safe from Bernard making those photos of her public. Cecily had turned down his marriage proposal in the field that day because she wanted to protect him from Bernard. And then changed her mind probably in the hopes that he could make her safe. It hadn't been grief alone those first weeks of their marriage; it had been terror, the terror of Bernard, and then terror of him. Her death had made her safe from both men.

Levi knew that in the end, he had been no different from Bernard. He had threatened her; she had even believed that he would use those photos against her. Cecily didn't commit any crime against him or anyone; everything Cecily had done, she had done because she had no other choice. She married him in fear. She married him to be safe, and he had never made her safe.

"I'll let you folks know when I need you," the sheriff said and took Cecily's picture from the desk and locked it in his drawer. "And I can assure you, Mr. Tucker, that no one will see that picture except the Judge and I. I'll get it back to you,"

"Burn it," Levi's words stopped the sheriff from speaking. "Send the photo to hell with the bastard that took it. I never want to see it again."

"You have my word; I'll do just as you say," the sheriff assure Levi before he left the office.

Grant followed his wife out of the sheriff's office and helped her onto her horse. "Grant," she said his name, and he looked up at her. "Would you mind if I rode a little way alone with Levi?"

"Why?" her husband asked he mounted his own horse.

"Because if he doesn't talk to someone, he's going to bust wide open. Didn't you see his face in there? I thought that he was going to have a bad case of my morning sickness. I think only one of us needs that complaint right now." She smiled into her husband's eyes, and he returned her smile. "I know that he's your friend, but he's been my friend all my life too. I would like to try and get him to talk to me. Please."

"All right, sweetheart, I'll hang back."

"Thank you, Grant." Clemmie kicked her horse into a run so that she could catch up with Levi.

Levi tried not to think about the past. He could not change anything now, and his stomach was tied in a knot and on fire. He could not think about Cecily. Blackmailed Cecily. Tortured by Bernard, Cecily. Torn apart by him. She had to run and hide from him. She had died having his child rip its way out of her body. A child that she did not want. He could not deal with this; the fires of hell were inside of his gut and killing him.

"Levi," Clemmie called his name as she caught up with him, he didn't look at her. "I have to tell you," she spoke on hoping he would glance her way, "that I'm sorry for slapping you yesterday."

"My God, Clemmie," Levi breathed her name. "I pushed and shoved and threw you out of my house. I was mean to you and to your best friend. What you should do is take a gun and shoot me, not tell me you're sorry." Levi kept his eyes straight ahead. He could not remember that day that he had thrown Clemmie out of his house; he had hurt Cecily that day.

"We both made mistakes, Levi. I thought that you knew what Bernard had done to both Cecily and me." Clemmie watched Levi's face; he still had not looked at her.

"What happened?" he asked after a few moments of silence.

"When?" Clemmie asked hoping that he did not want her to go into details about the day Bernard had taken her photo. She wanted to forget that day forever.

"The day that I got your photos and Cecily's photos from Bernard."

"Oh," Clemmie said and bit her lip. "Cecily was going to tell you about the photos. She was going to tell you everything,"

"What?" Levi looked at Clemmie, and she nodded her head.

"That afternoon she took me to her father's house, my father had kicked me out of our home, and Grant had taken back his ring, he believed Bernard too. I had nowhere to go so I went to Cecily and she said that she was going to tell you everything. She was upset she hadn't told you sooner. She said you would believe her because you loved her and you would get us both safe from Bernard."

Levi stopped his horse, got off and threw up. "Levi," Clemmie called his name and left her own horse to give him her canteen and a handkerchief.

"Cecily said that I could save her?" Levi asked after he rinsed his mouth out.

"She said that you loved her," Clemmie said simply as she stood and looked at Levi. "What happened to you Levi? You always treated us like you treated Sarah, well me anyway. I was your kid sister, and everyone knew how you felt about Cecily. Why did you turn on her like you did?" she saw him swallow hard and thought that he might be sick again.

"I believed Bernard's lies. The day before I got the photos and plates I followed her, I saw her give Bernard the broach I gave to her. I saw Bernard touching her."

"Bernard touched Cecily?" Clemmie cried out; she knew how Bernard had touched Cecily because Bernard had touched her too; he had grabbed her breast and pushed his body into hers. He had made her sick with fear.

Levi narrowed his eyes as he looked at Clemmie's face, "My God, Clemmie," he knew without asking that Bernard had touched her in the same way. Clemmie gave a cry and he pulled her into his arms. "I'm sorry," he said as he stroked her back. Seeing her face he knew she wasn't over what had happened and then he thought of Cecily. "I was so dumb. I believed Bernard's lies. I was jealous, everything I did was because I was jealous."

"If you are dumb then so is my father and Grant. They believed Bernard too." Clemmie pulled back from Levi's embrace and looked up into his eyes; his brows were raised as the truth dawned on him that he wasn't alone in believing Bernard. "My father put me out of the house, my mother wouldn't speak to me, and Grant took his ring back. And Cecily went to you, and you fixed everything for me, you and Cecily." Her words made Levi feel better, but not much. "Cecily was so scared of Bernard. I remember the night before her funeral; she was terrified out of her mind. She said that she needed money and that you had asked her to marry. I told her to marry you. And now that I look back I remember other times that she was afraid. She lived in fear, and I didn't know until Bernard did to me what he had already been doing for years to her."

"You told Cecily to marry me for my money?" Levi looked at Clemmie, and she almost laughed.

"Levi, your mother married your father for money, and theirs is the best-known love story in the whole state. Yes, I told her to marry you for your money.

"I think that my mother always loved my father,' Levi said softly while handing Clemmie her canteen and helping her to remount her horse, "I think that a lot of my parents' story was just made up."

"Cecily always cared for you, Levi. I thought of you like my big brother, Cecily never did. And she believed that you could save her. She was going to trust you with the truth, so you could save her, but it was too late, you had found out about the photos."

"And I ruined everything by believing Bernard Calhoun." Levi started his horse toward home with Clemmie beside him.

"Cecily should have told you the truth before she married you. I understand why she didn't though." Clemmie hoped she could make Levi feel better. Cecily was dead; nothing could hurt her now. But Levi was alive, and he was hurting, and no good would come from his suffering.

"I wouldn't let her talk after I found those photos," Levi glanced at Clemmie; she didn't look like she hated him. She should hate him for what he had done to Cecily. "What else happened that day?"

"Cecily got the photos from you and went for Grant; she told Grant everything, the whole awful story. They came to me at her father's house, and Cecily really did save my life. I had sliced open my wrist."

"Clemmie," Levi gave her a horrified look. "It was that bad? You wanted to die?" Levi's voice was hoarse and choked.

"It was worse than anything. I had lost my family; I had lost Grant. Bernard said that he would see my picture found its way into the Reverend Bidwell's bible on Sunday morning. I didn't have Cecily's faith in you. By the way, thank you for getting my pictures."

"I ruined Cecily's life, don't thank me. I killed your best friend." Levi couldn't look at Clemmie; he stared straight ahead.

"You didn't kill Cecily," Clemmie said softly and reached out to touch his arm.

"Yes, I did, Clemmie. She didn't want to have my baby; she told me so." Levi stopped his horse and looked at Clemmie when she had her horse still beside him. "That day, the day I put you out of my house," he stopped speaking and closed his eyes.

"What about that day, Levi?" Clemmie asked still touching his arm

"I raped her." Clemmie let go of his arm and stared at him in total disbelief shaking her head from side to side. "I raped her Clemmie. Right there on the parlor floor. There was no Ethan before that moment." He kicked his horse hard and left Clemmie; he could not stand to see the sick look of horror he had put on her face.

Cecily sat in a rocking chair holding her son, it was the first week of July, and she was packed to leave here, to leave her son and to leave Levi. Louise wanted to go, Louise wanted to take Ethan and run. Cecily was leaving Ethan to Levi. Her heart was breaking, it had been broken before, but it had never hurt like this. She had never in her life known this kind of pain.

"Your breast will be worse if you keep him on you like you are, Cecily. You need to stop feeding him now," Louise said as she sat down at the table and watched Cecily with Ethan. "We leave tomorrow; you do yourself no favor by feeding him."

"It's my last chance to have this with him," Cecily looked at Louise, her eyes pleading for understanding. They would be gone from here in just a few hours; she would never see her son again, never feed him from her body, never show him all the love she feels for him. She would pay the price later of her breasts hurting to have this last chance with her son.

"We should have run with him when we had the chance," Louise said as she poured herself a glass of water from the pitcher on the table.

"I've told you, I won't hurt Levi again," Cecily spoke firmly. "Besides, a son needs his father."

"A child needs both of his parents," Louise asserted. "Grow up, Cecily. You cannot leave Ethan; you must not leave this baby behind."

"I have too," Cecily said in a raw voice.

"You'll have no life," Louise said harshly

"I can't stay here, Louise. You know it's time we left."

"You love that blasted idiotic man! Just get up now and go to him, tell him you're as idiotic as he is and stays here with your child and with him. Do not leave here, Cecily. I'm begging you. You'll live to regret this for the rest of your life." Cecily's eyes left her son's face, and she looked at Louise.

"Levi doesn't want me. When he finds out that I lied to him again, he'll hurt me and with all the rights to do so. I can't stay here." She turned back to her baby. "And God help me, please, because I can't go."

"All right," Louise said in a calm voice. "Stay here for a few more days and think about what you are doing. Think about your choices. But stop sneaking into your husband's house at night and feeding this baby, if he catches you in the lie that way it'll be much worse than if you face him and tell him. Just think of your choices, Cecily." A knock sounded on the door, and Louise fell silent. Cecily reached down and pulled Ethan from her breast; he started screaming at having been taken away from his food and his comfort. Cecily handed him to Louise and rushed to the back of the house. She did not see Ethan's little arms reaching out to her, his mother.

"I thought I heard you talking to someone," Levi said as he came inside the house and took his crying son from Louise. Ethan became quiet in Levi's arms and started sucking on his own thumb.

"I was talking to the baby," Louise said when she wanted to say the mother's name and spill the beans and have this done. She would have too if she had felt that Levi wanted to hear his wife was very much alive.

"He and I have some really good conversations too," Levi said with a smile and bounced his son up above his head causing Ethan to giggle.

"You are a good father, Levi. And Ethan is happy with you. I'll miss you both very much." Louise reached out and touched Ethan's soft cheek.

"You will always be welcome here, Louise. I don't know what I would have done without you these past months. Honest, my home or this home is yours, come whenever you please and stay as long as you like. You're my family now." Louise tried to smile with her eyes full of tears. Levi handed her his handkerchief.

"If he ever wants or needs anything," Louise took a deep breath and looked into Levi's eyes, "If ever either of you need anything, promise that you'll let me know."

"You have my vow, Louise," Levi said and kissed her cheek as she kissed Ethan's cheek. "Thank you for my son."

Louise followed Levi out into the yard and held Ethan one last time before she left. Levi started to get onto his horse, but Louise reached out and grabbed a hold of his arm, he turned back to her and looked into her eyes. "Levi, what would you do if you could have another chance with Cecily?" She saw the pain in his eyes that her question had put there. "I don't mean to hurt you, but I have to know. If Cecily were here right now, if she could come back to you,"

"What are you doing to me?" Levi interrupted her, and she saw his eyes were too bright. "Cecily's not here. I won't have a chance to make what I did to her right. She's dead Louise. I really killed her," he looked so serious that she almost believed him.

"You didn't kill Cecily. No one killed Cecily," Louise said gently and touched Levi's shoulder. She saw him wipe at his eyes again.

"Believe me, Louise; I killed Cecily." Levi made a vain effort to fight the tears, he failed in his efforts, and they fell onto his cheeks. "Cecily married me because she needed money to be safe from Bernard Calhoun. I was so hurt and mad when I found out; I came into the house and heard her in the parlor talking to our friend Clemmie. She told Clemmie that I was dumb for loving her. I know that I'm dumb. I've always been dumb, and I got mad. She wasn't carrying this little one," he kissed Ethan. "There was no Ethan in her body. I raped her Louise, Ethan wasn't created from love; he was created from my revenge on his mother by being jealous when there was never any reason for me to feel that way. Cecily wouldn't be dead if I hadn't taken her against her will. I killed her."

"Cecily told me," Louise said softly, and Levi jerked his head up and their eyes collided. "Levi," she said his name and touched his shoulder. "Listen to me. Cecily wanted this baby. She loved Ethan before he was born and she never was sorry that you gave him to her. That's why she gave him to you." Louise thought of telling Levi right here and right now that Cecily loved him, that Cecily wanted to come home to him and work things out, but she didn't know if he would take Cecily in love, she couldn't let him put Cecily back in danger.

"Don't lie to me, Louise," Levi said as he turned around and faced her again.

"I'm not lying to you. Levi. I need to know; you have to tell me if Cecily were to come to you now, would you take her back with love? Louise held his eyes with her own and tried to see beyond his pain.

"I'd die if Cecily ever came back to me." He would rather be dead than hurt his wife again.

"Oh Levi, Why would you want to die? Cecily didn't want you dead; she knew that were killing yourself. Clemmie wrote and told me that you were wasting away, Cecily found the letter and the next day she went into labor, all the time she was giving birth, and it was a hard time for her, she kept begging me to bring Ethan to you so that you would have a reason to live. When Ethan was born, she cried out for you. She gave Ethan to you so that you would live, Levi. Cecily didn't hate you for this baby; she saved you with this baby. And I must know before I leave here, you must tell me. Would you take Cecily back if she were alive and here before you right now?"

"I don't know why you are doing this to me, Louise. Cecily is dead; she's gone. And she wouldn't want to come back to me even if she were alive. She's better off dead than with me." He mounted his horse and Louise stared up at him for a few seconds after she handed him the baby. "Just so you know, I love Cecily; I've always loved Cecily. If she were here right now, I would still love her. The answer to your question about taking her back. I can't give to you because I don't know what I would do."

Levi held tight to his son as he kicked his horse and trotted out of the yard and away from Louise Crandle.

"What did you say to him?" Cecily demanded to know when Louise came back inside the house. Louise could see that Cecily had been crying; there had been too many tears today. Someone had to put an end to this pain that Cecily and Levi were in. Louise could only wish that she had the answer to fix this mess these two young people had made of their lives.

"I asked him what he would do if you were here and came back to him," Louise said and went into the kitchen with Cecily at her heels.

"What did he say?" Cecily almost went to her knees in fear of Levi's answer.

Louise stopped and turned to look Cecily in the face. She didn't know how to answer this question. With all of her heart, she believed that Levi wanted Cecily back, but he had not told her that. "Cecily, the day that Levi forced himself on you, did you tell Clemmie that he was dumb for having loved you?"

"I would never call Levi," Cecily started to say and then closed her mouth as she remembered that day.

"Levi said that he's dumb, that you called him dumb for loving you and that he got mad and hurt you." Louise saw the emotions that crossed Cecily's face; there was pain certainly and confusion. "You did call him dumb," Louise said simply.

"He thinks that he's dumb because he couldn't learn to read," Cecily said in a low voice. "I didn't say that Levi was dumb for loving me, I just said that he was dumb. I was going to say that he was dumb for not seeing the truth. He came in and threw Clemmie out. Oh, Louise, the silence forced a miscommunication between us. And I started it by not trusting him when he married me and telling him everything.

"Cecily, I want you to think long and hard before you decide to leave here. I think that man would take you back and be glad to have you. Mind you; he didn't tell me that. He was too upset by my having asked him if he would take you back. He truly believes that he killed you. He feels that you didn't want his child and he believes that you died having his child."

"I told him once that I could never have his child, but I didn't mean it," Cecily whispered.

"Well, that is in the past. If you do decide to go back to him, you have to tell him how you feel. Everything you feel. You're going to have to open your heart to him. He can't see what's in your heart, Cecily. And he doesn't have one clue that you ever loved him. He honestly believes you only married him for his money.

"And I've loved him for as long as I can remember," Cecily cried, and Louise patted her back.

"But Cecily, he doesn't know that. He never knew that. He only believes you married him for his money."

"So what do I do? Walk over to his house and knock on the door and say, hello Levi, I'm home?" Louise gave a laugh and Cecily a quick hug.

"Better that than to have him find you hiding in a corner in the dark with Ethan at your breast," she teased. "Take a day or two and think about this, Cecily. We'll pray together and ask God to show the way. Don't go rushing over to him without some idea of what you're going to say to him. You both have hurt each other," Louise's tone was now serious. "And don't blurt out that you love him, you've withheld those words too long, and he might not believe you, he might think you want him only because of Ethan. Take time to show him your love; give him a chance to see your love." Cecily nodded her head and stared at Louise thankful for this kind woman.

"Cecily, I once thought that he needed to be brought to his knees for what he had done to you, but I was wrong. You were wrong as well; you should have told him the truth right from the start. But you didn't. So now I advise you this. When you go to him, go down on your knees, Cecily. Go on your knees before him and let him know that he is all you want and never his money, not your son, not anything other than him and him alone. Then when you do, you'll bring him to his knees. I'm certain he loves you and won't let you be alone in the sorry for the mistakes that were made."

"I'll never be able to thank you for all you've done for me, Louise." Cecily reached out and hugged her friend.

"Write me a letter when you've settled this. And remember, by going to Levi you get to keep Ethan, and I get to come often to visit and get all three of you."

"I just don't know how to go to Levi,"

"The heart knows the way," Louise advised. "Follow your heart."

Ethan had been cranky and irritable all night and into the day. Levi paced the floor with his son on his shoulder and patted the baby's back. That didn't help. He put whiskey on Ethan's gums thinking it was a tooth that might be trying to come in, that didn't help. He tried to give Ethan a bottle, but the baby just pushed the bottle away. Levi had never seen his son like this, and he was worried out of his mind.

"He's flushed," Levi said to Mrs. Liston. "I think I had better go for the doctor."

"He's flushed because you've had him near the stove," Mrs. Liston said.

"Well, something is wrong with him. He's crying all the time, and he won't eat." Levi tried bouncing Ethan on his lap, that did no good.

"Give him to me, Levi," Mrs. Liston said, and Levi handed her the baby. "What's wrong with the baby?" she crooned, but all Ethan did was tried to pull away from her. "This baby is trying to tell us something," Mrs. Liston looked at Levi's frowning face.

"What?" Levi asked her and went to where she stood holding his son.

"I don't know Levi. I never learned baby talk." Mrs. Liston shook her head as she walked out onto the porch with Ethan in her arms. "You know, Levi," she turned and looked at Levi as he had followed her onto the porch. "Every day you took this baby to Miss Crandle. He misses Miss Crandle. That's what is wrong with him — poor little thing. You would almost think by the way that he's acting that Miss Crandle was his mother. Mrs. Liston turned to go back inside. "We'll just have to suffer through this as Miss Crandle left yesterday."

Levi stood still on the back porch looking down the road that led to Daniel Walker's farm. Ethan was acting like Louise was his mother. Ethan wanted Louise. "If Cecily were here right now and came back to you, what would you do?' Louise had asked him the day before yesterday. "Cecily didn't want you dead; she knew that you were killing yourself, that's why she gave you Ethan. If Cecily came to you now, would you take her back?" Levi frowned as he kept remembering what Louise Crandle had said to him.

"Mrs. Liston, can you watch Ethan for me for a little while?" Levi called into the house.

"Yes, Levi. There's no reason for both of us to be miserable."

What was he doing? Levi asked himself as he saddled his horse. Cecily was dead, and Louise was gone. There was nothing for him at the Walker farmhouse; he was making a fool of himself by going there. At least no one knew what he was thinking or where he was going; only he would ever know what a fool he was.

A little while later, Levi stepped through the front door of Daniel Walker's home and stared at the shadows cast around the room. The place almost seemed haunted in its empty state. "Cecily," he called out not expecting any answer. This place was deserted, he knew. Louise had left the house clean, and in order, there was no sign anyone lived here. He walked down the hall to Cecily's old bedroom; he had been here once as a boy to tell Sarah it was time to go home for dinner.

He went into her room and saw all the books that filled the shelves. Cecily had been smart; he thought as he went to the window and looked out. Cecily had grown up in this room and looked out this window many times. But she wasn't here now; nobody was here now. And he had been stupid, as stupid as he had always known himself to be to come here thinking he would find his dead wife in this house.

Cecily came home from her walk in the woods and saw Levi's horse standing in the front yard. She stopped and stared, her heart beating crazily inside her chest. She had one of two choices right at this very moment. She could walk through that opened front door and face Levi and pray he wasn't so angry about this lie that he never forgave her, or she could run and hide from him again. She wanted her husband; she wanted her old Levi, she loved him. And her son, she needed her son. If she were going to lose them both, it would be with the truth. She had told Levi too many lies; it was time to face the truth.

Cecily entered the house expecting to see Levi in the parlor, but that room was empty. She then went into the kitchen, but that room was empty of her husband as well. She then started down the long hall looking into each room finally reaching her old bedroom. From the doorway she saw her husband looking out the window, his back turned away from her. Her heart dropped to her feet; she was so close to him, she wanted to be closer. With every breath she kept praying in her head, "please, please, please," she was scared half to death of his reaction when he saw her and what he would do.

Levi turned from the window, and with his eyes cast down to the floor, he started for the door. He stopped when he saw Cecily's slippers at the foot of her bed. It was almost like they were waiting for her to step into them. He wished that she could. He lifted his eyes from the floor; he saw her face and lost his breath.

"Levi," Cecily breathed his name, her hand over her heart, her eyes swimming in tears that when she blinked, they dropped huge and onto her face.

And then she was in his arms. He had rushed to her, lifted her off of the floor and was covering her mouth with his own. His mouth was begging for her mouth, and her mouth was begging for his. Cecily held on to Levi, and he held on to her. They were together, and she wanted him forever.

Levi found himself pushing Cecily down onto her bed and kissing her mouth, her cheeks, her eyes. He couldn't get enough of her. He had to touch her everywhere. He had to make sure she was real;

this wasn't a dream, this was really happened. Cecily was here, and she was alive. His heart was pounding, "Thank you, God, thank you, God, thank you, God," over and over and over again.

"Levi,' Cecily breathed his name again, and he jumped up and off her bed, looking at her laying still before him he raked his hand through his hair and looked around the room trying to calm down.

What was he doing? Was he going to rape her again? He backed further away from the bed and Cecily. He didn't see her now on her knees, her hand reaching out to him.

Cecily saw her husband's beautiful face. He didn't look mad at all, she thought. He looked scared and worried. He had wanted her before; she would make him want her again. He had taught her how to please him. He could not leave her now. She wouldn't let him.

Levi watched in total disbelief as Cecily left the bed and started pulling off her clothes. His breath was caught in his lungs, his heart was pounding hard inside of his chest, and he felt weak all over. And then his wife was before him; her clothes piled up on the floor around them, her small hand was reaching up to undo the buttons of his shirt. He reached down and started to help her to remove his clothes. He could not believe that this was happening; he was dreaming. He would wake up in just a few minutes. He didn't want to wake up too soon. He had to have her.

His clothes were piled up on the floor with her clothes and Cecily took her husband's hand and pulled him to the bed. "I need you," she whispered. "I want you, Levi."

"I never want to hurt you again," Levi said, and his voice broke. "Please, darlin', don't ever let me hurt you again."

"You aren't going to hurt me, Levi," Cecily said weakly. She was breathing hard, so was he. She pulled him down over her, and he let her. "I want you," she begged, and Levi touched her, she was being honest, she wanted him, and he hadn't even laid a finger on her. "Now," she begged as his mouth covered her mouth and he laid her back, his tongue entered her mouth, and he almost cried out, he loved kissing her. "Now," she pleaded as her mouth went to her husband's cheek and she felt him move into her and lost her breath.

When Levi regained his senses, he pushed himself up onto his elbows and stared down into his wife's crystal clear blue eyes, eyes that he thought only to see when he looked at his son for the rest of his life. Cecily was warm, she was soft, she was beautiful, and she was alive beneath him. He wanted to take her home. Home to Ethan. Home for himself. Home forever.

Levi left Cecily and got up off of the bed. She watched him with wide eyes, and he tried to speak to her, but he could think of nothing to say, his mind was a blank. And then he thought of a million things to say to her but didn't know where to start.

Cecily watched the play of emotions that crossed Levi's face. He looked relieved; he looked tired, there was no anger in his deep dark blue eyes. Nor was there any pain to be seen in the windows of his soul. She wanted to say something, anything, but the silence held her in a firm grip, and she could not fight to be free of that silence.

Levi reached down for his pants, and Cecily jumped up off the bed. He was going to leave her. He didn't want her anymore. She couldn't let him go without taking her with him. She would die if he left her now. "Levi, please," the silence was gone from her at last. She was free. "Don't keep Ethan from me." Her husband frowned down at her. "I'm begging you, Levi. I love Ethan too." Cecily fell to her knees and looked up at her husband, her hands clasped as though she were in prayer. "Don't take my baby away from me, please Levi, I beg you," she gave a soft cry, her eyes glued to his eyes. "I gave him to you when all I wanted to do was keep him for myself. I watched you through the window feeding him from a bottle with my breast aching in horrible need of him. I died a thousand deaths thinking that I would have to leave him forever. But I can't leave my baby, Levi. I need him; I need my child. I'll do anything you say, anything you want. It'll all be your way, please."

Levi grabbed a deep breath and pulled Cecily up off of the floor by her shoulders. He felt sick. She thought that he meant to keep her from Ethan. She still thought that he was the monster that he had been before she left him. "Cecily, I don't want to take Ethan away from you. I would never keep him from you. What I want is for you to get dressed and go get on my horse and come home with me." Cecily sagged against him in relief. "I want you to be Ethan's mother and my wife." He could be good to her now, Levi thought. He would have a second chance. A chance to correct the mistakes he had made with her. For a moment he looked up to the ceiling and thanked God for this chance, he wouldn't fail this time. He would make her love him too. She wanted him in her bed; she felt desire for him; he had something to build on. Even after what he had done to her, she wanted him.

Cecily wasted no time. She was dressed and out of the house waiting on Levi while he was still sitting on the edge of the bed pulling on his boots. She had gone down on her knees as Louise had told her to do, but she hadn't told him that she loved him. It was too soon for him to believe her. But she would tell him. She would find the right moment, and she would tell him everything, and he would listen and believe her. She would make him happy. There would be a forever for them.

Levi joined Cecily in the yard and lifted her up onto his horse before he climbed on behind her. She lay back against him and held his arm that he had around her waist. He couldn't believe that she was here with him, that she was alive, and he was beyond thankful to be holding her close. Levi wanted to say something, but he was afraid. He was afraid to break the tender hold that they had on one another right now. And Cecily was quiet as well. He wished that he could read her mind. He wished that she could read his mind.

Hell, he thought, he didn't have a mind. He had lost it when he had turned and seen her looking at him in the bedroom doorway.

Cecily was relieved that Levi hadn't rejected her, she was so relieved that she could barely breathe. And she knew, she would live by his rules, she would live his way and do anything that he wanted her to do. She would do anything to stay with him and Ethan. Maybe in time, he would forgive her. Maybe he would love her again. She would make him know that she loved him, that she had always loved only him; and she would have her tender Levi back. She wanted his concern, his caring; she wanted his heart.

Cecily heard Ethan screaming his little head off as they pulled up into the yard. She turned and looked up into Levi's eyes while his arm moved from her waist, and she slid down the horse and ran into the house and to her baby. Levi left his horse standing in the yard and followed his wife into the house, he saw Jamie out of the corner of his eye and knew that his horse would be taken care of; he also knew that everyone in the county would know that his wife was not dead and had come home before tomorrow morning. If Jamie didn't tell everyone, his mother would.

Mrs. Liston stood wide-eyed and staring at Cecily as she twirled her baby around the kitchen. Ethan wasn't crying anymore now; he clung to his mother as she clung to him both laughing and crying at the same time. Levi watched Cecily before he turned and told Mrs. Liston that she could go home for the day, he wanted to be alone with his family. A full minute passed before Mrs. Liston moved.

Ethan nudged his mother's breast and cried and suddenly feeling shy, Cecily left the kitchen and went into her old bedroom. She opened her blouse and put Ethan to her full and aching breast before she sat down in the rocking chair. Levi was shocked as he stood watching his wife from their bedroom doorway. His son was at his wife's breast, and he knew, Cecily had had Ethan for three hours every day of the week since she had given Ethan to him. Then he thought of the night he had been hurt from the fall off of his horse, she had been here, she had been in a corner feeding their baby son. All along she had been nursing Ethan; he was certain in the night, she was sneaking in and taking care of their baby.

"I'm here, baby. Mama will never leave you again Ethan," Cecily said as she rocked in the chair and held her son. "I'll never leave you again, not ever. I love you."

Levi moved out into the hall and leaned against the wall. She hadn't come here for him; she had come here for Ethan. And God help him, he knew he should go to her now and set her free, tell her she could keep Ethan and go wherever she wanted or needed or felt safe enough to go, be it her father's place or back to Louise Crandle's home in Georgia.

He closed his eyes and tried to stop the tears that burned to fall. She had pleaded with him on her knees for her son. She had let Levi use her body so that she could have their child. She was selling herself, and he was buying. He had to let her go. But he knew that he could never let her go. As long as she would stay, he would keep her. As it was before, it was again, Levi would take Cecily anyway he could get her.

Cecily put Ethan to bed and went to find her husband. She had to start opening up her heart to him as Louise had told her to do. She had to show him her love for him and this time she had to make him see that she loved him with all her heart. She found Levi sitting on the porch smoking a cigarette. She wondered if he was regretting letting her come home with him. Would he send her away? Or would he turn to her now and be mean and angry and hurt?

"Levi," she said his name, and he turned to face her. "May I speak with you?" His eyes held no anger; Cecily saw and took a deep breath in pure gladness before she saw the hurt in his eyes. She did not want to hurt him ever again. She couldn't hurt him ever again.

"Please, Cecily, don't say anything tonight. Why don't you go take a bath and go on to bed? It's getting late, and Ethan gets up early." Cecily started to speak to him anyway, but the hurt look in his eyes made her hold her silence. He wasn't angry. She would do as he asked her to do. She had told him that it would all be his way.

All through her bath, Cecily pleaded with God to not let Levi be mad with her anymore. She wanted her Levi back. She prayed so hard that her head ached when she left the tub. If she could just get him to listen to her, if only he would not make her stay quiet, she would tell him everything, and he would hold her and keep her safe as he did in the first few weeks of their marriage. He could not force her back into that silent world they both had lived in for too long. The silence made no sound.

Cecily pulled on one of Levi's shirts as she didn't have any nightgowns here and went to check on Ethan. Her son was sleeping peacefully. Levi entered their bedroom and saw his wife touch their son's soft cheek with her lips; he was holding her to him with his son. And God help him, he was jealous of the love that Ethan got from her. A love that she had never given to him.

Levi went into the bathroom and closed the door. He looked at his face in the mirror and felt dirty and awful. If only she could love him. If only he could make her love him. He filled the tub and sank down into the steaming water. He could not be jealous of his own son, he thought. He knew that he was. Ethan had what Levi never had from Cecily. Ethan had what Levi wanted. Levi wanted Cecily.

The room was dark when Levi left the bathroom. He had pulled on his robe before leaving the bathroom, but he pulled it off when he reached the bed. Cecily moved, she was still awake, he realized. He wondered if she wanted him, he knew that he wanted her. He wished that she would give herself to him, the reason why be damned.

Cecily had been waiting for Levi to finish with his bath and join her. He may not hear her words of love, but tonight he would feel her love, her body would say what her voice could not say.

Cecily put her head on his shoulder, her hand on his chest and she smiled when Levi took a deep breath. Her touch still affected him as his touched affected her.

Levi couldn't wait. He turned and pushed Cecily onto her back. She may not love him, but she wanted what his body could do to her. And he had to have her. He pushed open his shirt that she wore and stared down at her body. Her breasts were larger, her waist smaller. She was beautiful. Still, she was breathtaking. He put his mouth to her breast and tasted what Ethan tasted. He suckled at his wife's breast as his son had earlier and he wished that she would tell him that she loved him as she had told Ethan.

Cecily held Levi's head tightly to her breast. His hair was longer than it had been before, she liked it longer; she liked the feel of his mouth sucking the milk from her breast. His mouth was hot, so hot, she thought and moaned arching her back up to get closer to him. She felt his lips move down her stomach and place gentle kisses upon her body before he moved lower still and she shattered within moments into his mouth

Levi entered his wife tenderly; slowly he drove her mad as he made love to her, his body one with her body. She was here; he thought while plunging into her and then pulling out. She belonged to him and the reason why didn't matter. She wanted him. She was begging him for more; she was begging him to move faster, reaching out to him and pleading for him to move faster and faster still. He wanted her happy; he wanted to give her this; he wanted this from her and so much more.

"Do you feel me touching your heart? I'm touching your heart, darlin'," he cried out, and she did as well. He plunged within her once more, and she fainted, Levi almost fainted with her.

Chapter Twelve

Levi held Cecily in his arms until Ethan's cries woke them. Cecily left the bed and pulled on Levi's shirt that she had worn for a brief few moments last night. Levi had taken her to heaven; he would always take her to heaven. She had almost cried out that she loved him twice; the only thing that stopped her was the knowledge that it was too soon for those words. The time wasn't right to confess what she felt for him, not in the bed.

Levi propped himself up on his elbow and watched Cecily feeding his son. He saw Cecily look up and meet his eyes for a brief second across the room before she quickly looked away. He wondered what she was thinking. "You look beautiful with him at your breast," he said, knowing that they had to talk; he had to let her talk as she had asked him the night before. Regardless of her words and the pain they caused, he had to listen to her; he had to tell her that he knew everything that Bernard had done to her and that he was a fool for believing Bernard's lies.

"You're a perfect mother," he said in his low husky voice and saw her look at him again quickly, her face losing all color. What was she thinking? He wondered with a frown and saw the pain fill her eyes. And then he knew just what had caused her pain and he sat up while shaking his head. There had been another time when she had held his baby in her arms, a time that he had said something mean and cruel to her. "Don't Cecily, don't remember," he whispered.

"We need to talk, Levi," she said while looking him in the face.

Levi left their bed and went to her, down on his knees before her as she'd gone on her knees before him the day before. He had been intent on letting her talk to him only a few moments before, and now he knew; he could not hear her tell him that she wanted to take their baby and go. Cecily's words to him always hurt. He couldn't stand any more pain. She had to give him a chance to make her happy; if she only would, he would make her happy forever.

"Listen to me, darlin'," Levi held her eyes with his own. He wanted to wake up every morning for the rest of his life and look into those crystal clear eyes. He couldn't let her leave him. He wouldn't let her go. He would win her love. She had to love him. "I did some thinking last night. We aren't going to make it together if we drag up the past. One of us is going to lose Ethan." He didn't notice that she became very still because of his words. "Today can be a whole new beginning for us. Whatever was done, one to the other in the past can all be forgotten. Forever." Don't leave me; his heart cried out, don't leave me his, eyes silently pleaded with her not to go. Don't let the pain that I caused you before drive you away from me, his mind screamed loud and long, and he wished she knew how he felt.

"But is the past forgiven, Levi?" Cecily asked in a near whisper, the fear consuming her heart and making her feel sick inside. If she tried to talk to him or tell him anything that had gone on before, he would take their son from her; he would send her away.

"By me, it is," Levi said while nodding his head. He laid his head on her lap, and she stroked his hair. He was forcing her back into the silence. She would lose her son and him if she didn't live in the silent world that Levi was sentencing them both too. She loved him. She had promised him it would be his way less than twenty-four hours ago. And he had forgiven her at last. Maybe he would love her again. Her only wish was that he would hear her heart, that he would know she loved him. That he would know she always loved him. The silence filled the room.

Levi felt Cecily stroking his hair; he reached up for her hand and placed a kiss on her palm. They could start all over again. He would do everything right this time and make up for having caused her any pain. Cecily wouldn't leave him, and he would hold her close and make her love him, make her see that she was nothing without him as he was nothing without her. His heart dripped tears of blood for the love that he had for her and for the love that she had denied him.

The news of Cecily Tucker's being alive and at home with her husband and child spread like a wildfire throughout the community of Cherry Lake thanks to Mrs. Liston and her son Jamie. Everyone knew that Levi had brought Cecily home the night before and that she had danced around the room with her son in her arms. Many people wondered where Cecily had been and why she had sent her son home to her husband and not come home herself. The twins, Eva and Althea Bidwell declared to one and all that now that Bernard Calhoun was dead, Cecily felt safe enough to come home. The whole community knew that Bernard had assaulted women in their community and Lydia Masterson had put an end to Bernard attacking innocent women. Eva insisted that Bernard had driven Cecily away, and Levi had let her go knowing he couldn't keep her safe. Hadn't he tried the day of her father's funeral when he broke Bernard's nose? Levi Tucker had always loved his Cecily; he would have done anything to protect her. The speculation and rumors were endless, but all ended with Levi being like his father and winning his true love, Cecily's heart.

Clemmie burst through the front door of Levi's home and called out for Cecily; they hurled themselves into one another's arms. "Aunt Louise told us that you had died giving birth to Ethan,"

Clemmie had said as she laughed and cried at the same time. Cecily kept looking at Clemmie's round stomach and knew that their children would grow up together as she and Clemmie had.

"I almost did die having Ethan," Cecily said after they had finished hugging and were able to sit facing one another on the sofa in the parlor. She told Clemmie how she had found the letter from Clemmie to Aunt Louise and read about how ill Levi was. She knew that Levi would live for his son, so she had sent Ethan home to his father. "I knew that he was dying because of the hurt that I caused him," Cecily said and leaned back on the cushioned sofa as she remembered and told Clemmie all that she had done these past months. "When I left here, it was because I was hurting him. I never dreamed just how badly I hurt him. Levi gave me everything, Clemmie; I didn't want him dead. So I finally gave him something other than lies and a total lack of trust. I gave him Ethan, and he lived."

Levi came into the house and heard his wife's voice. He stopped and stood still remembering another time that he had come and eavesdropped on his wife with her friend. He did not want to stay and hear Cecily's words to Clemmie, but he could not move. He could not go away and not hear what Cecily said of him to Clemmie. He held his breath as he waited for Cecily to tell Clemmie that she wanted to take Ethan and leave him.

"Cecily," Clemmie looked at her friend and saw Cecily's eyes meet her own. "Levi told me what he did to you here in the parlor," Clemmie's voice was low, but Levi heard what she said to his wife. "He said that he," Clemmie stopped talking when Cecily put her fingers on her mouth.

"Levi said that we are not to talk about the past, Clemmie. What happened is forgotten and forgiven," Levi frowned in the hall where he stood. Cecily wasn't going to tell Clemmie that she wanted to leave him, but he heard the fear in her voice. He didn't like hearing that fear.

"Cecily," Clemmie pushed aside Cecily's fingers so she could talk.

"I cannot tell you anything about the past," Cecily said in an urgent voice. "I have to forget everything that happened from when I was here before. Levi let me stay. He let me stay here with my baby, that's all I care about right now.

Levi held his breath and leaned against the door. He had been right, Cecily had only come for Ethan, she still didn't want him, she didn't even care about him. Ethan was what mattered and what he was using to keep her with him.

"Has he hurt you in any way?" Clemmie asked, and Levi stood up straight waiting for the answer.

"No, Levi isn't hurting me," Cecily said and thought that he was, he was killing her by forcing her back into that world of silence again. "I will lose Ethan if I talk about the past. I have to forget everything that happened Clemmie. I can't lose what I have right now.

What did she mean she could lose Ethan? Levi thought with a frown. He gasped when he remembered his words to her this morning. She believed that he would take Ethan from her if she spoke of the past. She thought that he had been threatening her with losing Ethan if she talked of the past because he had told her one of them would lose Ethan if they dragged up the past. She was staying with him here for Ethan, she would forget everything that he had done to her so that she could keep her son, and he allowed her to believe just what she believed. He had never meant for her to take his words as a threat. He would give her Ethan; he would never let her lose her child. He would never hurt her again. He couldn't hurt her.

Levi didn't know what to do. He should go into that room right now and tell her that Ethan was hers, that he wouldn't use their son ever against her. But she would leave him. She would take Ethan and go, and he would never have the chance to teach her to love him. He would never be able to show her that he could love her enough for the both of them. He had to have a chance; he would make her give him that chance. He would do anything for just a few weeks in which to love Cecily and try to make her love him.

Clemmie saw Levi enter the parlor with Ethan; the baby's eyes were swollen as though he had just woken up. "Someone wants his mama," Levi said and handed Cecily her baby; she excused herself and left the room to nurse the baby. He turned to Clemmie and smiled. "Hello Clemmie, how are you?" he saw her nod her head, her eyes narrowed, and he smiled, gave her a wink and said, "A child always stays with his mama." He saw Clemmie relax physically and he nodded his head to her. "Always safe with his mother."

"You're going to make everything good for Cecily aren't you, Levi?" He nodded his head, and his smile grew. "You're in love with her still."

"With all my heart, Clemmie. I won't ever hurt her again. I just need a chance to show her, just a little time to earn her trust. You have my word, I swear, I won't ever hurt her again." Clemmie believed him.

Levi came home at dark from the mill and found Mrs. Liston gone. Cecily was putting dinner on the table, and he noticed only the one place setting and felt sick as he remembered all the times that he had ordered her to eat in the kitchen. She had married him to be safe, and he had hurt her worse than Bernard ever had. And now she thought he meant to take Ethan away from her. He would make everything up to her now; she had to let him take the wrong that he had done to her away.

Ethan lay on the floor on a blanket in the dining room watching his mother and Levi went to the baby and picked him up before going to the chair at the table where he held Ethan on his lap. Cecily looked at her husband and chewed on her bottom lip while thinking that he meant to keep Ethan in here with him and send her to the kitchen. Her heart was in the pit of her stomach pounding painfully at the thought of being sent away again.

"Here Levi," she said and reached out for her baby. "Let me hold him while you eat your supper."

"Yes, hold him for me," he handed her Ethan, reached out and turned her around and then forced her to sit down on his lap. "We'll all eat together," he said close to her ear, hoping that she was not remembering the many times that he had forced her from this very table in anger.

Cecily sat still as Levi put a spoon of mashed potatoes in Ethan's mouth. He filled the spoon again and held it for her. He was being so kind and gentle that she felt tears form in her eyes. He gave Ethan a string bean to chew on then put a bean into her mouth half way and bit off the other end, his lips brushing against hers. He was seducing her at the dinner table with their son on her lap; she thought as he put another bean halfway into her mouth and again shared the bean with her.

Ethan began to fuss after a little while, and Cecily tried to stand, Levi wouldn't let her. "I have to feed him," she said in a weak voice, Levi's mouth had just left her mouth, she was burning for his touch but had to feed the baby.

"Feed him here," Levi said and began to undo the buttons of her dress.

Cecily put Ethan to her breast, her eyes never leaving Levi's eyes until he bent his head to her free breast and began sucking. She closed her eyes and felt his hand reach under her dress and touch her. Levi sucked at his wife's breast, kissed her mouth with her milk warm on his lips and drove her mad with his fingers stroking her. He felt her stiffen on his lap and the breath caught in his throat. "Feel me, Cecily, feel me darlin'," Cecily went weak on him, and he thought that she might pass out, so he reached out and held on to Ethan.

"He's asleep," Cecily said a few moments later. Her arm was around Levi's neck; her face was buried against his neck.

"I'll put him to bed," Levi said, and Cecily stood, and she gave him the baby.

Levi left the dining room with Ethan and Cecily sat down in his empty chair and tried to catch her breath. Her husband had taken her to heaven again. If only they could talk as well as they made love. Everything would be perfect if she and Levi could just talk without her being afraid. She did not want to be afraid of this man she was in love with.

Levi came back into the dining room and saw his wife; her face had the sad look he had seen before. He wanted to take the sadness away. He wanted to make everything right. She had to let him make everything right, he thought desperately.

Cecily looked up at Levi, saw that easy smile on his face and stood. He had given her pleasure, he always was giving to her, and she was always taking. She wanted to give it to him. She hoped that he would let her. She went to him and undid the buttons of his trousers and pulled him free, holding him in her hand as he had taught her all those months ago. She could see that he still liked for her to hold him in her hand and smiled up into his eyes. She knew him well, she knew what he liked, and she would give him what he wanted. She heard him suck in his breath hard and fast when she went down on her knees before him.

"Cecily," he cried her name softly when she pulled him into her mouth. He reached down and held the sides of her head guiding her as he use too, even lost in his anger he had been sure that he never let her gag on his hardness. "You have to stop, darlin'," he begged of her, but she would not let him push her away. "Cecily, please!" he cried out and pushed on her harder; she clung to his thighs and wouldn't let him force her away from him. He gave to her; now she would give to him.

Levi tried to avoid what he knew he could not avoid. He threw back his head and cried out her name and knew it was too late. His wife had just had all of him; she had wanted all of him. He had tried to stop her; she wouldn't let him. He looked down into her eyes, and she smiled up at him, her lips moist from his body. He wanted to tell her that he loved her. He wanted to tell her that he could never live without her. Instead of saying anything that he wished to say, he pulled her up off the floor where she knelt before him and kissed her hard and fast.

"Thank you, Cecily, thank you for that." He held her close and thanked God for bringing her back to him; he would thank God forever that she was here with him, that he was having this chance.

"Can you take me to bed now, Levi?" she asked as her head rested on his shoulder, and she trembled in his arms. He started to laugh; she laughed with him and wondered what was so funny. It didn't matter; she had made Levi happy. She would make him happy for the rest of their lives. And she felt like she almost had the old Levi back. Maybe he was right, and they could start fresh. Maybe they didn't need to talk. Today could be a whole new beginning.

Levi swung his wife up into his arms, his mouth finding her mouth. He would win her love. He would fill her full of himself and make her love him and not able to live without him. Her body would belong to him; she would be enslaved by this passion that they had for one another. Love would come later. Love would come.

Levi spent every spare moment that he had with Cecily. They didn't talk much; he felt they didn't need to. They ate together with Ethan and enjoyed being with one another. He held her on his lap in a chair in the parlor, and she read to him stories from the newspaper. They rode their horses, and she even raced with him and laughed when he let her win, and she knew had done so. They took walks around the lake, he held Ethan, and he held her hand. He touched her all of the time; he couldn't get enough of her, a lifetime wouldn't be enough time for Levi to touch his Cecily. And she didn't mind him touching her, Levi thought, she wanted him as much as he wanted her. They didn't need to talk of the past ever; what had happened then wasn't a part of the here and now.

Every night before bed, Levi would take her out to the porch and sit her in a ladder back chair, and he would sit in a chair behind her and brush her long hair. Sometimes she would sit feeding Ethan, other times the baby would be asleep and the brushing would turn to lovemaking as he would pull her into his lap facing him and ask her over and over as he moved within her, "Can you feel me touching your heart? I'm so deep; I'm touching your heart. Can you feel me touching your heart?" Cecily would only nod her head and beg him for more which he always gave her. What he wanted from her was the words he long to hear her say, "I love you, Levi," but the words never came.

The sadness was still in Cecily's eyes, but not as it had been in the past. And the sorrow was from the silent world that Levi was forcing them to live in. Unable to speak of the past wrongs and help set them right and the fear that she might not follow Levi's rules and be sent away from her baby was almost unbearble for her. Though the hurt and anger were never seen in Levi's eyes. He had found a place of peace and happiness and hope for love with his Cecily and with Ethan beside them.

Levi thought that maybe his mother had married his father for his money and maybe, just maybe, she had fallen in love with his father. Maybe his father had really made his mother fall in love with him as Levi was working to see that his Cecily fell in love with him. She had to fall in love with him because he knew; he was nothing without her in his life.

Levi had kept Cecily all to himself for nearly two weeks, but today he was taking her to church services. Cecily was nervous about what might be asked of her or said to her, but she kept her fears to herself. The past days with Levi had been heaven, his easy smile was back on his face, his laughter was often heard, he was her old Levi, and she hoped and prayed she could do the right thing and always have him happy.

Levi wasn't dumb to his wife's fear that Sunday morning as he helped her into the buggy, he could feel it in the way she trembled beside him and chewed almost constantly on her lower lip. He had tried so hard to make her happy since he'd brought her back home. He had done everything that he knew to do to give her happiness, to make her see that she would be safe with him and that he would never use anything against her again, including their son.

When the services were over, Levi looked back down at his wife's face and saw the sadness was back in her eyes. He stood holding Ethan on his hip and her hand with his free hand. He thought of what he had done to bring about the fear he could see so clearly in her eyes and he let go of her hand and tilted her chin up, so her eyes met his. "What's the matter?" he whispered, and she looked away, he saw her taking a deep breath, and he knew, he had lost her, but then, he had never had her, he knew that in his heart. He was holding her to him with Ethan as Bernard had held her with those photos and he couldn't do that any longer. He would let her go. He would give her their son, and set her free. He never really had the right to her after what he had done.

Cecily watched as she and Levi and Ethan drew closer and closer to the church doors and the Reverend Bidwell. She had never told anyone, but she was terrified of the man. He wasn't just stern; he was judgmental and often cruel. She expected this morning to be publicly humiliated by him because she'd left her husband first and second has allowed everyone to believe she was dead. She felt Levi let go of her hand and she looked up quickly to see the hurt in his eyes, she hadn't seen his pain since she'd come back to him. "Levi," she said his name in a begging tone, and he looked back down at her right as they reached the Reverend Bidwell.

"Well, young woman," the Reverend Bidwell spoke to Cecily in his booming loud voice and Cecily saw the crowd in the churchyard turn and stare at her. "You have certainly made a scandal of yourself." Cecily felt her face heat up at the Reverend's words. "First you abandon your husband, then your child and you lie to everyone by letting us all believe you're dead. I hope you are truly ashamed of yourself and realize how lucky you are that your good and kind husband has done the Christian thing and taken you back.

Levi looked down at his wife's face, she was red one second and then she was pale, almost white. His Cecily, his perfect, innocent wife that he took in anger and fear was being blamed for his sin, for his guilt and for his shame. Everything that had happened between them was his fault. He knew the truth, all of the truth. She had never once done anything wrong. She came to him pure, and he nearly destroyed her. She had married him to save herself, Clemmie was right, that's what woman have to do. And he, her husband, should have saved her instead of hurt and punished her. And now, now he had her back, and he had again forced her into the world of silence, and yes, she was still trapped in the fear that she'd been in for years. He put her back in the silence because he was selfish, because he didn't want to talk of how horrible he had been to her, how wrong, how judgmental as this Reverend was being now.

"Cecily never," Levi's voice was louder than the Reverend Bidwell's voice, and if someone hadn't turned to hear the Reverend's words, they turned to hear Levi's. "Ever at any time abandoned this baby," Levi's eyes locked with the Reverend Bidwell's eyes. "I drove her away from our home. I hurt her," his voice broke as he turned and looked down at his wife, "and she did the Christian thing, she shared our son with me after I hurt her. She forgave me for what I did to her, and I have never done anything to earn her forgiveness. I never even told her I was sorry for all I did to her." He looked back at the Reverend Bidwell and spoke even louder; he wanted everyone to hear his words. "I'm the one that is lucky. I'm blessed because Cecily came back to me even after I had hurt her. And I'm so glad she's by my side. I love her more than life itself." He was talking to the crowd one minute and her the next, the palm of his hand cupping her face. "My sweet darlin' Cecily, always so sweet." He saw her turn her face into his hand and kiss his palm and he pulled her close. "I'm so ashamed of how I treated you, Cecily, of every harsh word I said to you. And God have mercy on me for what I put you through. Please, forgive me. I know you were always innocent."

Cecily burst into tears; Levi hadn't expected her to do that. "We need to talk," he said and took her hand into his pulling her from the church. Clemmie and Grant were just outside the door looking at him, he knew they, along with everyone inside and outside the church had heard his words to the Reverend Bidwell and then to Cecily. "Here," he handed Ethan to Grant who passed the baby to his wife. "Take care of him for me for a little while," Levi said and saw Clemmie nod her head.

Levi pulled Cecily under a tower oak tree in the churchyard away from the crowd; she was still crying tears but not making any noise. "I'll give you your father's house," he said gently. "And I'll give you more money; you'll never want for anything the rest of your life. I swear you won't want for anything darlin' not one thing. And Ethan is yours too, though I would like to visit him from time to time if that's all right."

Cecily fell back away from him, and he gasped, she looked like she did when he had hit her that one time. "Why? Why are you throwing me away? What did I do wrong?"

"Throwing you away?" Levi shook his head hard knowing he wasn't throwing her away.

"I made a mistake, Levi. Well, I made a lot of mistakes." The time had come, Cecily realized. Here was her chance to tell Levi everything; she had waited too long to tell him everything.

"Bernard gave me a glass of tea when I went to have my photo made for Daddy. I didn't pose for those photos; I was asleep, I was drugged. I didn't even know what he had done until he came to Daddy demanding money. I never loved Bernard. I never wanted to pay court to him, honest I didn't. He blackmailed me into doing everything he wanted me to do; he used those photos to make me his puppet on a string. I should have never let Daddy pay him one cent, Levi. I should have told you and Clemmie, she's like my very own sister, but I didn't and Bernard did to her what he had been doing to me. And you, I should have told you everything before I married you. I was just so afraid of what you would think of me; the photos were so awful. I deceived you; and I lied to you. The only mistake that I didn't make was the day I married you. And you loved me, Levi, we might have been happy together if I been honest with you. All of the mistakes were mine.

"I use to come to church every Sunday and sit in the front row in the hopes that God would help me with Bernard. And then one Sunday, God threw me into the lap of my savior where Bernard was concerned, and I was too blind by fear to see, I was too blind by fear to trust you. I'm sorry, Levi. I know you don't love me anymore, and I don't blame you. But if you'll just give me a chance, I think I can make you happy."

Levi knew in that moment in his life that he really was dumb. And he probably looked like a complete idiot standing here in the churchyard staring down at his beautiful wife with his mouth hanging open. "You didn't make one single mistake, Cecily," he finally said, and she let go of the breath that she had been holding. "You did just what you had to do, what was best. Everything you did, you did because you had no choice. I'm the one that messed everything up for us darlin'." He moved to her and took both of her hands into his own."I treated you like a prisoner in our home; I wouldn't let you tell me the truth when you wanted too. I gave you horrible rules, and I made you wear your hair down when I love it twisted up like it is now. I said awful things to you that I'll never forgive myself for." He hung his head, he couldn't look at her face as he confessed his many sins to her. "I roughly took your virginity. My God, I raped you." He fought to breathe with his last words and Cecily saw his struggle and the pain that he felt for what he had done to her.

"Cecily, I tore you apart in the daylight and again in the darkness. I know what I did to you." He looked again into her eyes. "I shamed you. I dishonored you when all I ever wanted to do was love you. All the mistakes were mine. Everything that went wrong between us was my fault because I believed Bernard's lies of you. Because I was jealous of Bernard."

"Levi," Cecily looked up into his deep eyes. "If I hadn't let you force me to tell the worst lie of all, none of what you did would have ever been done."

"What lie are you talking about?" Levi took a step closer to her, getting lost in her crystal clear eyes.

"The one about my having married you for your money," Cecily answered, and Levi shook his head.

"It's all right; I know you married me to pay Bernard for his silence about the photos. That doesn't matter to me anymore, darlin' honest it doesn't."

"It does matter to me, Levi." She took the last step that separated them. "You have to know, you have to believe me, it's the truth, and it's always been the truth. I love you. But for Bernard's blackmail I would have married you and gladly. Daddy knew how I felt about you; he was sick that I wasn't free to marry the only man I've ever loved. Levi, every one of the box lunches of mine that you bought, I made for you, only you." Levi stared at her in disbelief; she saw that disbelief in his eyes. "I'm telling you the truth. I was fourteen, you were nineteen, and you were chasing me down by the lake, well you were chasing Sarah and Clemmie and me with an old garden snake and then you were running just after me and I looked back over my shoulder and saw you and I knew, I was in love with Levi Tucker. All my girlhood dreams were of you, to marry you, to have your children, to grow old with you. I'm telling you the truth and you have to believe me. Bernard ruined me for you; that's why I put you away from me. I shut you out because of Bernard when all I wanted was to be with you always." He was holding her in his arms, and she felt him laughing against her. "Did I say something funny, Levi?"

"Sort of Cecily," He pushed her back and looked down into her eyes again. "That day at the lake when I was chasing you girls around with that snake, and you looked back at me, that memory is carved in my mind. That was the day I knew I would wait for you to grow up. I never married or courted any girl, because I was in love with you. That's in large part why I was mad, I wanted you to love me, and I believed you didn't. I didn't want to live without you and I thought you didn't love me. I was mad all over."

"You were mad," Cecily confirmed. He was so close to her that she had to tilt her head back to look up into his face, he was almost on top of her. "And then you took me to bed, and I thought if I only had known how good that would be between us, I never would have kept you from my bed. I was wrong, Levi."

"I was too, darlin'." Cecily was so close to him now that he could feel her warm breasts touching his chest.

"After you found the photos and forced me to silence I tried to show you, my love. You were so mean; you wouldn't even let me eat with you."

"You're right, you're so right, I was awful to you. I beg you to forgive me." Levi closed his eyes. "And I did worse you need to forgive me for.

"I thought that you hated me," Cecily cried.

"Never," Levi reassured. "You should hate me forever."

"That day in the parlor, I just wasn't ready for you. You always kiss me, and I turn to liquid flame when you do. And when I said I didn't want your baby, that wasn't true; I want a whole house full of children with you. I was just afraid if I had a baby by you and then you divorced me one day over the photos then I'd lose my child."

"I'm not sorry that Bernard is dead," Levi said in a thick voice, if Bernard were alive, his life would be in danger.

"After I left you I wasn't sorry I was going to have a baby, Levi. I rejoiced. Something of us was created that wasn't a lie or shameful. I'm glad about what happened in the parlor, Ethan came to us. I was going to keep him and never tell you of him; then I read Clemmie's letter to Louise saying you were dying and I knew, our baby could save you. I really did almost die having him.

"Levi, everything went wrong because I was silent; I didn't trust you at the start. And then when I wanted to tell you everything, you put me back in silence." Cecily gave a deep sigh of relief. Finally, at long last, the silence that had held her for too long was gone. She was opening up her heart to her husband, and he was hearing her words and seeing her heart. "I thought you didn't want me, that there was no place in your world for me and every night I snuck into your home and hid in a darkened corner and nursed our baby. You were both my life, and I knew, without you, I was truly dead. I was getting ready to come to you when I found you in my room."

"Cecily, I thought your words would break me. I thought you'd leave me and hate me forever in the leaving." He stared down into his wife's eyes and heard her words and knew they weren't hurting him; he should have let her talk long before now. "I still can't believe you're alive and here with me. I heard you talking to Clemmie the other day, and I knew that you were afraid that I'd take Ethan from you. I thought I was holding you with Ethan as Bernard held you with those photos. And I never meant to threaten you with our son. I was afraid of losing you so, I spent the past few days trying to make up for any kind of threat that you thought I meant to make."

"No more silence, Levi. From now on we have to trust each other with our thoughts and fears and our truths. We have to share everything. We have to talk."

"I promise darlin'; the silence is nearly what destroyed us. I knew that and forced more silence on you in my fear of losing you.

"So Ethan and I aren't going to Daddy's house, we're staying with you? You love me still?" Cecily saw his head nod and the easy smile that touched his eyes.

"The only place you're going is home with me and Ethan too if we can get him away from Clemmie," he nodded his head in the direction of the church yard and saw Clemmie on a blanket playing with Ethan, Grant was with her.

Cecily looked back at her husband and sighed again. "Levi, I love your mouth on me. I love your hair long like it is now. I love wearing your shirt to bed and having you take it off me. I love you, Levi, I've loved you all my life."

Her words broke Levi's hold on her hands. He grabbed her and covered his mouth with his own; their bodies were so close that he didn't know where he started and where she stopped. Gently, Levi made love to Cecily's mouth with his own, and she moaned into his mouth and he into hers, they each wanted more, to be home alone, just the two of them.

"There are two things that I need you to do for me," Levi said when he lifted his mouth from Cecily's mouth and looked again into her crystal clear eyes, eyes that he would look into every day for the rest of his life.

"And they are?" Cecily asked, still standing close to her husband and looking up into his eyes. He loved her again and he knew that she loved him and she hadn't had to go to her knees to make him believe her.

"First, you let me put my betrothal ring and wedding band back onto your finger," he said gently and reached into his pocket pulling out the rings. "I've been carrying these around with me for two days," he said as his wife looked down into the palm of his hand where the rings lay.

"Done," Cecily said and held out her hand for him to slide the rings onto her finger forevermore. "And the second thing?"

"Write a letter to the Prichard's in Jacksonville and tell Ollie that you're home. She wouldn't come back to me until you did." Cecily laughed softly.

"Done, the instant we get home."

"No," her husband said, and she frowned. "The instant we get home, I'm pulling you into my bed for at least an hour. And then we are going to talk some more. You can write Ollie tonight." Levi made love to her with his eyes before he bent his head and kissed her again. When he finally looked up and over her head, he groaned out loud.

"What's the matter?" Cecily asked of his groan, and he looked back down into her eyes.

"The whole church congregation is staring at us, darlin'." Cecily groaned louder than he had a second earlier.

"What should we do?" She asked him in her soft sweet voice with a worried frown on her face and Levi gave her one of his easy smiles. He knew that he would never fear the sound of her again, from out of Cecily's silence he had found the love that he had been dying to have for more than six years.

"You could tell me that you love me again," he suggested. The tenderness that Cecily had always known to be in her Levi's eyes was back, and she gave him a smile that his heart had put upon her lips.

"I do love you, Levi. I was afraid that when I married you, I was taking you to hell. And you told me that you would take me to heaven every time you held me in your arms. I didn't believe you.

I was falling into hell and pulling you down with me. And then you held me in your arms, and instead of falling into hell with you, I fell into heaven. Every time you hold me, I fall into heaven within your arms."

"Dear God, darlin'," Levi said as he held her face with the palms of his hands and placed gentle kisses on her forehead, he loved her words to him. He had won, Cecily was his. and she was happy to be his. "I love you so much." He heard her soft moan before she leaned against him, her arms tight around his waist and her cheek on his chest. He looked back at the churchyard full of people and smiled. "I think that our story will put more little girl's to sleep than my parents' story ever did." Cecily looked back up at his beautiful face. "Everyone in the churchyard is grinning at me."

"I love you, Levi Tucker," his wife whispered, and he again covered her mouth with his own and pulled her close.

They forgot that they were being watched; when they remembered they didn't care. From out of the silence Cecily had her Levi back, and Levi had his Cecily…

NO SOUND THE SILENCE MAKES,
QUIET IS THE SUN AS IT AWAKE,
I THOUGHT WHEN I MARRIED YOU
I WAS TAKING YOU TO HELL
YOU HELD ME IN YOUR ARMS AND
TO HEAVEN WE FELL

The End

www.ingramcontent.com/pod-product-compliance
Lightning Source LLC
LaVergne TN
LVHW021220080526
838199LV00084B/4298